W9-BTO-223

# THE
# CRIPPLER

# THE
# CRIPPLER

## CAGE FIGHTING AND MY LIFE ON THE EDGE

**CHRIS LEBEN**
**WITH DANIEL J. PATINKIN**

Skyhorse Publishing

Skyhorse Publishing books may be purchased in bulk at special discounts for sales promotion, corporate gifts, fund-raising, or educational purposes. Special editions can also be created to specifications. For details, contact the Special Sales Department, Skyhorse Publishing, 307 West 36th Street, 11th Floor, New York, NY 10018 or info@ skyhorsepublishing.com.

Skyhorse® and Skyhorse Publishing® are registered trademarks of Skyhorse Publishing, Inc.®, a Delaware corporation.

Visit our website at www.skyhorsepublishing.com.

10 9 8 7 6 5 4 3 2 1

Library of Congress Cataloging-in-Publication Data

Leben, Chris, 1980-
    The crippler: cage fighting and my life on the edge / by Chris Leben, with Daniel Patinkin.
        pages cm
    ISBN 978-1-63450-566-6 (hardcover: alk. paper)—ISBN 978-1-5107-0135-9 (ebook) 1.
Leben, Chris, 1980- 2. Mixed martial arts—Biography. I. Title.
    GV1102.7.M59L43 2016
    796.8092—dc23
    [B]

                                2015029058

Cover design by Rain Saukas
Cover photo: AP Images

Printed in the United States of America

# CONTENTS

# INTRODUCTION
# PERSPECTIVE

Some people think I am a hero; others think I am the anti-Christ. Some people consider me the biggest dumbfuck who ever put on pants; others consider me an insightful person with a worthwhile perspective on the world. Some view me as an important trailblazer in the history of the sport of mixed martial arts; still others view me as a loudmouth thug who gained notoriety by being in the right place at the right time and by behaving like a reckless nutcase.

Some portion of each of those viewpoints—maybe even all of them in their entirety—are true at the same time. I acknowledge both sides of my coin without shame and without hesitation. I am a man, and I am a monster. I walk on that curved line that divides the yin from the yang. I am Chris Leben. I am the Crippler. And, like it or not, I exist on this planet.

For over ten years, I was a notable fighter in the MMA universe. During that time, almost eight years of which were with the UFC, I compiled a record of 22–11. That's not, by far, the best record ever strung together by a mixed martial artist. However, I can say that, quite honestly, I squared off with some of the most skilled and dangerous hand-to-hand combatants to ever walk the face of earth. Some of them I bested, even knocked out. Others kicked the piss out of me. That's the fight game, after all. Drive a car long enough, and you're gonna get in a wreck. Sooner or later, no matter how great you are, your number will come up. The fight will end with you on your back, or with plasma dripping from your face, or with your head hung in shame because you just didn't have what it takes that night. An MMA fighter must deal with this painful inevitability.

I think it is fair to say I was a very good fighter—maybe even a great fighter—at times. But I was never the best, no matter how hard I tried or how badly I wanted it. As a result, you may be wondering why you should give two shits about what's contained in the next couple hundred pages. When the shelves are stocked with biographies and autobiographies of athletes who truly stood head and shoulders above their furious competition, why should you take the precious time to read a whole book about a not-quite-championship-caliber fighter who has pissed off as many people as he has pleased? Why not clap this book shut and find the nearest Barnes & Noble that has Ronda Rousey's book or B. J. Penn's book or Georges St-Pierre's book in stock?

The simple answer is this: none of them are me. Regardless of my shortcomings (of which there are many), I can boldly and confidently claim that there has never been another human being who has experienced life quite the way I have. In a world where the vast majority of people eke out a living, get laid a few times, and then die, I have made it my mission to forge a path all my own. To collect the most extreme of experiences. To suck the hot, sticky marrow from the bones of our inexplicable existence. What you read here might disgust you, shock you, terrify you. Or it might amaze and excite you. Probably all of those things. But I think when you make it through to this book's final words, you will agree with me that I've done to this thing called life in an obscenely unique way.

When I first announced on Twitter that I was writing this book, one of my followers replied with a hilarious tweet:

*I got drunk a lot. The end.*

I laughed my ass off at that. The "drunk a lot" part is very true. Yet, this mockery demonstrates how little most people know about me aside from the parts of my public persona that have reached the surface. My goal in writing this book is to give my readers an inside look at my erratic life. I want you to share the ups and downs, the hard choices and celebrations, and the victories and failures of a multilayered, highly emotional, and flawed human being who had the guts (or maybe the idiocy) to pursue his dreams with reckless abandon. Because, at the end of the day, I think we all embody these shortcomings and challenges, although most people don't express them with the kind of madness that I have.

You *will* have a reaction to this book, one way or another. I guarantee that. And my hope is that after you put this book down (or throw it out, or burn it . . .), you will feel compelled to reflect on your own life and on the lives of others. I want it to force you to wrestle with issues of morality and fear and insanity and love that you have never had reason to wrestle. One word sums it up: perspective. I want this book to give my readers perspective they've never had before. The human experience is an ocean of confusion and complexity, and I think that the best way to navigate is to get the broadest lay of the land you can. You'll have a better chance of reaching your desired destination if you have a 360-degree, high and low, backward and forward viewpoint than if you are just looking through a periscope. And, as you allow your gaze to sweep the terrain, sometimes you'll witness a glorious sunset over majestic mountaintops. Other times you'll get a close-up look at a festering pile of dogshit.

Now, a little something about the writing of this book. I did not personally put any of the words on the pages. My writer, Daniel Patinkin, did all of that. We met for the first time in early 2014 through my manager, a crazy little Persian-Swede named Bobby Cavian. The reason I gave Daniel 100 percent of the writing duties is pretty simple: I can barely write. In fact, I think that until my early twenties, I would have been classified as illiterate. So, of course, taking it upon myself to put all of my experiences and thoughts on paper was out of the question. Instead, over eighteen months, Daniel and I spent hours and hours together—in person, on the phone, and over Skype—recounting the wild shitstorm that is my life. I think, in all, Daniel recorded something along the lines of forty hours of interviews for this book. In the process, I believe he grew to understand me almost as well as anyone.

So I would tell Daniel stories and stories and stories. He would do his best to efficiently structure our interviews, a task that I do not envy. I definitely have a healthy dose of ADD, and Daniel struggled to keep me on the train tracks. Sometimes he would even fly out to stay with me for a few days in order to really get the full Crippler experience. Then, after collecting a big mess of information, Daniel would head off into his writer's cocoon or wherever and bang out a chapter or two. Some time later, we'd reconvene to review and revise the material. But, because I can't read well enough, Daniel would have to recite everything he wrote to me. Most of what Daniel wrote I loved right off the bat. Plenty of it, however, we scrapped. It has been a long, emotional, and painstaking process—a labor of love.

I should also take a moment to point out that everything in this book is true. Or, more precisely, in these pages I am telling the truth *to the best of my ability*. Keep in mind that I made a living by getting punched in the face, and that I have done enough drugs to kill a herd of wildebeest. I'm sure that many of my brain cells have been wiped out. And the ones that are left don't always function perfectly. So, while the occasional detail might be out of whack, if there's one positive thing that I can say about myself it is that I am honest to a fault. Telling the truth has set me free. It has also gotten me in a lot of trouble when a little white lie or some silence would have done the trick. To be clear, although Daniel did a lot to bring these stories to life and to fill in the blanks when our interviews or my recollection did not provide all of the flavor we needed, I never allowed him to embellish in a way that would inappropriately distort the truth.

That said, some people might remember differently some of the anecdotes that you will read in this book. Hell, I get tripped up from time to time when I attempt to relive my history. There's a lot of fog in my past. I know, for example, that I once gave an interview in which I recalled trashing a public bathroom in the Hard Rock Casino prior to my fight with Brian Stann. In reality, that episode occurred before my fight with Patrick Côté, and you will read about it in detail in the first chapter of this book. I preemptively apologize if I screwed up the order of some events or misremembered a fact here and there. It's definitely not intentional.

I also want to let you know that there are many omissions in this book. There are plenty of stories that Daniel and I discussed that were left on the cutting room floor, as they say. There are several reasons that this might have happened. First of all, sometimes there just wasn't a place for the story. The book, of course, had to have a reasonable flow to it, focusing on a limited set of themes that deserve special attention. As much as I like to tell stories, I couldn't turn this book into a tedious accounting of every somewhat interesting moment in my life.

I also left some things out to protect people, including myself. I've been behind bars more than a dozen times in my life. So it should come as no surprise that a fair share of my friends and I have made a habit of breaking the law. I definitely want this book to be a success and to generate some buzz, but I don't want it to jeopardize the reputations and livelihoods of the people that I care about. In order to protect the innocent (and the guilty) I had to let some sleeping dogs lie. In some instances in this book, I have even used fake names.

So, here it is: all that's fit to print and a whole heap of shit that isn't. I hope this book fucks up your world!

Chris "The Crippler" Leben
July 2015

# CHAPTER 1
# VS. CÔTÉ

The alarm went off, ruthlessly and repeatedly, until I awoke from my drunken haze and peered through bloodshot eyes at the bedside clock. 8:04 AM. Fuck. I slapped the clock off of the nightstand and it crashed to the floor. The blaring ceased. Another knockout, I guess, though not a hard-fought one.

As consciousness slowly took hold of my body, so too did a growing sense of agony. I had been hungover countless times before, but this episode had a ripe kick to it. My eyes struggled to adjust to the morning sunshine that wedged in through the curtained window. I was in a hotel, for sure, but for the moment I could not recall which one or why I was there. Both the present and the recent past were a blur. Then I noticed a sour and utterly disgusting odor—one I was not a stranger to. Fully clothed, I rolled over and found myself in a broad puddle of my own vomit.

Fuck.

The phone rang, sending shockwaves through my head. I contemplated tearing it out of the wall and giving it the alarm clock treatment but could not summon the energy. So I let it ring and forced myself to sit up. My feet found the floor, which was also glazed with puke. It seeped between my toes, and I fought back the need to retch again. I stood up and wobbled over to the window. I pulled the curtains apart and sunlight washed over me like an unholy baptism.

I shielded my eyes with my forearm for a few moments until I could finally take in the bright world beyond the window. A busy airport stretched out to my left. In the distance, cars and trucks zipped up and down a wide interstate. And, in the foreground, an imposing black pyramid. It was coming back to me now. That was the Luxor Hotel, and further to the right were the Excalibur and New York, New York casinos. Sin City, of course. Below me, already active at this early hour, was the fabled Strip. I squinted to read a billboard that towered over Las Vegas Boulevard.

> *Ultimate Fight Night*
> *August 6, 2005*
> *Cox Pavilion—Paradise, Nevada*

Son of a bitch, it was fight week. Wednesday, to be precise. And in just three days I would be stepping into an eight-sided cage for my thirteenth professional mixed martial arts fight.

For the uninitiated, mixed martial arts (MMA) is a combat sport that features one-on-one fights between athletes enclosed in an open-top cage. The Ultimate Fighting Championship (UFC) is the leading organization in the world that produces and promotes MMA contests. Whereas in boxing punches are the only allowed offensive maneuvers, in MMA the fighter can attack with punches, kicks, grappling techniques, chokes, throws, limb manipulation, and more. World-class experts in karate, kickboxing, freestyle wrestling, Brazilian jiu-jitsu, boxing, judo, taekwondo, Sambo, and Greco-Roman wrestling have all appeared in professional MMA events.

Is MMA the same as or similar to professional wrestling? I get asked that question all the time, and the answer is flat-out NO! The kind of professional wrestling that is produced by organizations like the WWE—though physical and somewhat dangerous—is not real improvised combat. It is a choreographed performance of stunts and acrobatics with, for the most part, a predetermined outcome. An MMA fight, on the other hand, is actual hand-to-hand battle between highly trained, modern-day gladiators. The knockouts are real. The blood and bruises are real. The pain is real. Nothing is staged or faked.

The phone stopped ringing. I stood there, mostly covered in bile and regurgitated booze, wondering if I would be in condition to perform that weekend. Would I be able to make weight on Friday? Would my body recover from this epic hangover in time for me to survive a three-round brawl against a world-class striker? And how the hell did I allow myself to get so wasted in the first place? Actually, I didn't ask myself that last question. There was never a need to justify getting absolutely smashed. It's something I had been doing, almost on a daily basis, since I was about fifteen years old.

My whereabouts were coming into focus, but I couldn't exactly piece together what had happened over the past twelve hours or so. The last thing I remembered was meeting my brother Tyler at a margarita stand near Caesar's Palace. He worked there four nights a week those days, blending low-quality tequila, crushed ice, and margarita mix. He was like a minimum-wage medicine man, enthusiastically distributing the potent cocktail in plastic yard glasses to tourists eager to tie one on and forget about their shitty lives back in suburban Ohio and Little Rock, Arkansas. In short, at twenty-six years old, with a meth problem and not a pot to piss in, my brother was an aimless degenerate. But I didn't judge him too harshly. That was par for the course in my family. I was a degenerate, too, after all—just not so aimless.

I stripped off my soiled clothing and stepped into the shower. I cranked the water temperature as high as I could bear in the hopes that the intense heat would somehow detoxify my blood and ease my nausea. This, again, was not foreign territory for me. During the two-month training camp leading up to this fight, I had shown up hungover to most of my early practices. I actually harbored a deranged sense of pride in the fact that, chemically impaired, I was able to complete the grueling strength and conditioning sessions that coach Matt Hume put us through each morning. My teammates there in Seattle at the American Martial Arts Center (AMC), for the most part, wouldn't have considered drinking more than a glass of wine the night before one of these sessions, much less three or four sixteen-ounce tallboys of malt liquor, as was my regular practice.

I let the hot water fall heavily onto the top of my head, its rumbling spray soothing my skull. Despite the pain, I was not ashamed of myself—not consciously at least. I come from a family in which, truly, beer is a breakfast item. I'm not kidding. On the weekends, if you didn't have a can of Schlitz in your hand by 10:00 AM, then you were either in bed with pneumonia or you were a fucking weirdo as far as we were concerned. My mother was a big time drinker. My brother Tyler, my uncles, my aunts— all outrageous boozehounds. I was raised to get drunk in the same way that regular boys are raised to brush their teeth. It was daily, encouraged, and routine. So, until well into my adulthood, shame was not even a recognizable part of that equation.

But depression was.

In the past few years I have come to realize that I have suffered from recurring depression since about the age of ten. And, though I did not understand it that way, as I stood in the MGM Grand Hotel shower, a creek of scum flowing into the drain, I was depressed. I could not put my finger on it, exactly, but my emotions were off-kilter. And I was pretty sure that it had to do with the murky proceedings of the night before. I was three days away from my second fight in the UFC. Spiritually, though, I would have preferred to curl up in a ball in a dark room for a month. To be clear, I was not suicidal. There was no way I was ready to take my own life (at least not at that point). However, I did have an unhealthy preoccupation with death. I frequently thought about whether I would kill myself one day and, if that day came, precisely how I would do it. I imagined, even fantasized about, putting the barrel of a Smith & Wesson in my mouth or hanging myself from an oak tree. I learned later that this is called "suicidal ideation," and that it is a basic symptom of depression.

When I stepped out of the shower, the phone began to ring again. Goddamn, somebody really wanted to reach me. I hurried back into the bedroom, avoiding the patches of barf that marked the carpet in various spots, and grabbed the receiver.

"Hello?"

"Chris?" It was a woman's voice.

"Yes?"

"This is Anne at the UFC. What are you doing in your hotel room?"

She was urgent and concerned. My mind began to race. Was something wrong? It was so early in the morning. Why were they calling me?

I replied, "I was just . . . er . . . showering. Is there a problem?"

"Well, yes, there is," she said. "We're waiting for you here at the Cox Pavilion. You were supposed to be here at eleven for your photo shoot."

I looked at the alarm clock I had smacked to the floor. It read 8:20 AM. I was confused. Did I incorrectly set the time in my drunken stupor the night before?

"What time is it?" I asked.

"Eleven forty," she replied with irritation.

Before every event, the UFC conducts a photo and video shoot of each of the participating fighters. The photos from these are then used on promotional materials, broadcast within the arena during events, and shown between bouts on the television broadcast. When I finally arrived on set for my shoot, the first person I bumped into was UFC president Dana White. He rolled his eyes and shouted for all to hear, "Thanks for finally rolling out of bed, Leben! We're happy to stand around waiting for you, princess. Don't mind us!"

Though I grew to like and respect Dana, he was frequently as surly as he was bald. Then again, running an MMA promotion and overseeing dozens and dozens of hard-ass fighters most definitely requires a certain disposition.

Embarrassed and still feeling garbage slosh around in my belly, I took my place in the makeup chair. I would have felt even shittier except my good pal and fellow Team Quest fighter Nate Quarry was also there waiting his turn.

"Don't worry," he said sarcastically, patting me on the back, "I don't have any other obligations until Saturday."

Nate and I were on the same team during the notorious first season of a reality show known as *The Ultimate Fighter*. And now, we were both appearing in the UFC's very first *Ultimate Fight Night* event. He, as you will learn, has been a voice of reason throughout my adult life.

As the promotional team finished their work with me, my impending opponent, Patrick Côté, arrived. Though I had never met him, Côté seemed like an impressive dude. A French-Canadian Muay Thai kickboxing specialist, he had a 6–2 professional MMA record by the time we crossed paths. This included three knockouts and a submission by rear-naked choke. He was training at the Brazilian Top Team in Quebec alongside the likes of Georges St-Pierre—who would go on to be the greatest UFC welterweight champion of all time—and tough middleweight David Loiseau.

Côté had recently battled the former UFC light heavyweight champion Tito Ortiz to a decision. During that fight, which took place at 205 pounds, he actually once dropped Ortiz with a right hook. Though Ortiz arose and won the fight, the MMA world was shocked by the Canadian's chin and ability to throw a punch. Patrick Côté was not the greatest fighter in the world (no, I would fight the *greatest* fighter in the world three years later), but he was a tough bastard who could put mean men to sleep with his hands. In fact, Côté went on to fight for the middleweight championship (against, yes, that very same *greatest* fighter in the world).

I had seen Côté conduct an interview earlier in the week and noticed how clean-cut and well spoken he was. For a moment I thought to myself, *This guy doesn't seem that tough*. But then I remembered that, in mixed martial arts, such thinking is a cardinal sin. The saying "don't judge a book by its cover" does not come close to expressing the pitfalls of assessing an MMA opponent by his baby face or his haircut or, for that matter, his physique. Legendary fighters like B. J. Penn, Nate Diaz, Lyoto Machida, and Martin Kampmann probably wouldn't raise many eyebrows walking down the street. But they are each world-class warriors who would beat you to a pulp if you stepped into the cage. My friend and training partner Myles "Fury" Jury looks like a fucking mama's boy who would be more comfortable in a book club than a bar fight (sorry to say it, Myles!). But, I would not be the least bit surprised if he wears a UFC title strap one day. Likewise, Patrick Côté, as it would turn out, was one of the grittiest, most hardnosed fighters I ever went toe-to-toe with.

On my way out of the building after the photo shoot a young reporter approached me, holding out an audio recorder. He was short and heavyset with big black plugs in his ear lobes. These grungy punk types were always at the core of my fan base, and I was happy to have them. Unfortunately, I can't remember this particular reporter's name or what publication he represented. However, during those days, when the sport had only a marginal fan base, it was unlikely that he worked for anything more significant than a popular regional fighting blog.

"You were very emotional and erratic during your stint on *The Ultimate Fighter*," he began. "How has your mental approach to the sport changed in the past six months?"

"I have my emotions under control, now," I replied, lying through my teeth. "I've grown a lot."

Many UFC fans remember my infamous role in the very first season of *The Ultimate Fighter* (*TUF*), a reality show about a group of MMA fighters who live and train together while they vie for a contract with the UFC. I won't discuss it in too much detail in this chapter except to say that, by conventional standards, I was an out-of-control emotional mess during the two months of filming. And, truth be told, I had taken no steps since that time to address my psychological issues. In fact, the problems seemed to have grown worse.

When the reporter finished his line of questioning, my brother appeared. In a wrinkled shirt and blues jeans that were long overdue for a wash, he looked as haggard as I felt. But, as always, he had a mischievous smile on his face.

"Dude, last night was epic!" he exclaimed.

I grabbed him hard by the arm and told him to shut the fuck up. Dana White was somewhere nearby, and the last thing I needed to do was broadcast the details of my wild partying of the previous night. Tyler quieted down and we headed down the street.

"I don't think I've ever seen you so fucked up, bro," he continued.

"What happened?" I asked.

"You nearly tore apart the whole fucking Hard Rock Casino! I figured you'd be in jail right now. But somehow, you're standing here."

Tyler went on to explain in great detail how a group of fanatical Irishmen joined us at the margarita stand before moving on to a bar at the Hard Rock. Those Irish, as we all know, have livers like industrial garbage disposals. And many of them love nothing more than to drink through the night and cause a ruckus. Until early the next morning we told stories, talked shit, and consumed all sorts of booze—beer, whiskey, tequila, rum. Egged on by the mickies, I seemed to be gunning for a personal record. Then, Tyler revealed, at some point I got up and stumbled to the bathroom, where I shattered a sink and kicked down three marble toilet stalls.

"I hardly remember any of that," I said.

"Well, it happened, bro. We can go survey the aftermath at the Hard Rock right now if you want."

Tyler and the Irishmen only realized that something was amiss when they saw two security guards marching me across the casino floor, my shirt torn and my hands in steel cuffs. The guys tried to intervene, but the security guards warned that if my drunken pals didn't back off they'd find themselves joining me in the jailhouse.

"That's why I'm surprised to see you here, man!" Tyler continued. "I figured that was felony property damage and that you'd be behind bars 'til someone posted a shitload of bail for you!"

But, as far as I knew, the only cage I would see that week would be the UFC Octagon. To this day, I'm not exactly sure how the situation resolved itself. Somewhere, in the back of my mind, I seem to remember trying to bribe my way out of the situation. Maybe someone else did the bribing for me. Or perhaps the security guards turned me over to a sheriff who was a big fight fan. Could Dana White have gotten involved, using his powerful Las Vegas influence? Who knows.

"Fuck, Tyler," I lamented. "I can't believe you let me do that. Do you want me to get kicked out of the goddamn UFC?"

"Since when have I ever been your babysitter?" he retorted.

I couldn't argue with that point. Tyler was eighteen months my senior, but he had never looked out for me. Not once. In fact, throughout a big portion of our childhood, he was a cruel bully.

"What set me off?" I asked. "Why was I tearing up that bathroom?"

Tyler lowered his eyes—a rare display of shame.

"I told you about Dad," he said.

"What about Dad?"

Tyler seemed hesitant to reveal anything more, justifiably so considering my previous reaction. But then he came out with it.

"He wants to come see you fight."

And, as I stood there outside of the Cox Pavilion, my heart dropped into my gut.

My father is, for the most part, a no-good son of a bitch. He ditched my mother when I was two years old and skipped town, leaving her to tend to two young boys in a shack on the dirty side of Portland, Oregon. He never paid child support and never made an effort to contribute to our upbringing. In fact, I blamed him for most of the heartache and misery I had experienced in life up to that point. At the age of twenty-five, as I readied to fight Patrick Côté, I had only actually met my father once, when he unexpectedly reached out to me the previous spring while I was auditioning for the first season of *The Ultimate Fighter*.

In March 2004, the UFC contacted me through Matt Lindland to invite me to Las Vegas to try out for the show. Matt Lindland was one of the founders and head coaches at Team Quest in Portland. I trained there for years during the early part of my career. Not only did Matt have a notable MMA career in the UFC and other promotions, he was a silver medalist in Greco-Roman wrestling at the 2000 Olympics in Sydney. When he gave me the phone message, I could hardly believe my ears. I returned the call of the UFC representative, who made it extremely clear that the audition process was to remain completely secretive. I could not share the news with my friends or family. I had to sneak down to Vegas, do my thing, and keep my mouth shut. But, it didn't exactly turn out that way. As I boarded the plane from Portland to Las Vegas, I ran into my good buddy and training partner Ed "Short Fuse" Herman. He, obviously, was headed down there for the same reason, and there was no point in bullshitting each other about it. We spent the flight talking about what might be the best strategy for earning a spot on the *TUF* show.

Once we arrived, the UFC immediately sequestered each of us in our own rooms at the MGM. They didn't even provide us with room keys because they wanted us to come out of hiding only for scheduled events and meetings related to the *TUF* tryouts. I was supposed to be there for four days: one day of interviews followed by two or three days of physical performance assessments and fighting evaluations. Soon after I settled in, I was called down to a meeting room in the MGM. A woman led me inside, where there was nothing except for a video camera on a tripod facing an unoccupied wooden chair. She explained to me that, for this part of the audition, my job was to talk to the camera and tell it why I would be an excellent selection for the television show. It sounded like an awkward thing to do, but if there's one thing that my friends know about me, it's that I am never at a loss for words—especially when the topic is *me*! The only thing faster than my hands, I've been known to say, is my mouth!

The woman left the room. I took a seat on the chair and immediately broke into an enthusiastic speech about why I was a tough motherfucker and why the viewing public should give a shit about me. In my last two fights—against Mike Swick and Boyd Ballard—I had delivered two massive knockouts. I was riding high and felt invincible. As I recall, I shouted at the camera about the thunder in my left hand, and about what a dangerous man I was. I may have even pounded my chest at one point. (At least, that was the kind of mood I recall being in.)

Suddenly, in the middle of my rant, the door on the far side of the room swung open. In walked Dana White and one of the producers of the show. Obviously, they had been watching my performance and they were laughing their asses off. Dana came up to me, put an arm around my shoulders and said, "Enough! We've seen enough! You're a madman and you're definitely going to be on the show."

I could hardly believe it. I was just getting warmed up, but, apparently, that was sufficient for them. They did not even require me to participate in the physical and fighting portions of the tryouts. I had my golden ticket. They congratulated me and sent me back to my room.

That was one of my proudest moments as an adult. It was the first time I learned that I actually had value in the world. Sure, I had done well as a high school wrestler and had won a half-dozen or so professional MMA fights. However, I was making peanuts, and only handfuls of people in the world had even heard of me. This was different. Not only was the UFC going to pay me a little bit of money to appear on *TUF*, the show was going to be broadcast to the entire country on the Spike TV cable channel. Finally, I had been given a moment in the sun. I was on cloud nine when I got back to my room and flopped down on my bed. Smiling to myself, I imagined that I would become a national hero and, just as importantly, get laid a lot.

Then my cell phone rang.

I checked the caller ID, but did not recognize the number. I debated whether to answer before finally giving in to my curiosity. Hesitantly, I flipped open the phone.

"Hello?"

"Chris?" came the reply.

"Yes?"

"Chris, it's Frank Ellis . . . your father."

For what seemed like an eternity, I froze. I stopped breathing and felt my face go numb. It was as if a comic book super-villain had come to life and was saying my name. After a long silence, my father continued speaking. His voice was abrasive and deep, just like mine, but tinged with a quiver of humility. The sound of it immediately sent me back to my childhood. Although, when he was last a presence in my life I was too young to form long-term memories, I think his voice had embedded itself in my subconscious brain. As I lay there in bed, the phone pressed to my ear, a wave of powerful and disturbing emotions washed over me. Clearly, whatever remnants of my father still clung to my psyche were completely destructive. My hand shook and my mouth went dry. And, as he went on to explain that he lived not far from the

MGM and that he hoped we could have a drink that night, all I could do was fight back tears and listen.

Finally, my father finished speaking. Against my better judgment, and apparently mesmerized by his unexpected reappearance in my life, I agreed to meet him.

Throughout my life, my mother has told a handful of stories about my father, virtually all of them negative. They had a very turbulent marriage before he ditched the family. Both he and she were alcoholics, he an especially unpredictable one. His frequent use of coke and crystal meth further stoked the fire. Many a dish was broken during their arguments. My dad hardly provided for the family even during my mother's pregnancies, choosing instead to blow the bulk of his earnings in the local saloons and at the horse track.

In my dad's absence, the only father figure I knew during my childhood was a Harley rider named Dave, who linked up with my mom when I was a tot. He was a decent guy and a hard worker. And, although Dave and my mother never married, he helped provide for us for about five years. Reminiscing on Dave, I often find myself smiling. He was a great storyteller, a party animal, and ready with a hug when I needed one. But Dave passed on when I was in third grade, and the remainder of my formative years was spent in a mostly empty house with a terrorist of a brother and a stressed-out mother who was only occasionally present. It would have been nice to have a decent male role model during that time. It would have been nice to have a friend.

After ending the conversation with my father and hanging up I felt paralyzed. I didn't know what to do, where to go, or how to react. A tornado of thoughts and emotions swirled in my mind. A big part of me wished nothing but misery on this faceless man who was little more than a sperm donor to me. However, another part of me was filled with curiosity and, yes, even optimism. Maybe I would learn that my father had turned his life around and we would be able to forge a new relationship. I imagined that he might become a source of support for me, guiding me through the rough patches of life, maybe providing a couple of bucks here and there when times were tight. Hell, to this day I'm the last person to deny someone the benefit of the doubt or the faith that a guy can change.

My heart jumped with the hope that my dad and I could one day make up for lost time and, though he was never a father to me, that he could be a grandfather to the kids I would bear. But then I slapped myself in the face. "Be more realistic, Chris," I told myself cynically. "When have you ever had that kind of good fortune?"

As I lay there marinating in emotional confusion, I felt like I was on the verge of a mental breakdown. I needed to talk to someone, and that someone happened to be down the hallway. I jumped out of bed and ran down to good ol' Eddie Herman's room.

Adjacent to the rows of armchairs, side tables, and ashtrays that furnish the sportsbook betting area at the MGM Casino, there is a small bar where young party guys or emphysemic old ladies can grab a quick beer or shot in between wagers. This is where I was supposed to meet my dad. However, I wasn't going to do it alone. I had been able to convince Eddie to accompany me for moral support even though hanging out in the casino was a violation of the rules the UFC had laid out for the *TUF* audition week. He's a good guy like that. As Eddie and I approached the rendezvous point, we debated about whether I should hug the old man, shake his hand, or just keep my hands in my pockets. As it turned out, we had plenty of time to think about this issue. My father didn't show up until nearly forty minutes after our scheduled meeting time. So I had a beer or two to calm my nerves. I insisted that Eddie do the same.

Before we knew it, a stocky middle-aged man suddenly appeared before us. He smiled weakly, and it was almost like staring into a tarnished mirror. Except for a tooth missing here and there, along with blotchy, overexposed skin and advanced male pattern baldness, he shared many of my features (and even more of my brother's). Neither of us offered a handshake. Neither of us moved in for a hug. It was like we were two deer shining flashlights in each other's eyes, until, mercifully, Eddie broke the ice and suggested that we all have a shot of whiskey.

That did the trick. After throwing back our shots, everyone relaxed a bit. The conversation that followed was underwhelming, but my mind—desperate for my father's affection—seemed to add special significance to it. As we sipped our beers, the old man and I didn't even broach the subject of our family's past—the divorce, the abandonment, the twenty-three years of absence. Instead he filled me in about his job as a construction worker in Vegas, and about the small house he had not far from the Strip. He told me that, though he hadn't witnessed any of my fights, he had heard from Tyler that I was a hell of a brawler.

"He says you're tough as nails, Chris. That makes a father proud."

Wow. The approval of my father. That was the first time I had ever felt the warmth and satisfaction that a father's pride creates. Though, in retrospect, his gruff words may have been the manipulative ramblings of a selfish, unfeeling dickhead, I was on top of the world. The three of us threw back another shot or two, shared with each other a handful of offensive jokes and obnoxious stories, and then decided to call it a night. I paid the tab.

Though the meeting provided little upon which to base a lasting relationship, I was optimistic about the future. My father seemed like a decent guy who had long ago atoned for his sins. Most importantly, he was funny and shared my loud-mouthed, demented sense of humor. We shook hands, and he patted me on the back.

"Chris," he said. "You turned out well."

"Thanks," I replied earnestly. "It's good to see you. Hopefully, you'll be able to watch me kick some ass on TV."

"I'm confident you will. You, too, Ed."

"I haven't won a spot on the show yet, but I'll do my best," Ed replied.

My father smiled and hesitated for a moment before speaking again.

"I hate to do it, but I have to ask you a favor," he said.

"Sure. What do you need?"

"Just a few bucks to get me through the weekend. I get a check on Monday and I'll pay you back." My father looked at his feet and shifted back and forth. Out of the corner of my eye, I could see Eddie's jaw drop.

"How much?" I asked.

"A hundred," he said without hesitation.

With the benefit of hindsight, I now recognize that my father, on the very first night after a two-decade absence, was taking advantage of me. If he tried to shine me on like that today, I would tell him to go fuck himself. At least, I like to think I'm older and wiser to that kind of bullshit (which probably is not the case). But back then, a few sheets to the wind and with the wool pulled over my eyes, I didn't think twice. I pulled out my wallet and went straight to the ATM.

Then fourteen months went by without a word from the old man.

What had caused me to go on my restroom rampage a year later on the Tuesday night before my fight with Côté was not only the fact that my old man wanted to come to the fight but also Tyler's revelation that he had actually taken up residence with that bald bastard in Las Vegas. The news, of course, initiated a massive crying and yelling argument right in front of the bawdy Irishmen. I had no interest in seeing that conman again. He had his chance. The fucker could drink himself into a hole as far as I was concerned. And, on top of that, I was pissed that my brother was dumb enough to link up with that bastard. I felt betrayed.

But Tyler explained that my father felt horrible about borrowing that money from me, and was too ashamed to call me and tell me he couldn't pay me back. He wanted to come to the fight because he finally had some dough to give me. But, more importantly, he wanted to support me in the hopes that our relationship could be salvaged.

"I wouldn't cross the street to spit on that guy," I told Tyler.

"But he's your dad," Tyler replied.

"I don't care if he's the fucking Pope."

Tyler eyed me carefully.

"You've never made a mistake that you wished someone else would forgive?" he asked.

And, with that, my shell cracked. I, of course, had made countless mistakes in my past that I regretted immensely—screw-ups that had hurt my friends and family. I paced and rubbed my head, knowing that I had lost the battle.

"If he fucks up again, it's all over," I warned Tyler. "I won't give him a third chance." But as the words left my lips, both Tyler and I knew that, if it came down to it, I'd give Dad many more chances than that. An abandoned heart is a weak heart.

I agreed to ask for a special favor from Dana White: to provide me with two front-row tickets to the fight, for Tyler and my father. But it was not going to be easy sailing. After my antics on *TUF 1* and my late arrival to the photo shoot that morning, I was pretty sure I was on Dana's shit list. The last thing the boss man owed me was a favor.

I should mention that all of this emotional turmoil and debauchery was occurring during the very time I was supposed to be supremely focused on my weight cut for the fight with Patrick Côté. Generally, in the week leading up to a fight, I would drop around twenty-five pounds via diet and dehydration. Because such extreme measures are exceptionally damaging to a fighter's body, especially the kidneys, we (I mean, most fighters) tend to be very careful to put only pure and natural foods and beverages into our systems during fight week. I'm sure that the doctors who are reading this book, if any, are pulling their hair out at the revelation that I was drinking heavily while at the same time undertaking a massive weight cut. That could have been a death sentence.

Needless to say, when Friday rolled around I was still in bad shape from my Tuesday-night bender. I woke up at eight o'clock feeling like death warmed over. Then I spent the next four hours on the treadmill and in the sauna, sweating out as much water as possible. At noon, with the weigh-ins just an hour away, Nate Quarry noticed that I had big black circles under my eyes. He was concerned that my appearance would generate scrutiny from the Nevada State Athletic Commission (NSAC). If their doctors deemed me unfit to fight, I would have had to bow out and give up my purse. (Actually, I was in such a wretched state at the time that this did not seem like a horrible option.) However, scratching the fight not only would have hit my pocketbook hard, it would have been a severe setback in my career. More importantly, my dad was coming to the event. I couldn't pull out. I had to show him that I had grown into a real man—a man's man.

So I did the next logical thing: I had a friend buy some eyeliner at the Walgreens and I went to work darkening the edges of my eyelids. Not only did it look rock-and-roll, the makeup, I figured, would draw attention away from the fact that the rest of my face could have belonged to a corpse. Also it fit well with my hair, which, as usual, I had dyed a fiery shade of red. As I waited for the weigh-ins to begin and mingled with various other fighters, UFC representatives, and, yes, officials from the NSAC, I felt straight-up ill and ready to collapse. But nobody was the wiser.

The announcer called my name and I emerged from backstage for my public weighing. The crowd that has assembled for the spectacle went berserk as I climbed the stairs to the stage. I felt wobbly and was concerned that I would keel over in front of everyone. However, the overwhelming energy of the fans held me up. I had never yet experienced that kind of roaring adoration. This was my first real fight in the Octagon since completing my stint on *The Ultimate Fighter*. Though I'm not sure I deserved it, it was now clear that, since *TUF* aired, fans were starting to back me in a big way. What a feeling! I took my place on the scale and weighedin at 185.5 pounds, just a half pound below the limit. Patrick Côté and I squared up on stage, nose-to-nose, jostling each other and talking shit. The photographers snapped away and the crowd absolutely ate it up.

Saturday, August 6, 2005, was fight day. By the time I stepped outside of the MGM that morning at nine o'clock to track down a decent cup of coffee and have a chew of tobacco, the Las Vegas air was as hot as dragon breath. Walking along Las Vegas Boulevard, I thought about how interesting this period of time was for fighters in my 185-pound weight class. My division, middle-weight, was not yet a top draw within the UFC in the way that the 205-pound class was. That roster had household names on it such as Randy Couture, Vitor Belfort, Tito Ortiz, and, of course, Chuck Liddell. Millions of people knew, loved, and followed these men. By contrast, back then you'd have a very hard time finding anyone other than a diehard fight fan who could name a premier 185-pounder. In fact, the UFC middleweight belt was vacant for more than three years until Evan Tanner TKO'd David Terrell to capture it in February of 2005.

However, now the UFC was setting up for an aggressive growth phase, cobbling together the middleweight division by dipping into *The Ultimate Fighter* reality show talent pool, and by poaching athletes from other organizations, including the WEC and Pancrase.

Things were changing—and fast. Tanner lost the belt on his next outing, absorbing one of the worst sustained beatings in the history of the UFC at the hands of the great Rich Franklin. When the doctor mercifully called an end to it in the fourth round, Tanner's eyebrow was split open and his head was as lumpy as a sack of potatoes. That was just two months earlier, on June 4.

So a sense of excitement grew among the middleweights on the UFC roster. The division was gaining momentum. Rich Franklin was our first burgeoning superstar, and the fans were taking notice. On top of that, the belt was within reach of a good number of fighters. Yes, Rich looked exceptionally tough and multidimensional in his four-round drubbing of Tanner. However, I was tough, too. And I was multidimensional. And by that time I had finished nine of my eleven professional opponents by knockout or submission. I knew that a win over Patrick Côté would not only give me the foothold I needed within the UFC but also propel me into the thick of the title hunt. There were only a handful of guys who were particularly deserving of a shot around that time, among them David Loiseau, Jeremy Horn, and Nate Quarry. That meant that with even the briefest of win streaks—two in a row perhaps, maybe three—I could find myself in the Octagon battling for the belt. I spent much of the day contemplating that notion and visualizing my glorious triumph over Côté.

There were eight match-ups on the fight card for *Ultimate Fight Night 1*. Chronologically, my scrap with Côté was sixth, right in the middle of the main card. Before the time came for me to make my way to the cage, I was able to watch the preceding fights on a monitor in my prep room. Kenny Florian, a welterweight back then, did enough damage to Alex Karalexis to get the doctor to intervene and stop the fight. Josh Koscheck, my nemesis (or so fans like to think), choked Pete Spratt until he submitted. Then my boy Nate Quarry finished Pete Sell with a punch in less than a minute. Overall, five of the bouts that night resulted in finishes—not a bad ratio for a UFC event.

To stand out from the crowd, I was going to have to put on one hell of a show against Patrick Côté. My hope, of course, was to put him to sleep with my left fist. However, my Brazilian jiu-jitsu skills had come a long way by then, and I had no doubt that, if it went to the ground, I could lock in an armbar or a choke. Côté was not known for his wrestling or grappling, so there was a fair likelihood that I would take him down and put a stop to it there. Either way, I knew that the Canadian they called "The Predator" would come out with guns blazing.

Finally my time arrived. The UFC hype man Burt Watson appeared in the door to my prep room. He escorted me down a long, desolate hallway with my cornermen following behind and shouting encouragements. I emerged from backstage and the crowd erupted. Fans screamed and waved and applauded and stamped their feet. They grabbed my hand and patted me on the back as I walked toward the cage. A videographer walked backward pointing his camera directly at my face, tracking my entrance. I heard one woman yell, "I love you, Crippler!" An older man shouted, "Knock that Canadian asshole out!"

But the one member of the audience that mattered to me most that night was, of course, my father. I was going to show him how far I had come, alone, without him. I was going to make him regret the day he ever walked out on our family, abandoning my mother, my brother, and me. But most most of all, I was going to make him proud. He'd see me in my most natural environment, at my best. And he'd realize that he'd want me to be part of his life, and him of mine. That night, I remember thinking, would start the healing process on two decades of paternal negligence that had scarred me so deeply that, as a child, I soaked my pillows with tears countless times before falling to sleep. That night, in the cage, and in my father's mind, I would leave no doubt.

I arrived at the staging area next to the cage and was met by famed MMA referee Big John McCarthy. I was so revved up that he kept telling me to keep still while he checked my hand wraps and frisked me for contraband. Assured that all was in order, he then sent me on my way into the cage.

When I entered the Octagon, I looked across the cage at my foe, Patrick Côté. He was bouncing and boxing the air—relaxed and ready. When our eyes met, we both smiled broadly. I wagged my finger in his direction and Côté chuckled appreciatively. That brief interaction communicated a clear mutual understanding between us. It meant, *Let's give these people what they paid for!* I took my place at the opposite side of the cage. No more waiting. It was time to smash. My smile grew bigger.

Octagon announcer Bruce Buffer took to the center of the cage and introduced us with the pomp and circumstance that only Bruce (and his famous brother, boxing ring announcer Michael Buffer) can muster. It was "The Predator" versus "The Crippler"—quite the battle of nicknames. Having whipped the crowd into a frenzy, Bruce stepped away, and it was referee Herb Dean's turn. Herb took a position in the center of the ring and asked Patrick and I, in succession, "Are you ready to fight?" Of course we were. "Let's go then!" shouted Herb.

We squared up in the center of the cage and evaluated each other briefly. I marched forward and, wary of my heavy left hand, Côté backed up. I charged and he threw the first punch of the fight, a hard right cross. But that was what I was expecting. I ducked under it and drove my shoulder into his gut, pinning him against the cage. I worked for the takedown, but, to my surprise, Côté's wrestling wasn't half bad; in fact, it was nearly as good as mine. He must have put some extensive work in with a wrestling coach or spent some extra time on the mat with the UFC's greatest wrestler—Georges St-Pierre. Côté pummeled under with his right arm and prevented me from getting a proper grip of his hips. We struggled in the clinch for the first part of the round, during which he threw a hard elbow and I responded with a left uppercut. He repeatedly drove strong knees into my midsection, and I responded by jacking his ribs with my left fist. After a while, the clinch became a stalemate and we separated and moved to the center of the cage. We circled briefly before Côté landed a straight right on my chin that made my legs wobble. I immediately countered with a left hook that smacked off of his cheek. He backed up, stunned. It was a nasty exchange that left us both clearing the cobwebs. I extended my fist as if to say, *Let's show them more of that.* Côté tapped my fist with his. The crowd loved it, and the fight continued.

The rest of the first round was an active back-and-forth scrap. We clinched against the fence and then separated to exchange punches. With about a minute and a half left, it really heated up. Côté decided he wanted to bang in the center of the cage. We started throwing everything we had behind our punches from both hands. He caught me with a nice left hook and a right hand, and I backed him up with a series of left hooks. We swung away until the round ended to a roar of appreciation.

I walked over to my corner and put my hands up on the cage. I knew it was a hell of a round and I wanted to see my father's reaction. So I looked over to the seats that I had obtained for him and my brother.

Tyler sat there, alone. My father was nowhere to be seen.

Tyler and I made eye contact and I gestured with concern, pointing to the empty seat. He shrugged his shoulders and shook his head shamefully. Perhaps my dad was off getting a beer somewhere. Or maybe he was taking a piss between rounds. Or maybe . . . Fuck. I knew the truth. He was a no-show. That motherfucker begged for a seat at my fight and then bailed. He was a worthless prick after all. And I was the numbnuts who had naively put faith in him. I immediately despised myself for it.

This was the worst possible mental state I could have experienced in the midst of a fight. When I should have been focused and motivated, I was instead distracted and crestfallen. I felt detached from my body, numb like someone had pumped me full of anesthetics. On autopilot, I nodded my head as my cornermen gave me instructions. Tears welled in my eyes.

Then my coach Robert Follis smacked me in the face. I looked at him.

"Where the fuck is your head, Chris?!"

"I'm fine," I lied.

"Focus on what's inside the cage, not what's out there!" he shouted. Robert was livid with me. He knew how susceptible I was to emotional instability. I had less than a minute to snap out of my funk or that heavy-handed Canadian would come out and steamroll me.

"You're right," I said spiritlessly.

He smacked me again.

"Chris! Let's go!" He was desperate to charge me up again. "This is your time! *Your* time! No one else's."

That last comment echoed in my ears as my cornermen gathered up the stool and water and headed out of the cage. Everything seemed to be happening in slow motion. I looked across to see Côté stand up to ready himself for the continued battle. *This is your time.* I heard those words again, allowing them to sink in. Then I said it to myself. *This is your time.* And in those few seconds, I began to believe in the truth of that statement. Goddammit, it *was my time.* I made it here through hard work and guts. I made it here through morning after morning of sacrifice and day after day of unwavering determination. Most importantly, I had made it here *without* my father. I simply could not allow him to unravel everything that I had woven together. I gritted my teeth as Herb Dean called a start to the second round.

The second round, to everyone's amazement, began even more wildly than the first ended. I backed Côté up to the fence, and we began trading haymaker after haymaker, one after another, our fists bouncing off chins and cheekbones. It was an offensive explosion. And, although that exchange only lasted five or six seconds, it felt like a full minute. When we finally separated, the entire crowd was on its feet. We spent the remainder of the round dirty boxing in the clinch and separating to throw heavier strikes.

I took him to the mat in the center of the cage and did my best to inflict some damage. But Côté's defensive guard was, like his wrestling, better than expected. And when the action stalled, Herb stood us back up. Finally, with five seconds left in the round I threw a kick and, in doing so, dropped my hands. Côté took advantage of the opportunity, firing a crisp left-right combo that dropped me to my back. He jumped on top of me, but the horn sounded, ending the round before he had a chance to deliver any real punishment.

I wobbled back to my corner and, this time, opted not to look toward my father's empty seat. Follis told me that I had to win the final round at all costs. By his count the fight was tied one round to each man. The fighter who performed in the final five minutes would steal the victory. My skull was ringing, but I remember saying to Follis, "Man, that guy has a head like a cinder block." Later that week, I learned from one of his cornermen that Côté made almost the same comment about me during the fight.

Herb started us up for the third time and the brawl continued. We clinched and then went toe-to-toe, lighting each other up. The offensive output was grueling. I pressed Côté against the cage and looked for a takedown. I barely had the energy to execute it, but finally he tripped, and we went to the floor. I knew that this was my chance to impress the judges and maybe even finish the fight with a TKO. So, from the top, I did everything I could to connect with fists and elbows. I used my anger as a weapon. *Fuck it!* I shouted inside my head as I dropped an elbow on Côté's forehead. *Fuck the depression. Fuck the drinking. Fuck the pain!* I pounded on his temple with a hammer fist. *Fuck the anger. Fuck that sperm donor who calls himself my dad.* And, for the final minute of the fight, I poured every ounce of energy and emotion into pummeling my foe. Then the final horn blew.

Under the current UFC fight-night bonus system, at the end of every UFC event Dana White awards $50,000 bonuses to the individuals that he deemed to have participated in the most exciting and competitive fight of the night. Unfortunately, that system was not put into place until after Côté and I danced. And it's too bad because, even though our war ended in a decision and not a knockout, I'm sure the two of us would have walked away from the Cox Pavilion with fat pocketbooks to go with our fat lips.

Bruce Buffer took to the center of the ring one more time to announce the decision. Herb Dean grabbed Côté and me by our wrists, positioning us at his side in preparation for the declaration of a winner.

"Ladies and gentlemen," Bruce bellowed into the microphone, "after three rounds of action we go to the judges scorecards for a decision. John Schorle scores the bout 29–28, Leben! Roy Silbert scores the bout 29–27, Côté! And Dalby Shirley scores the bout 30–27 for the winner by split-decision . . . 'The Crippler' Chris Leben!"

I threw both arms into the air, almost completely overwhelmed by the moment. I had triumphed—both emotionally and physically—in the toughest battle of my life. I marched around the cage, celebrated with my team and shared a well-earned embrace with Patrick Côté. There were no hard feelings whatsoever. Together we had fearlessly put on the best fight of the event. In its aftermath we respected each other more than ever.

UFC broadcaster Joe Rogan came into the cage to congratulate and interview me.

"Chris, that was a really tough fight," said Joe. "What do you think made the difference?"

"When somebody starts throwing at me," I shouted in reply, "I just want to throw back. That's how it oughta be done."

Those words weren't premeditated. They just came out in the spur of the moment. And, although that comment was by no means brilliant or poetic, it was probably the clearest expression of my personal worldview I have ever voiced. My entire life has been a struggle—an assault from all sides. And, in each of the dark moments, when it seemed like I would be out for the count, I had to make a choice: either curl up in a ball, or give it back harder than I got it. I've always fought back, and I will never stop. You can say a lot about me, much of it negative, but at heart you will find a fighter—a pure fighter.

Joe finished his interviewing duties and the crowd gave me one final ovation. But when the cheers subsided and I made my way out of the cage, the celebration ended. My father's seat was still empty.

The following morning I woke up in the desert. Literally on the ground in the sand. As was becoming all too frequent, I had no idea how I got there. I had pissed myself and I absolutely reeked of booze. A crushed cigar and a nearly empty bottle of vodka were on the ground next to me. My clothes looked as if someone had dragged me behind a freight train for miles. That's how I felt, too. Perhaps somebody took me for a ride and dumped me here. Or maybe this was near the last stop on the bus route and the driver had kicked me out. Again, who knows? I stood up to get my bearings and immediately heaved a bellyful of stagnant booze into the sand.

I was not far from civilization. About fifty feet to the west was a road that ran north-south, and about three miles beyond that were the high-rise casinos and hotels of the Strip. I touched my face, which was swollen and bruised from the many hooks and crosses that Patrick Côté had landed twelve hours earlier. Behind me, the sun had just begun to peek over the rugged Nevada landscape. I reached into my pocket and, though my wallet was predictably missing, found a pack of Marlboro Mediums and a lighter. Thank god. I lit a cigarette, took a puff, and slowly staggered back toward Las Vegas.

# CHAPTER 2
## AWOL

*T*he plane swooped and banked hard, left then right, before descending sharply and banking again. I clutched the straps of my parachute rig. This was one fucking wild ride. On the opposite side of the plane a baby-faced soldier vomited into a paper bag. Another wrung his hands and seemed on the verge of tears. As the craft wobbled and shuddered, even one or two of the higher-ranking officers couldn't hide their looks of concern. I laughed to myself—not because I found humor in the plight of these suffering soldiers, but because this shit was insane! It was "jump week" in the US Army Airborne School at Fort Benning, Georgia. We were about to execute our final training jump, this one at nighttime. So sixty-four of us had been herded like condemned sheep onto a bulky, gunmetal gray Boeing C-17 Globemaster III. The pilots, too, were training, practicing sharp evasive maneuvers and other wild aerial tactics. We were all learning the hard way that this massive military transport plane was very nimble in the air. And, although my intestines felt as if they had wrapped themselves into square knots, I was loving every second.

I began singing an old cadence song to myself. "C-130 rolling down the strip! Recon ranger gonna take a little trip. Stand up, buckle up, shuffle to the door. Jump right out and count to four . . ." I would have shouted it at the top of my lungs, but my brothers in arms would have thought that I was a total douche bag.

*As if on cue the plane leveled out and a red light came on, illuminating the fuselage. A siren sounded.*

*"Outboard personnel stand up!" shouted the jumpmaster. And, as practiced, we stood up, stowed our seats, and formed a line. Shortly came another command: "Hook up!" I clipped the cable from my parachute to the anchor cable that ran above our heads. "Check static lines!" This command meant that each of us should double-check our own connection and that of the man in front of us. However, on this particular training run, I was the first jumper in line. So I instead adjusted my gear and made sure that it was strapped on tight. The jumpmaster smiled at me in a dickish way. Then he took a position next to me, yanked a lever, and lifted the side door of the craft, sliding it upward like a garage door. The air inside was sucked violently out of the plane, almost dragging me with it.*

It is no secret that I spent a short time in the United States Army. However, people who know me—my friends, my fans—are always shocked by that revelation. I know it's because they generally consider me an unbridled wild man. I train hard. I party harder. And I leave everything on the table. I dye my hair bright red. I wear black nail polish. And I'm mostly covered in colorful tattoos. Though I have devoted my adult life to the rigorous practice of martial arts, I am, at the same time, notoriously hard to control. I've done more than my fair share of partying and experimenting—more than the vast majority of people who are walking around on this planet, I'd bet. And so you could say that I am not the typical "breed" of man that mother army normally hopes to bring into her bosom.

My wild nature first had a chance to shine when I was just a child in Mount Hood, Oregon. My mother, my brother, and I relocated there in 1990, when I was in third grade. It is an unincorporated, blue-collar community in the shadows of the actual Mount Hood, which rises 11,249 feet above the northwest region of the state. Previously, the three of us had lived in an area of southeast Portland known as "Felony Flats." That nickname wasn't just catchy; it happened to be a very accurate title for the neighborhood. Felony Flats was an underclass sector of the city that was characterized by dilapidated tweaker houses and a disproportionately high crime rate. My neighbors were small-time crooks, druggies, wannabe gang-bangers, and general miscreants. If I recall correctly, at one point in time Felony Flats had the dubious distinction of boasting the highest per capita percentage of sex offenders in the United States.

We lived there for two reasons. First, my mom was born and raised there and never really made it out. Actually, I think that most people of my socioeconomic status get stuck for life in the same shithole where they first sucked from a baby bottle. Second, of course, my mom couldn't afford anything nicer. I'd like to say that my family was a cut above the riff-raff that populated our neighborhood. But with my mom's heavy drinking and occasional meth use, we definitely didn't stick out like a sore thumb.

What prompted the relocation to Mount Hood was a drive-by shooting next door. We didn't know much about the guy who lived there other than that he was a belligerent drunk and a Gypsy Joker. The Gypsy Jokers are a hard-living motorcycle gang and crime syndicate based in Oregon. On a regular Tuesday night, I was playing with some toys in my bedroom when an extended volley of gunshots rang out. It sounded like there was a whole brigade of guys lighting the dude's house up with shotguns. It probably lasted only twenty seconds, but it felt like much longer. Thinking my brother had found some firecrackers and was having fun outside without me, I went to the window to take a look. But, right then, he and my mother rushed into my room, and we all huddled on the floor next to my bed until we were sure it was safe to come out.

When all was clear, my mom called 911. However, she didn't want anyone in the neighborhood to know that she had notified the cops. So we turned off all of the lights and hid in her bedroom for the rest of the night. The cops knocked on the door a few times, but my mom told us to stay quiet. After a while they left us alone and finished their investigation. To this day, I don't know whether my neighbor lived or died. But, when I went out to survey the scene in the morning, the front of his house looked like Swiss cheese.

So, a few weeks later, we packed up our rusty '85 Toyota 4Runner and headed eastward to a new home in the forested foothills. I still am not sure how my mother chose Mount Hood as our next port of call. Maybe she thought it represented the polar opposite of our previous experience. Or maybe she thought that my brother and I would have a better chance in life if we spent our days exploring the woods and the river rather than stepping over discarded needles. Regardless, it was nice that we didn't have to worry about stray bullets or molesters any more.

On the downside, the shack we moved into was actually an architectural downgrade. It had a leaky roof, no heat, no hot water, and the plumbing was so bad that for a period of time we had to bathe in the creek instead of the tub. When we first moved into the place, there was a skunk living in the crawl space under the house, and it sprayed like a motherfucker. My mom did her best to get rid of the smell by washing us with tomato sauce, but it didn't do much. In fact, Tyler and I stunk so bad we smelled up our entire school. They ended up spraying the whole place with an industrial deodorizer!

Soon, my mom got a job at the nearby Brightwood Tavern as a bartender. To give you an idea of how much time she spent working (and not working) there, I still know the phone number by heart some twenty-five years later. And that's the *only* phone number that I remember from my childhood (or from my adulthood, for that matter). While my mom did her thing in the saloon, my brother and I were left to run wild around Mount Hood. We explored and roughhoused and discovered countless ways to get in trouble. We linked up with a group of neighboring boys, who were just as out of control. During this time, for example, one of our favorite pastimes was to engage in running "rock wars" in which we split into teams and attempted to pelt each other with walnut-sized stones. This resulted in as many broken windows and split foreheads as you'd expect. Some of those lacerations deserved stitches, but that would have meant pissing off mom by asking her to drive us to the hospital in town.

Yeah, I would say that my mom was maybe a little too laissez-faire during our upbringing. Let me rephrase that: she hardly gave a shit. Yes, she loved us. And, yes, she wanted us safe and healthy. But, unless it was a world-shattering emergency, she really couldn't be bothered. Once, Tyler and I came up with the brilliant idea of using an old mattress as a punching bag. He told me to hold it up so that he could work on his boxing. But instead of throwing a punch, he took a running start and jump-kicked the mattress. I went flying against a boat trailer, crushing my forearm. When my mom came home from the bar later that night, I showed her my swollen and discolored limb.

"My arm's broken, Mom!" I announced with tears in my eyes.

"Jesus, Chris," she said, examining my arm briefly. "You just bruised it. You'll be fine."

So for the next three days, I suffered quietly and waited for my arm to get better. Due to the injury, I couldn't climb into the upper bunk bed where I slept. So, I spent those nights on the floor. On the third night my mom came into our bedroom and discovered me lying on the carpet in pain. This made her realize she had fucked up, and so she took me to the hospital. Sure enough, an X-ray showed that I had snapped my radius bone in half. I remember the doctors were pissed at my mother for waiting three days to bring me to the hospital. They lectured her angrily, and I'm pretty sure she had to beg them not to call child protective services.

I'm not purposely being hard on my mom. I'm just trying to tell it like it was. And I don't mean to imply that she was a total fuck-up of a parent. Hell, the whole story is that my mom wasn't perfect, but with what little she had, she made efforts to give us a decent childhood. Whenever she could, she would send me to sleep-away camp over the summer. Generally, she couldn't afford the fees they charged. However, some of the camps had spots for poor kids and would allow them to participate for free. One such camp that I went off to involved a week-long tour up the coast of California to learn about sea life. We took school buses and made various stops at campgrounds along the route. All of the kids had to buddy up with a partner for the trip. The parents were instructed to send money for daily food and snacks. The camp counselors told us to take turns buying food for our partners. Unfortunately, my mom sent me off with food stamps instead of cash. And when it came time for me to pay for the goods, the grocery store we had stopped at wouldn't accept the stamps. Needless to say, my trip buddy—a middle-class kid who had never even heard of food stamps—thought I was really weird. I felt like a total loser. When I got home from camp I gave my mom shit about it for weeks.

Not long after we settled into Mount Hood, my mom's boyfriend Dave died in a horrible car crash. They had been together for a good part of my childhood, and it is clear, in retrospect, that this incident had a traumatic and lasting effect on her. That man was the love of her life—the only man she had really connected with. And you know what? He was a damn good guy. Somehow, my mom had reached her hand deep into the garbage pail that was blue-collar Portland and pulled out a shiny apple. Dave, as I mentioned earlier, was a biker. Not a gnarly Gypsy Joker, but a regular badass who looked tough in a black leather Harley Davidson jacket and who had a heart of gold. Unlike any other grown man I had known to that point, Dave tried to be a role model for my brother and me. He did the best he could to make us happy and to protect us.

There are a lot of great stories that I can recall about Dave, but I'll only relay just a few here. There was the time that, in an effort to make the Fourth of July extra special for the kids, he put a match to a pile of gunpowder that he had poured onto the street. It blew up in his face and sent him to the hospital burn unit.

There was the time Dave had a party, and a bunch of drunken dudes from the neighborhood showed up. I was maybe just seven years old, and some guy started roughhousing with me a little too aggressively. He picked me up over my shoulder and swung me around dangerously. I started screaming. Dave yelled, "Put my fucking kid down!" When the man ignored him, Dave whipped a full can of Budweiser across the yard and it exploded on the man's forehead. We both went tumbling and the guy took off down the street with his tail between his legs.

And there was the time I got in a fight at school. The principal called Dave at work and made him come pick me up. Dave was fuming and I was crying, and it was an ugly scene. We drove home in silence and he punished me by making me do a whole sink full of dirty dishes. But, about a half hour after I started the chore, he came back into the kitchen and stared at me. I looked at him and noticed a gleam in his eye.

"So," Dave said. "Did you win?"

Then he gave me a friendly nudge, and I couldn't help but smile.

After Dave passed, Mom spent an increasing amount of time getting drunk at the Brightwood Tavern and, I believe, ramped up her use of methamphetamines. While my mom binged, the house fell into an even worse state of disrepair. It was constantly and completely filthy, with dirty dishes piled in the kitchen, garbage spilling out from bins onto the floors, and rumpled clothes in nearly every corner of the house. Often my mother forgot to pay the utility bills (or couldn't pay them), and we would be without electricity or water for days at a time. The plumbing in the house was all but useless, and rather than properly dispose of our trash, we burned it in stinking piles right in front of the house. At the age of nine, none of this seemed out of the ordinary to me. My sense of "normal" was completely demented.

In a few years we moved into a different house in Mount Hood. This one should have been fucking condemned. My mom pulled my brother and me out of school for three weeks to help my Uncle Gene with renovation efforts. We had to repair the roof, patch walls, and paint. Also, the house had no foundation and was sinking into the ground. So my Uncle Gene came up with the idea to jack the house up and straighten it out. Unfortunately, during this process the front wall detached from my second-floor bedroom. It pulled away and created an open-air gap that started near the floor and widened to about eighteen inches near the ceiling. Bugs, birds, snow, squirrels—you name it—made their way into my bedroom as the seasons changed. During the two years we lived there, that dangerous defect was never repaired. And I was not in the least bit fazed by it. This kind of crazy negligence was a familiar sight throughout my childhood.

Uncle Gene really led the charge when it came to our trashy, hillbilly lifestyle. He was ever-present during this phase of my life. In addition to heavy drinking (the national pastime of everyone in my family), Uncle Gene's hobbies included hunting without a license and dumpster diving. In the back of his property, he had a big storage shed that housed the countless items he had fished out of the dumpsters of local grocery stores. The guy had everything: fruits, vegetables, loaves of bread, sausages, old cinnamon buns, bagels, cheese. Half of it, of course, was rotten and covered in fungus, and you could smell the mess a quarter-mile away. To this day, there are two things that I cannot put in my mouth—that I cannot even think about—without retching: fruitcake and deer meat. Fruitcake made that list because, one January, Uncle Gene hit the post-holiday jackpot and brought home something like six-dozen spoiled fruitcakes. When I refused to eat, he literally pinned me to the ground, pried open my mouth, and shoved in a handful of that putrid shit. He forced me to chew and swallow, despite my gagging and sobs. You may get a laugh out of this anecdote, but as a little kid, this really fucked me up. It made me feel subhuman.

The reason I convulse at the mention of deer meat? Well, that's an even more disgusting story, and it has to do with Uncle Gene as well. One day when I was twelve years old, my brother Tyler and I got in trouble for breaking yet another window. As punishment, my mother grounded us and demanded that we clean the kitchen. This was a futile assignment, however, because the house never remained tidy for more than a few days. So, despite our protests, we spent a whole Sunday afternoon sweeping and mopping and scrubbing the countertops while my mom and a couple of aunties and uncles got their drink on at the Brightwood Tavern. (When you grow up in the backwoods like I did, everyone your mom knows—friends, neighbors, coworkers—are known as "aunties" or "uncles.") By sundown, the kitchen looked decent—not great, but decent. We had done the best a couple of unrefined school kids could do without any instruction. Shit, the kitchen would have even smelled OK if it weren't for the fact that not far away, out on the porch, hung a skinned deer carcass.

The carcass had been there for two weeks. It was covered in patches of white and green fungus, and it smelled like the asshole of hell. Uncle Gene and my cousin had gunned down this doe and its fawn on a recent hunt in the backwoods. Actually, Gene did all the shooting. When my cousin didn't have the nerve to kill the fawn, Gene took care of it. Of course, they didn't have the foresight to plan transportation for the game once they bagged it. All they had was a rusty Honda Civic. So they stuffed one of the deer into the trunk and strapped the other to the roof of the car. Because they did not have a permit to bag two deer on a single trip, they decided to drop one of the carcasses off at our house before getting on the highway. They skinned and gutted the thing, wrapped it in one of my bed sheets (thank you very much), and strung it up on our porch.

Apparently, Gene forgot about this particular trophy until he and my Uncle Tiny returned from the tavern the night my brother and I had finished our cleaning duties. At around midnight, Tyler and I awoke to loud thuds and the sounds of drunken laughter. We walked out onto the porch in our underwear. Uncle Tiny had the deer carcass laid out on the gravel and was unsuccessfully attempting to hack the limbs off with a splitting maul. Uncle

Gene held the deer steady while my mom, clearly fucked up, leaned against the house and laughed.

"See!" Gene announced, "This here is good meat, boy! We ain't letting a spot of this go to waste."

"No, sir!" Tiny echoed before taking another bloody whack at one of the haunches.

Soon it became apparent the axe method was not going to get the job done. So Tiny scooped the thing up in his arms—its filthy juices soaking into his Levi's jean jacket—and lugged it into the kitchen. Meanwhile, my mom retrieved our Sawzall sabre saw and the food processor. The men dumped the rancid deer onto the freshly scrubbed kitchen table, gore splattering onto the spotless linoleum floor. My brother and I looked at each other with helpless shock. Uncle Gene plugged in the electric saw and began buzzing off chunks of moldy, disgusting meat. Flesh and rot sprayed throughout the kitchen, sticking to the refrigerator and stove I had taken so much care to disinfect.

"We gonna eat good fer a week!" Tiny shouted over the hubbub while firing up the stovetop burners.

My mother scooped up the chunks of deer carcass with her hands and dumped them into the whirring food processor. When the meat was sufficiently chopped, she poured the mess onto the countertop, where Junior formed it into patties. He then flopped the patties into a greasy pan on the stovetop and voila! Venison burgers.

Tyler and I quickly retreated to our bedroom in the hopes that the adults would forget about us. We turned out the lights and pulled our blankets up tight. "Pretend you're sleeping," Tyler advised. So I did. But, sure enough, Uncle Gene soon swung the door open and staggered in. He grabbed me by my feet and dragged me out of my bed and onto the floor. Resistance was futile. He sat me at the kitchen table, the remains of the carcass under my nose, and forced me to consume a sizeable, medium-rare deer burger. I spent the rest of the night taking turns with Tyler, heaving into the toilet. Ah, the memories.

*With the door open, the howling wind was like a siren beckoning me into the abyss. The night sky was violent and freakish, filled with towering thunderheads and sheets of rain. Distant lightning streaked through the sky from time to time, offering brief glimpses of the patchwork farmland that stretched out two thousand feet below me. My jumpmaster gave me a nudge and I hesitantly stepped out on to an eighteen-inch-wide ledge on the side of the aircraft.*

*I had to hold that position for a good five minutes before it was my time to leap. It was a death-defying perch behind the left wing. I was literally hanging halfway out of the airplane. Despite the tremendous noise and the stomach-turning vista, and despite the fact that I was on the outside of an aircraft traveling nearly three hundred miles per hour, this was a rather calm position. This plane was designed with aerodynamic features that directed wind completely away from the side door. Standing there, my jumpmaster gripping the back of my jump suit so I didn't tumble away, there wasn't much more than a stiff breeze playing against my face.*

*A flash, and I turned to see a bolt of lightning zap from the side of a storm cloud about three miles to the east. It would have been accompanied by a heavy bang of thunder, I'm sure. However, two roaring jet engines were attached to the bottom of the nearby wing, drowning out all other sound. Rain poured onto my head and ran across my forehead and into my eyes. Although I may have looked like I was crying, I had never before felt so alive. I smiled and then opened my mouth and roared into the black sky.*

As you might expect, my roughneck, unfiltered upbringing did not prepare me well for the military lifestyle. But, upon graduation from high school, my options were rather limited. Although I was a highly regarded wrestler at the time, and various colleges had expressed interest in me, I was essentially illiterate. That's right—I earned a diploma from Benson Polytechnic High School in Portland yet could barely read or write. Don't ask how I pulled that off. But, I'll tell you one thing: it takes guts to make it all the way through high school without being able to read. It is a character-building experience, and I applied some of the savvy I developed during this time to my fighting career.

Nonetheless, the academic demands of a college education—and four more years of floundering—were not something I wanted to get on with. So, when my friend Benny told me that he had met with an army recruiter, my ears perked up. I had always loved war movies, *Platoon* being one of my favorites. I thought that kind of action—gutsy, macho, military training—would suit me well. It would definitely be a step up from my childhood rock wars. But more importantly, I had no other options at this point in my life. The choice was simple: either get a job pumping gas or roofing or sweeping floors and spend my free time smoking meth like many of the kids I grew up with, or enlist.

Beyond that, I had already developed an interest in aviation maintenance. It was the focus of my education at Benson Polytechnic High School in Portland, and I showed some promise in that field. Despite my reading problems, I was particularly good at following step-by-step instructions and working with complex diagrams. As a senior, I even won a statewide mechanics competition, for which the prize was an awesome toolset. In considering the army, I figured I could I could get my training in helicopter mechanics as a soldier and then work for a private aviation company when my six-year service obligation came to an end.

The next day, Benny drove me over to the recruitment office. The recruiter, Master Sergeant Alvarez, had shiny black shoes and perfectly pressed slacks. With a smile, he walked me through the process of enlisting and what would follow after that. Of course, Alvarez's description of the army experience highlighted the most appealing aspects: the action, the camaraderie, the travel.

"This gig could take you all over the world, my friend," he said. "And let me tell you . . . there are some wild women out there." He winked. "I can see that you're a wild man. You'll love it."

Admittedly, that all sounded damn good. And, when I pressed Alvarez, he assured me that I would be a welcome addition to the army wrestling team. He even told me that, according to his records, the army wrestling coach had seen me perform in high school and was impressed. That's what sold me. The only place I had *ever* experienced a sense of belonging or a sense of validation was on the grappling mat. Fuck, I wouldn't have even stayed in high school through graduation if it weren't for that sport.

My wrestling coaches in high school had a big impact on my life. They could tell that, even though my home life was such a mess, I had a drive and grit that set me apart from most of my peers. Head coach Lawrence always reminded me that my heart could take me far in life. On my graduation day, I remember him saying, "Chris, no one ever expected you to graduate from this school. A lot of the teachers figured you would have been done and gone by your junior year. But here you are. I believe in you, and I'm proud of you." I'll never forget that. It's a good lesson for adults out there: sometimes just saying the right thing to a kid will influence him for the rest of his life.

The wrestling team was more than a team. We hung out together. We rooted for each other. We backed each other up when we got into trouble. And, boy, did we get into some trouble. I'll never forget the time we had a meet against rival Jefferson High School. One of our 142-pound fighters, a kid named Morgan, pinned his opponent using a figure-four maneuver. In that move, Morgan wrapped his thighs around his opponent's head so that Morgan's crotch was right in the kid's face while he pinned him. That alone was pretty funny. But then, when the referee called an end to the bout, Morgan basically rubbed his balls on the kid's head while standing up. The kid shoved Morgan off, and it almost caused a brawl right there on the mat. Coach Lawrence stepped in to calm things down and smack Morgan on the head.

But, as it turns out, a brawl was inevitable—it was simply delayed by a few hours. After the meet ended, a few of us were carrying the wrestling mats to a storage room in the mezzanine area that wrapped around the gym. While we were up there, a bunch of the Jefferson kids started roughing up Morgan. One of the kids was an especially large heavyweight wrestler who looked like he could have absolutely crushed Morgan with one hand. I jumped into the fracas and jacked one of the kids in the face. Immediately the rest of the Jefferson guys jumped on me and started beating on me. I could tell that they wanted to throw me over the mezzanine rail onto the basketball court twenty feet below, so I grabbed on to a nearby pole and hung on for dear life. The big heavyweight kid started stomping on my head.

The next thing I knew, the entirety of both wrestling teams had jumped into action and were mobbing each other. It was like a forty-on-forty riot. I was on the bottom of a pile of kids who were just beating the shit out of me. Then, out of the corner of my eye I saw Coach Hugh barreling toward me. This dude was a three-hundred-pound Hawaiian, and when he plowed into the pile of kids it was like a freaking atomic bomb went off. They all went flying. I finally got back to my feet, and the place turned into a goddamn battle royale. Kids were punching each other in the face, kicking each other, just going nuts. I was throwing haymakers, laying out people left and right. The teachers and family members who had attended the wrestling meet could only watch in horror from below.

I know that story makes my wrestling buddies and I sound like a bunch of meathead assholes. And to some degree we were. But that brawl was one of those experiences that brought us all closer together. We had shown each other that we had each other's backs. Even the coaches had gotten their hands dirty in rushing to our defense. For the weeks that followed, there was a sense of unity among us that I had never known before. These guys were much more like family to me than my own family.

Given this background, the thought of joining the army wrestling team was so exciting to me that I hardly gave any attention to the other variables that should come to the forefront when evaluating a military career. So, even if it meant committing six years of my life to Uncle Sam, the decision was a no-brainer for me. I signed on the dotted line and, weeks later, flew across the continent to Fort Jackson in Columbia, South Carolina.

My army career began, as it does for all new recruits, with Basic Combat Training (BCT). Almost immediately after that phase began, I knew that I did not belong in the military. The rigorous physical demands of the training were not the problem. In that regard, I was exactly what the army was looking for. I flew through the ten-week regimen and scored a perfect 300 on my physical fitness test. Moreover, I performed at the "expert" level as a marksman in firearm evaluations. These high performance marks were the reason I was one of only four soldiers in my company selected for Airborne School. If it were not for the fact that I had already signed on to a track to become a helicopter mechanic, I would have aspired to become an Army Ranger. Oh yeah . . . I also had a tendency for insubordination.

I have always had a problem with authority—with someone else telling me what I can or cannot do. Now that I think about it, even my mom barely ever told me what to do. This isn't because I didn't listen. It's just that she was either too busy or too fucked up to dole out orders. Unfortunately, authority is the name of the game in the military. It's all about following instructions and staying in line. As soon as I realized how few choices I would have in the years to come, my heart was no longer in it. In fact, very early on I began contemplating a way out.

I had numerous unfavorable run-ins with the higher-ups. I often absentmindedly put my hands in my pockets during formation, or forgot to salute my superiors. My issues flared up, for example, during an early morning fitness session during BCT. A drill instructor named Murchison commanded us to complete a set of twenty push-ups. Unfortunately, when I dropped to the ground, I put my hand right on top of an anthill. As I pressed up and down, the ants started swarming up my forearm. I stopped, knelt, and began to feverishly swat them away.

"What are you doing, private?!" Murchison shouted.

"My hand was in an anthill, sir!" I replied.

"That's not my problem, soldier! Did I tell you to stop doing push-ups?"

"No, sir!"

"Don't call me 'sir,' goddammit!" Murchison bellowed. "I'm not a 'sir'! I work for a living!"

"I'm sorry, drill sergeant!" I replied.

"Why did you stop doing push-ups, private?!"

"Because there were ants crawling up my arm, drill sergeant!"

"Ants crawling up your arm?" He was incredulous. "Do you mean to tell me that, if you're in the middle of the shit, and you're in a firefight, and your army brothers and sisters are counting on you to carry your weight and to do your part, you'll put down your gun like a candy ass because there's an ant crawling up your arm?"

I didn't put much thought into my answer before announcing, "It was a whole colony of ants, sir . . . er, drill sergeant! And this is push-ups, not a firefight, drill sergeant sir!"

Murchison didn't like that response one bit. He immediately yanked me out of formation and led me across the yard to his office. I stood at attention while he sat down at his desk and began to write.

"Leben, I'm sick of this shit. I'm recommending you for a platoon for dysfunctional soldiers."

"Dysfunctional?!" I shouted back. "There were fucking ants!"

"You will not speak to your superior that way!" he shouted back, standing up from his desk.

My eyes began to water as I sputtered, "You're not my superior. I don't have a superior!"

He sprang toward me and grabbed me by the lapel, bellowing directly into my face, "You will contain yourself, soldier!"

That settled me down. I wanted to get the fuck out of the army, but I knew that having a meltdown in my drill sergeant's office wouldn't be the best path. I shut my mouth and stood at attention. He backed off and lowered his voice.

"You think there's an easy way out of this, Leben. Well there isn't. I don't care how much you try and fuck up. I'll recycle your ass as much as I have to. You'll spend a year in basic for all I care. Try me, son."

And I knew he was telling the truth. I had done a bit of research prior to shipping out. An enlistee can't simply change his mind and drop out of basic training. Bad behavior and resistance usually result in an extended BCT. Only in extreme cases does discharge become an option, and even then it takes months for the process to run its course. I was a dickhead, but, as much as I wanted to be, I wasn't an extreme case. Mouthing off would only make things less bearable for me, and the drill instructor was throwing down the gauntlet. So, after that incident, I did my best to calm down and stay out of trouble. The remainder of BCT wasn't without incident. But at least I finished in the platoon that I had started with.

*The Boeing C-17, began to descend sharply. I steadied myself by gripping the door frame. I didn't want to tumble out of the plane before we had reached the jump zone. Complicating the issue was all of the gear I was wearing; in addition to my bulky parachute, I was carrying a seventy-pound rucksack and, of course, my M16 rifle. As planned, we were dropping to a dive height of around 1,200 feet. The purpose of this was to unload the soldiers as close to the ground as possible without overly exposing the aircraft to enemy fire. Fortunately, as this was a training jump, there would be no bullets zipping past and ripping holes in my chute.*

*The plane began to level off, and I knew it was jump time. I readied myself and listened closely for a shouted "go" instruction from my jumpmaster who stood behind me inside the C-17. But that instruction never came. Instead, without warning, he shoved me hard in the middle of my back and I flopped out of the craft and into the air.*

*The first seconds of an army skydive are always the scariest because those are the moments of uncertainty. Our jump altitude was so low that, if my primary chute failed, I would only have a matter of seconds to deploy my reserve. As I dropped away from the plane, I held my breath tightly, hoping for a sharp backward jerk that would indicate my parachute had popped open. But, due to the way I was pushed out of the plane, I was spinning like a top. It was hard to gauge which way was up, much less determine whether my chute had deployed properly. As I streaked away from the plane, the icy rain pelted my face like a million tiny needles and, not far away, a bolt of lighting lit up the sky.*

After Basic Combat Training, I moved on to six months of Advanced Individual Training, known as AIT. For that I was stationed in Fort Eustis in Newport News, Virginia. There I trained to become what is known as a "67 Tango"—a Blackhawk helicopter mechanic crew chief. Of course, my top priority was to harass my superiors about the wrestling team. At first they told me to check again at a later date. When that time came, they told me that I wouldn't have my chance until I finished AIT and was assigned to a duty station. I was starting to get really pissed off. But I bided my time, and completed my training without serious incident.

Next I moved on to Fort Bragg in Fayetteville, North Carolina—"Fayettenam" as the grunts called it. This was my duty station. I was assigned to a phase crew in the Eighty-Second Airborne and began servicing Blackhawks. Again, I submitted a request to join the wrestling team. And, of course, weeks went by without an answer. It was around this time that a sense of hopelessness set in. The work was much less interesting, and much more soul-sucking than I hoped it would be. In my mind, it was slave labor. I was on the clock for twelve hours a day, five or sometimes six days per week. I felt completely stifled, trapped, stripped of my individualism. Hell, I would have preferred they send me to the frontlines of a fucking war. I had always figured I would die young; might as well see some action before it's all said and done.

Not surprisingly, I continued drinking regularly—every night in fact. Usually it was a fifth of 5 O'Clock Vodka, an especially shitty but cheap bottle that I could pick up at the local convenience store. The booze helped me escape just a little bit before bed time. Often (again, not surprisingly) I overdid it and suffered the following day. I even once missed a company formation—a major no-no. My roommates saw me sleeping in and presumed I had the day off. In actuality I had slept through my alarm. Though I could have been punished in a big way, maybe even stripped of my rank, my platoon leader covered for me at the role call. Afterward he chewed me out and put me on restriction for two months. That meant I was given additional duty hours and was allowed to spend my time only at work or at home. This made life twice as unbearable.

When I wasn't on restriction and had days off, I did my best to go wild. I had cobbled together a handful of friends and we often escaped for the weekend to Virginia Beach. There we hit the bars and clubs, chased girls, and got fucked up. For Labor Day weekend of my first (and only) year on duty, my friend Buck and I joined a group of guys who were heading to an all-night rave. We each snorted a few lines of coke (my first time, actually), took a couple of tabs of ecstasy, and rolled until the sun came up. Getting smashed like this was quite risky in the army because of the frequency of drug tests. Every few months we were subjected to piss tests, and, after a three-day weekend it was almost sure to happen. A failed drug test could mean a variety of punishments—demotion, hard-labor assignments, denial of weekend passes, even dismissal from the army if the violation was significant enough. I already had enough dings on my record. A drug violation would have sent me up shit creek.

So, upon returning to base after the rave, Buck and I headed straight to the sauna. Our move was to spend four hours guzzling water and sweating out the toxins. The other guys didn't think this was necessary, or maybe they were just too hung over to tolerate the heat. They went back to their bunks and slept.

It turned out our paranoia was warranted. We were all tested early Tuesday morning. As I pissed into the little cup, I was so nervous I could barely aim. Later that day our first sergeant called a special formation for the whole company, nearly two hundred soldiers. We lined up in the yard for inspection. The captain himself then appeared and marched back and forth, staring into our eyes. It was like he was trying to conduct his own visual drug test. I could have sworn his gaze paused on me longer than on anyone else. Finally, he barked two names.

"Fitzgerald and Hixon, step out!"

The two of them stepped forward. Fitzgerald was right next to me and I could swear that I saw sweat bubbling up on his forehead. I held my breath. The captain scanned the formation one more time, and I was certain that he was going to call two more names—Leben and Buck.

"Soldiers!" he shouted. "These two miscreants failed their drug tests today. There is no place in my army for druggies!" He approached Hixon and ripped the stripes right off of his shoulder. He then did the same to Fitzgerald. In front of so many peers, it was incredibly demeaning. They both looked ready to cry.

Then the captain continued, "While these boys report for processing, the rest of you get to enjoy a five-mile run around the yard. Say, 'Thank you, dirtbags!'"

We all shouted in unison, "Thank you, dirtbags!" And then we commenced our punishment. Buck and I had escaped by the skin of our teeth. I have never been a fan of cardio work, but that day I was thanking my lucky stars I would be going on a long run. I found out a week later that Fitzgerald was sent packing with a dishonorable discharge. Hixon was demoted two ranks and was put on restriction for four months. He spent much of that time mopping the barracks and cleaning toilets. Poor bastards.

About six weeks into my time at the duty station, the news came: there would be no wrestling team for me. My first sergeant explained to me that because 67 Tangos were in short supply, he simply could not afford to give me the time to train and travel with the wrestling team. I pleaded with him, but there was no budging. The decision had been made, and I was going to have to live with it. I walked out of his office with my head hung low.

In the weeks that followed, my dejection turned into anger. I had been recruited to the army with the promise that I would be able to fill a spot on the wrestling team. I had envisioned myself tearing through the competition and setting records, traveling around the country to compete, and encountering new people and places. But, upon learning of my first sergeant's decision, all of those ambitions went down the toilet. I woke up each morning with a gnawing pain in my stomach, terrorized by the idea that I had more than five more years of misery ahead of me in Fayettenam—five more years during which I couldn't do the one thing that mattered to me most. I hated the recruiter who had duped me into enlisting. I hated the superiors who denied me the opportunity to wrestle. I hated the army.

Finally, I made up my mind. I would get the hell out of dodge. I would go AWOL.

For a period of two months, I formulated my escape plan. I did research on what it meant to go AWOL and came across some disconcerting facts. First of all, I learned that there are two types of unauthorized absences, both of which are federal crimes. The primary distinction is between individuals who intend to leave service temporarily and those who intend to remain away permanently. The former is considered an AWOL—absent without leave—offense. There are all kinds of circumstances that qualify as AWOL violations. For example, showing up late for work or leaving work early without permission could fall into the AWOL category. Temporarily abandoning a guard post is another example. Skipping town for a few weeks and then returning to base, too, would be considered an AWOL violation. The punishment, generally speaking, is commensurate with the crime. A soldier who misses a day of work, for example, might simply have his pay docked. A soldier who goes AWOL with the intent to avoid field exercises or maneuvers, on the other hand, could get a few weeks in jail before being discharged.

AWOL violations are not as serious as the other kind of unauthorized absence: desertion. A soldier is considered a "deserter" if he leaves his post with the intent to remain away permanently. The absence could be for one day or for ten years. The key element is intent. However, generally speaking, there is something called the "Thirty-Day Rule." It states that a soldier who disappears for more than thirty days is automatically classified as a "deserter." His unit can replace him with a new person, and his information is entered into a "Wanted Persons File" in the FBI criminal database. This does not mean the soldier will ultimately be punished as a deserter, but it greatly increases the likelihood.

The punishments for desertion can be staggering—dishonorable discharge, up to five years in prison, etc. And, during time of war, a deserter can even receive the death penalty. (I was comforted by the fact that no deserter had been put to death since 1945.)

Also, I had learned that, since the army was likely to fill your spot after thirty days, if you really wanted to be discharged you had to stay gone for at least that period of time. If they tracked you down in less then thirty days, the army was more likely to try to force you to carry out your service commitment. Without a doubt my intent was to leave the army permanently. There was no way I was coming back voluntarily.

So, one weekend I packed up my sky blue Ford Escort with my modest belongings, which included a twenty-four-inch television set. One of the guys saw me carrying the stuff and asked me where I was headed. I explained to him I would be visiting a friend for the weekend and I needed to bring my TV with so that we could play video games. I told him I'd be back late on Sunday night. Then I got into the driver seat and drove away from Fort Bragg, never to return. Though, generally speaking, soldiers who go AWOL are viewed as the scum of the earth by much of our society, this may have been the best decision I ever made.

*After a second or two of uncontrolled, twisting freefall, my primary parachute engaged. However, my gear was fucked up and out of place. As I spiraled toward the ground, one strap was choking me while another was cutting off circulation to my left nut. Blackness started to fill my peripheral vision. I was about to pass out when, with one final desperate yank, I was able to dislodge the strap from under my chin and relieve the pressure.*

*Finally taking control of my descent, I was surprised, as I had been on previous jumps, by how fast I was falling, even with my parachute fully unfurled above me. Someone told me that, decades ago, an army scientist had determined the optimal rate of descent for a paratrooper. He calculated a speed that would allow for the evasion of enemy gunfire but limit injuries to soldiers when they hit the ground. I hope, for the soldiers' sake, it didn't involve too much trial and error. I'm not sure of the exact speed that he arrived at, but I do know it is a shitload faster than what you hit during a recreational skydive.*

*Dropping toward the landing zone, I had about a minute to enjoy the view. The thunderclouds were a safe distance away, their occasional flashes of lightning illuminating the leafy forest that surrounded the area. The C-17 rumbled away and climbed into the dark sky. Around me sixty-three other soldiers hung from their parachutes, their rucksacks dangling below their feet. Rarely in my life—either before or after that moment—had I ever felt so at peace.* Enjoy this moment, Chris, *I told myself,* because you may not have another one like it. Let it all go and see where the wind takes you.

I drove the nearly 2,900 miles from Fort Bragg back to Portland, Oregon, in about fifty-four hours. Back then ephedra was still legal and sold in convenience stores, so rather than sleep, I made frequent stops at the Flying Js and Circle Ks along the highway and stocked up on ephedra supplements and Mountain Dew. I thought for a minute about stopping somewhere and partying— Saint Louis, maybe, or Omaha. But, despite my liberation from military servitude, I was not in a celebratory mood. I was deflated and ashamed. I had failed. I didn't care about what my fellow soldiers thought of me or about the disappointment that my superiors at Fort Bragg were certainly expressing to each other. That shit didn't matter. Nor did I care that I would soon become a wanted fugitive. I couldn't have given a fuck about the criminal consequences. What ate at me—what burned painfully in my chest—was the knowledge that I had encountered a situation that I couldn't tolerate, that I couldn't live with. For the first time in my life, I had run away rather than face the music. And, more importantly, I had no clue what I would or could do next. The army was a means to an end, and, as I already mentioned, just about my only way forward after high school. By bailing on my military service obligation did I just fuck up my entire life? Was I destined to live a white-trash life in the sticks of Oregon, never to make anything of myself?

As my Ford rolled through cornfield after cornfield of the American Midwest, I repeatedly slammed the steering wheel with the butt of my hand and cursed myself.

# CHAPTER 3
# FIRST FIGHT

Portland.

I was back.

My stint in the army was already fading like a weird dream that doesn't make any sense in the morning no matter how hard you try to think about it.

Why return to Portland, you ask? Where the fuck else was I going to go? I hardly knew anybody elsewhere in the world. Plus, I was a wanted man at this point. I couldn't think of anyone who would take me in besides my loyal best friend Sam Songer or possibly my brother Tyler, who really didn't give a shit about much of anything. Also, in the back of my mind, I think I knew my days on the lam were numbered. I wanted to relax and have some fun with my old friends before Johnny Law came knocking.

I rolled into town around 3:00 AM and went straight to Sam's place, a duplex downtown that he shared with his mom, Kim. Kim and Sam were more like family to me than my own family. I had spent so much time at their house during middle school and high school that Kim sometimes referred to me as her "other kid." She fed me, helped me get to and from school, tried to get me to stay out of trouble. And Sam, for his part, was always there to get my back or to bail me out of a bad situation. Hell, if it weren't for those two I'd be on skid row. So it made sense to seek refuge there.

I banged on the door and hollered until Sam finally appeared at the entryway, disheveled and mostly asleep. He was in disbelief that I was standing before him. I had called him right before I ditched the army and told him I was coming home, but it was pretty clear he didn't believe I would really go AWOL. Sam was a welder and often had to be at work very early in the morning. Most people in that position would have been supremely annoyed that a hopped up madman was banging on the door in the middle of the night. But Sam, God bless him, smiled and welcomed me back. I was so fucked up and exhausted from the three-day drive I could barely talk. I made a beeline directly to his extra bedroom and slept until the next morning.

When I came to, I decided to make a visit to my mom's place in Felony Flats. Unbelievably, she had moved us all back there when I was in seventh grade. Having returned home, I didn't want to hang out in Portland too long without her knowledge. That would have made her feel like shit. When I showed up she gave me a huge hug and started crying, telling me she had been very distressed because she didn't know when she would ever see me again. Then she took me on a quick tour of the minor upgrades she had made to the house (which, to be honest, might have easily been considered downgrades). She made a special production of taking me to my bedroom, where, on the door, she had spray-painted the words *My beloved Chris has gone to the army. Aug 1998.* This was her modest tribute to me after I enlisted. God knows what compelled my mom to do that, but I'm pretty sure it involved a lot of drinking. It was touching in a weird, white trash kind of way.

I needed a permanent place to crash, but I decided not to impose on Sam and Kim at that time. They had put up with me enough in the past. And, although I loved my mom, I knew I would go nuts if I moved back into my old bedroom. So I had a beer with her, grabbed some clothes, and, against her protests, headed over to Tyler's place.

I pulled up to my brother's house, threw my duffle over my shoulder, and knocked on the front door. Even though my arrival was unannounced, I figured he'd be happy to see me in some way or another. The door opened and Tyler stood there shirtless, with bloodshot eyes. He stared at me expressionlessly.

"What's up, man," he mumbled listlessly as if I hadn't been gone at all.

"I'm back, bro!" I announced.

"OK," he replied with a yawn. And with that he retreated to his bedroom, leaving me standing in the middle of a sparse living room, no less alone than I had been for the last couple of days while driving across the nation I was supposed to be serving. Not much of a homecoming, but at least I wouldn't be out on the street.

I spent a couple of weeks snorting coke and playing video games before I accepted the fact that I would need to make some money and start living my life. I found a gig cleaning carpets, which sounds like shit but isn't half bad, especially when your clients include the occasional hot, single mom in yoga pants. But those good times came to a screeching halt just three days later when my boss Jerry called me early in the morning.

"Chris," he grumbled, "we got ourselves a big gig cleanin' the carpets for them Intel headquarters in Hillsboro." Jerry was in his fifties and was probably suffering from stage-three emphysema, so every time he talked it sounded like he was narrating the end of the world.

"Sounds good to me," I replied.

"Thing is," he continued, "they got some serious security protocols over there. They're afraid of industrial spies and such."

"OK." I really didn't give a shit about the details.

"The reason I'm telling ya is cuz we're gonna have to run a background check on all of our employees. That's the only way we're getting' in there."

Shit. Not good. The way Jerry spelled it out, it sounded like he had an inkling that there were some skeletons in my closet. He was spot on, of course. The one thing I couldn't let the old man do was look into my history. By now there must have been a federal warrant for my arrest on the books. Inside I started to freak out, but I played it cool on the phone.

"What do you need from me, Jerry?"

"I just need you to come down to the office and sign some paperwork. That's all."

"You got it," I replied with false confidence. "I'll stop by tomorrow."

I hung up knowing this would be the last time I ever spoke to Jerry. I never showed up to fill out the paperwork. He called me a few times in the next several days, but I didn't pick up the phone, and that was that.

This incident was a grim reminder I wouldn't be able to run and hide forever. At some point the AWOL thing was going to catch up with me. For the next few days I was a bit paranoid that Jerry would look into my background anyway and tip off the authorities. I imagined a bunch of squad cars screeching to a halt in front of the apartment . . . police officers assuming tactical positions and training their guns on the front door . . . a police captain shouting into a megaphone, "Come out with your hands up! Don't try anything funny. We've got you surrounded and we're authorized to use lethal force," and all that kind of shit.

Actually, part of me hoped that this would play out was sooner than later so I could just do my time and get on with my life. It sucks driving down the street knowing that if you get stopped by the cops you are going to jail. And, the longer I waited, the worse it was going to be. If I got popped for even a minor infraction— public drunkenness, or a baggie of dope, or whatever—then it was all going to be ten times worse. *This is what it feels like to be an outlaw,* I thought.

The smart move would have been to walk over to the nearest police station and just beg for leniency. But, as one might expect, I couldn't bring myself to do the smart thing. It was bad enough I had to throw in the towel and run off. The thought of admitting it publicly, voluntarily surrendering, and letting the army know they had gotten the best of me, was something I could not stomach. Plus, it would have been lame to turn myself in that way. I like to go down in style.

Not many weeks later my brother was able to hook me up with a sales gig at the same used car lot where he worked. It was called Auto Spot, or something like that, and it was located on McLoughlin Boulevard, just a couple of blocks from our apartment. I had never been a salesman of any kind before, but I did have the gift of gab, so I was optimistic. Best of all, they didn't need to run a background check in order to hire me. As you might have guessed, the used car business is not particularly selective when it comes to evaluating personnel.

Hell, I'll just come out and say it: being a used car salesman is a dirty, dirty job. The goal of it is to wring every possible cent out of your victims . . . er, customers. Negotiating a car sale is very much a shell game. As the salesman, you try to introduce so many variables that the customer can't keep track of the bottom line. I used a common technique called a "four square." I would divide a piece of paper into four quadrants in which I would write down 1) the customer's desired down payment, 2) the trade-in value for his existing car, 3) the overall cost of the car I was trying to sell him, and 4) what he could afford to pay per month. Then I would start shifting numbers back and forth, adding and subtracting, until we arrived at a configuration that appealed to the buyer. The thing is, when you factored in the financing, all of that maneuvering did almost nothing to the actual cost the buyer was going to pay for the vehicle over time.

And while working this ruse, I would yap and blabber and promise whatever I could to close the deal. Sales, I learned, is more about what you have to say than what you have to sell. I was much more likely to ensnare a buyer if I kept my mouth moving than if I stayed quiet. This didn't mean that I was telling a bunch of outright lies, but rather that I talked so much, and with enough enthusiasm, that the customer didn't have the breathing room to make a calculated, rational decision. My style was "buy or die"; either the customer was going to leave the lot with a car that I sold him or he was going tell me to go fuck myself and storm off with nothing. There was no in-between.

An exchange between a buyer and me might have gone something like this:

BUYER: This is really more than I can afford.

ME: Actually, it's not, because guess what—my boss likes your trade-in and he can give you top dollar for it. All you have to do is bump up your down payment just a couple hundred bucks.

BUYER: Well, that's good. But the thing is I've been saving for my kid's birthday. He wants one of those new Sony Playstations—

ME (interrupting): What would make your kid and your family happier? A video game or a hot new car to ride to school in? Think about it. If you want to give your kid a happy birthday, drive home in this Jeep today and take him for a nice long ride. He'll love you for it.

BUYER: Well, I guess that makes sense—

ME: Of course it makes sense, my friend! Now, let's talk about the payments. You said that you can afford two twenty-five a month. Bump that to two fifty and I think I can get my boss to sign off on this . . .

As it turned out, I was more than half decent at my job. I got addicted to selling, and the highs came from squeezing the customers for juice. My take was 20 percent of the profit. The profit on the car was calculated by subtracting the adjusted cost of the car from what the buyer ultimately paid for it. The adjusted cost was the amount that my boss acquired the vehicle for, plus a flat thousand dollars. So, for example, if my boss paid five grand for a car, then I got 20 percent of anything I negotiated above six thousand. If I sold the thing for nine thousand, then my take was six hundred. For the first time in my life, I started to make a fair amount of money. It wasn't long before I was pocketing four or five grand a month. That's not a lot of money for many people, but for me it was a gold mine.

Best of all, I had some folding money to pay for booze and drugs. I'd put in ten hours on the lot, and then I'd go out and get completely fucked up with my coworkers. We did this literally every night. Besides alcohol, the drug of choice for used car salesmen was pills: painkillers, especially OxyContin. We popped those things like jellybeans, and, I'm telling you, every last one of the guys did it.

Moreover, having a couple of bucks in a bank account gave me a level of confidence I never had before. Praise the lord, I even started to have success with the ladies. One night, my cousin Misty had a get-together at her house in Portland. The week before, she had told me there was a girl named Michelle who wanted to meet me. When I arrived, Misty handed me a beer and directed me right to Michelle, who stood leaning against the piano, sipping from a plastic beer cup. She was a cute brunette, sweet and quiet with a nice little body. There was a gleam in her eye that suggested a wildcat lurked beneath her shy exterior.

Michelle and I clicked right away and started cozying up. I went on and on about my crazy exploits in the army and on the used car lot, and she told me about how annoying high school was. She was eighteen years old, but still a senior on the verge of graduating. We started making out on the piano bench. (Before you freak out, keep in mind I was barely twenty years old at this point. It was all above board, my friends.) Then, as we got drunker and hotter, we migrated to the top of the piano. It was pretty funny and awkward. We didn't have sex, though, because everyone else was in the same room.

You should know this was a very exciting moment for me. I was by no means a Casanova, and, to be honest, my life to that point had been pretty grim in the pussy department. Benson Polytechnic was a vocational school. So the majority of the student body comprised dudes who were there to prep for a career in engineering or mechanic work or carpentry, etc. The handful of eligible girls that roamed the halls didn't exactly meet my standards. (And *trust me*, my standards were as low as fucking possible.) Moreover, although I was very popular, everyone there knew me as "Crazy Chris." I was the guy who got fucked up all the time, started fights, lived in Felony Flats, and sometimes drove a rusty motorcycle to school even though he didn't have a license. Not exactly boyfriend material, you might say.

The army, too, was a sexual wasteland. There were a couple of slutty girls my friends and I took turns with, but nothing worth writing home about. And when we went out on the town for the weekends, I typically came home empty-handed and penniless. This was mostly because, at the time, I was too insecure to approach chicks. Yeah, I had a few conquests. But usually the only way I got to see a girl naked was when my friends and I threw money into a pot and got a stripper.

Early on in my tail-chasing career I didn't know how to talk a good game, and really, I was too lacking in confidence to try in most cases. I guess, at heart, I knew I was a semi-literate hillbilly from the sticks of Oregon. I felt like that truth was plastered on my forehead. But that all changed in my early twenties when I started making notches on my headboard thanks to what I had been learning on the used car lot. I used the same "buy or die" approach with women that I used when trying to unload a Honda. Either they'd go home with me or they'd detest me.

I know this sounds bad, but I always started by offering the girl a complement paired with an insult. The kids these days call this technique "negging." For example, I'd say, "You're hair is really nice but you should do something about your teeth." This would typically make the girl angry and embarrassed. But, as we all know, love and hate are not opposites—they are closely related emotions. This risky move didn't always pay off, but often a girl's instinctual response was to try and win me over and prove that, in reality, I liked her. This required a very patient and calculated strategy on my part. At just the right point in our conversation, I would flip the script. I'd retract my previous insult and say something like, "On second thought, your teeth are kind of pretty. The lighting must have been off earlier." If I was lucky, that would be hook, line, and sinker, and she'd end up going home with me.

Yes, I'm fully aware that this kind of behavior probably qualified me as a sleazeball. But it was just about the only tool I had in my belt.

In November of the year of my return, some high school buds and I decided to drive down to Eugene for the annual "Civil War" football game between the Oregon State Beavers and the University of Oregon Ducks. It was a big annual event. Thousands of people would converge on the University of Oregon campus to take part in a rivalry that began in 1894. Wild parties were planned for the whole weekend, and I didn't want to miss a minute of it.

A couple of the guys I had wrestled with in high school—Kevin and Burt—were sophomores there and had rented a house together. On that Friday night they had a huge party. The place was packed from wall to wall with horny frat dudes and the girls that they were trying to hook up with. Well, soon enough I started talking shit to some guy. (At that point in my life, about 75 percent of the conversations I had involved some sort of shit talking.) We started shoving, and when Kevin came over to get my back, another dude busted a bottle over his head. The place immediately erupted into a massive brawl. Fists and beer went flying. More bottles were broken. I started bitch-smacking anyone who came near me. For half a second I thought about the implications this behavior might have with regard to my AWOL warrant, but, for the most part, I was too drunk to care.

The brawl raged on until the wail of approaching police sirens filled the air. I scrambled through the house and found an exit in the back. But by the time I busted out, it was too late to make a run for it. Eight police cars had taken up perimeter positions and officers were already emerging with big fat mag lights in hand. My only option was to dive behind some bushes and keep quiet. I was no stranger to police action, but this was a scary moment for me. Several months into my desertion, I was sure to get some jail time if remanded into military custody. And, for all I knew, I could be looking at six months in the slammer. So, as a bunch of hammered dudes and panicked chicks ran this way and that, I sprawled in the dirt and got ready to wait it out.

For about twenty minutes I watched as the cops slapped cuffs on people and shoved them into the back of a paddy wagon. Then, just when I thought they were about to head out, two of the cops walked over to an area near where I was hiding.

"Chris Leben!" one shouted. "We know you're back here. You've got a level-five warrant with the feds and there ain't no wiggle room. Don't make us search through these bushes and drag you out!"

Fuck. Someone had ratted me out. Most places I went, my reputation preceded me. Also, I had made more than a few enemies at the party. Maybe one of them had bargained his way out of an arrest by offering me up as a sacrificial lamb. I froze and considered my options, which were quite limited.

"Come out now! If you make us play hide-and-seek, we'll make sure this gets ugly for you."

I finally had a moment of clarity. Resistance would only extended my time behind bars. Moreover, in the previous weeks, the army had been calling my friends and my mom repeatedly, asking them to turn me over. It had become embarrassing and disgraceful. There really was no light at the end of this tunnel. The time had come.

I emerged from my bushy hiding place and put my hands above my head. The cops surrounded me, shining their flashlights in my face.

"Here I am," I announced. "You got me."

I was ushered into an isolation cell at the Eugene jailhouse. Like most jail cells, it was cramped and the only creature comforts were a chrome shitter and a thin, stained iron cot. I was there for three days. Except for mealtime, when a tray of lukewarm grub was slid into my cell by a faceless cop who would have put more care into feeding a hamster, I had nothing to do and no one to talk to. It was torture.

On Tuesday, when I expected to be transferred to the courthouse, I was instead transferred to the general population section of the prison, where they hold all of the hardcore thugs, rapists, and murderers. I didn't know what the fuck was going on or when I was going to be released, and nobody was giving me any answers until a few hours later when a corrections officer appeared. Unexpectedly, he released me on my own recognizance, instructing me to spend Thanksgiving with my family before reporting to an army base in Oklahoma for processing. He must have woken up on the right side of the bed that morning.

Of course, there was no Thanksgiving celebration to return home to. When I got back to the apartment, I found my brother and his buddy Mack semiconscious and sick on the floor. Shortly after I left town to head to the Civil War game they found my stash of "blue honey." Blue honey is a mixture of honey and *Psilocybe* mushrooms. These tiny little fungi contain two potent psychedelic compounds: psilocin and psilocybin. One of them causes crazy hallucinations and time distortions, while the other gives you an intense brain high, as if your head was plugged into a wall socket. When you put them in honey, it absorbs the psychedelic chemicals. Just spread a little smear on a piece of toast and you're in for a hell of a trip. Notably, *Psilocybe* mushrooms and acid are like steroids for skater dudes. In middle school and high school, my buddies and I would take a couple of shrooms and spend the whole night skating. It gave us laser focus. Man, I've seen some dudes land some insane skating tricks that never would have been possible if they weren't hopped up on the stuff.

Well, Tyler and Mack had guzzled a whole jar of blue honey over the span of about seventy-two hours. You aren't supposed to take mushrooms over and over like that because, in essence, they are poisonous. As a result, the guys were practically comatose when I found them. I was pissed not only that they ate my stash but also that I had to spend part of my last couple of days of freedom tending to them and making sure they recovered. Of course, I also found time to drink heavily and huff a bunch of lines of coke. I wasn't sure how long I was going to be incarcerated by the military, so I made sure to let loose a bit.

The army was nice enough to provide me with a one-way plane ticket to Oklahoma. I got offensively drunk prior to heading to the airport. Then I guzzled cocktails for the duration of the two-hour flight. When I finally stumbled out the terminal at Will Rogers World Airport in Oklahoma City, I was a stinking mess and nearly as shit-faced as I had ever been in my life.

In the airport there is actually a special office whose main purpose is to receive AWOL soldiers who are surrendering to the army. It's a tiny little hole in the wall, and there were two uniformed soldiers behind the desk when I arrived.

"Here I am!" I announced in the same way I had when I was arrested at the house party.

They glanced up at me and then gave each other a knowing look that seemed to say, *here's another drunk one to deal with.* However, the soldiers were nice enough as they placed me in handcuffs and escorted me to the transport vehicle that would take me to the Regional Correctional Facility at Fort Sill.

At Fort Sill a surly corrections officer instructed me to turn in all my personal effects and change into a military-issue prison uniform, which consisted of a lightweight jacket and fatigues that were about two sizes too big for me. He also handed me a tattered woolen blanket. These were the only possessions I would have for the duration of my stay. Then he sent me to my quarters.

The facility did not have barred cells as you might imagine, but rather small sleeping rooms. Everything was housed within crumbling barracks that dated back to the late nineteenth century. The personnel consisted of two or three low-level officers who did little more than play cards and keep an eye out for trouble. The only creature comfort I ever came across at Fort Sill was an obsolete TV that we were almost never given the opportunity to utilize. To top things off, I began my sentence in December, and the facility did not have adequate heat. It was fucking freezing. My blanket did very little to keep me warm. I barely slept a wink the first night, but at least I had a roommate (a "celly") to talk to. His name was Derrick and he was a nice enough guy.

That first morning, the jail staff roused us at five and marched us into the frigid courtyard. I think there were about twenty of us, and pretty much everyone was doing time for AWOL-related violations. We spent about two hours kicking rocks until, finally, the brawny master sergeant appeared and told us to stand at attention.

"Good morning gentlemen," he boomed. "Many of you are new today, so there is some important information that I have to share. And I want you to pay attention."

The master sergeant swept his arm to direct our attention to the dense forests and rolling hills that surrounded the facility.

"Look around you. Go ahead. Look around you." He seemed to fill with a sense of pride as he, too, took in the vista. "Fort Sill was staked out in 1869. That's more than a century and thirty years ago. Many a good man has trained and operated here. And many a misguided man has taken residence in our correctional facility. I'll have you know that this Fort Sill facility sets a high bar for the whole military correctional system."

Damn, I thought. This place was in disrepair. The rest of the military correctional system must have been god-awful.

The big man continued. "You may have also noticed, looking around, that there isn't much going on around here, outside of our gates. So, if you get an itch to make a run for it, keep in mind a couple of things. First of all, most of you are here for only a short time—weeks, months maybe. Attempted escape from a military correctional facility will earn you another twenty years behind bars, guaranteed. Twenty years during which you'll be doing mostly what you're doing now, standing in the freezing cold or in the heat and listening to an old man bark. If you've done time before and think that you can handle a long stretch like that, think again. Military jail is different from civilian jail. We aren't hamstrung by silly regulations that are supposed to make you boys comfortable.

"Second, the next town is about twenty miles away. You could try to hitch a ride, but ain't many people around here dumb enough to pick up a straggler. So, you'll have to hoof it. But, remember, there is a very active artillery training program here. So, you'll be dodging tank and mortar fire as you make you way. And you'll be tiptoeing around undetonated ordinance. As it is, if you do survive the bombardment, you'll probably die of exposure before you find someone to take you in and give you a glass of milk and a cookie. So, my friends, think long and hard about whether you want to take that chance."

Of course, by the time he had finished talking, I knew I was staying put. I had learned my sentence was only going to be three weeks. I've had hangovers that lasted almost as long, and withdrawal kicks that lasted longer. This wasn't going to be the most painful challenge of my life.

Each morning, after a long stand at attention, we were transported in cattle trucks from the yard to the chow hall. There we stood in line, at attention, for an insufferably long time as we inched along and were served one-by-one. Typically, when I had finally received my portion and sat down, I had only five minutes to scarf down the slop before it was back on the cattle truck, and back to the freezing cold yard for another two or three hours of moping around. Then it was another ride on the truck to the chow hall, a quick dinner, back on the truck, into the yard, and a final two hours of listless yard time to close out the day. Returning to my room was a joyous occasion every night. As rickety as my bed was and as tattered my blanket, I grew to love my meager quarters because it was a sanctuary from the painful misery of each day.

Those three weeks felt like three years. I was finally released and my god-awful commitment to the military was over.

Now, while Uncle Sam is generous enough to fly you in to begin your incarceration, they seem to be a little stingier once you've paid your debt and are ready to head back home. On the return trip they provided only Greyhound bus fare. And from Fort Sill back to Portland would run me about forty-two hours. Fortunately, my celly Derrick was headed in the same direction so we made our way to the bus stop together. The first leg of the ride only took us as far as Amarillo, Texas, about two hundred miles away, where we had a fucking twelve-hour layover. So Derrick and I grabbed two fifths of Jack Daniels, posted up in the bus station there, and got to work pickling our livers.

We were in an ugly state when the bus we were waiting for finally pulled into the station. Derrick and I put on sober airs and quietly found a place in the back of the bus. But we were too wasted to fly under the radar. Before we even left the station, Derrick dropped his bottle and it clanked among the seats. Apparently the beefy Texan bus driver had no patience for drunkards. He immediately stood up and stomped back to where we were seated. He picked up the bottle and looked square at Derrick.

"Are you drinkin' on my bus?" he demanded. "This your bottle?"

"What's left of it," Derrick replied, showing an impressive lack of respect.

"Then you ain't goin' anywhere."

"What are you talking about, man?" Derrick was so drunk he sounded like he had a mouth full of marbles.

The bus driver bent down to put his big chin right in front of Derrick's blurry face.

"What I'm talking about is there ain't no drinking on my bus, and you're gonna have to drag yourself off it before I feel the need to get my hands dirty."

"Fuck," moaned Derrick. "When's the next bus to Portland?"

"This time tomorruh," replied the bus driver.

Derrick looked like he was ready to cry. Slowly and reluctantly, under duress from the bus driver, he grabbed his duffle bag and stumbled off the bus. But the bus driver wasn't done. He turned back to face me.

"You drinking too?"

"Fuck, no!" I replied without missing a beat. The bus driver gave me the stink eye. "I mean, hell no, sir."

He stared at me for another few seconds before turning slowly and returning to the wheel. As the bus pulled away, I looked out the window to see Derrick sitting on the curb. He was crying and taking swigs from his bottle. It was a pathetic sight. I felt so horrible for that bastard. If I had to wait another twenty-four hours for a bus after suffering at that goddamn correctional facility for the better part of a month, I probably would have had a complete meltdown. That was the last time I ever saw Derrick.

Life resumed. I got a gig at a different used car lot, and I kept selling cars and getting by. Michelle and I had moved in together and were living in a house with my friend Jordan in Milwaukie, Oregon. I began taking classes two nights a week at a community college in order to get my English and math up to the level required to become a certified electrician. I didn't have the most success in that. My algebra grade, for example, was a D+. So at this point, my life and plans were certifiably blue collar. I was kind of headed nowhere fast until one day, as I was laying on the couch and playing video games, my brother called.

"Chris!" he shouted breathlessly. "You gotta get down here!"

"Down where, dude?" I didn't feel like moving.

"The place where I'm working now!" Tyler had previously told me that he found a new gig, but the news had gone in one ear and out the other.

He continued, "Matt Lindland and Randy Couture are in the back beating the shit out of each other!"

"Say what? What are you talking about?"

My brother didn't have time to explain. "Just get your ass down here, dude, or you're going to miss something awesome."

Matt and Randy were legendary wrestlers, and growing up I had paid attention to their careers. Matt took home a silver medal in Greco-Roman wrestling from the 2000 Olympics, and Randy was a three-time alternate for the US Olympic team in the same event. More importantly, by this time in 2003 they had both become big-time UFC fighters, and cage fighting, as we all know, was right up my alley. In fact, I started telling people I wanted to be a UFC fighter when I was only about twelve years old. Of course, at that time, middle schoolers did not have the opportunity to train in MMA. We pretty much had wrestling, and that's about it. Things are different in this day and age, though.

So I got directions from Tyler and headed over to Matt Lindland's USA Auto Wholesale at 182nd and Stark. Matt made a little bit of money in MMA, but he paid the big bills back then with his dealership income. I made my way to the back of the property where I discovered that part of the mechanic shop had been converted into a crude fighting area. There was still an oily concrete floor. They had ripped out some of the sheet rock to make room for an arrangement of shitty grappling mats, and they had a heavy bag in the corner. By this time, Matt and Randy had wrapped up their sparring session and were having a laugh with some of the guys who had gathered for the spectacle.

"We're going to be doing this a lot," said Randy. "So if any of you want to start learning MMA or just want to get in shape, just let Matt know. Maybe something cool will happen here."

And that was the birth of the renowned fight gym known as Team Quest.

Randy had me at hello. I borrowed seventy-five dollars from Sam to join the gym and started training the very next day. I was the twelfth student in the history of Team Quest and, some would say, the most gung-ho. For a long time I participated in almost every class. I typically trained three hours in a row every day: kickboxing, then grappling, then boxing. At that time, Robert Follis was the head coach and, along with Dennis "The Piranha" Davis, ran all of the classes. Within a week of beginning my training, I started asking them to set up an amateur fight for me.

"Hey coach! Have a fight for me?" was my daily inquiry.

And Follis would say, "As I told you yesterday, and the day before that, and the day before that, I am looking for an opportunity for you and will let you know."

He wanted me to hold my horses, but I was insatiable. All I could think about was getting into the cage and seeing what kind of balls I really had.

One night I came home and told Michelle I was going to stop taking college classes at night.

"Great!" she replied. "That means you can spend more time with me!"

That's not what I had in mind.

"Not exactly," I told her. "I'm going to start training at Team Quest every day, twice a day. That's the only way I'm going to get good enough to be a real fighter."

And that's exactly what I did. I stopped selling cars because I really didn't have the time for it. I moved into Sam and Kim's basement and paid them $200 per month. To earn enough to live and party I split my time between working with my friend Jordan at his father's painting business and working with Sam, remodeling old Victorian houses. It was basically nine-to-five stuff. So I'd put my eight hours of hard labor in, head home for a quick shower, and then zip over to Team Quest for three straight hours of training. After that, of course, I would go out and drink until the wee hours of the morning. I barely ever saw Sam because I was usually returning home drunk as he left for work. And, when he returned from work, I was at the gym training. I maintained this kind of schedule for a good three or four years. Michelle fucking hated it. Needless to say, we didn't last very long.

But this was the first time since high school I really felt I was part of a team. Yeah, they emphasize teamwork in the army, but that's forced shit and I didn't like most of the people I enrolled with. Plus, I was always a square peg in the round military hole. Team Quest in the early 2000s was different. I became very close with the guys I trained with, especially Eddie Herman and our friend Jason. Team Quest was a place where I had a role and a sense of value and purpose. It was like being back on the wrestling team, but we—my coaches and my teammates and I—had even bigger goals in mind.

The first two amateur fights that Follis rustled up for me fell apart because my opponents pulled out. So I was going nuts. Then, to make me even crazier, that sneaky bastard Eddie got to get in the cage before I did. As much as I love that guy, we have always shared a healthy competitive angst. Because we started training around the same time and went through a lot of the same motions in building our careers, we often compared ourselves to each other. Eddie had the first amateur fight, which pissed me off. But then I made it on to the first season of *The Ultimate Fighter*, which pissed him off! We've even had fans mistake us for one another on several occasions.

Eddie was notorious for his temper, and I was notorious for egging people on. Eddie was once banned from the gym for two weeks because he flipped out and smashed some lockers after I had repeatedly kicked his thigh too hard during a kickboxing session. On a different occasion, Eddie mocked me ruthlessly for tapping out too quickly when I was caught in a triangle choke. He laid into me so much I vowed never submit again, no matter what kind of predicament I found myself in. And, you know what? I never did over the course of my eleven-year professional career.

Another time, early in our careers, the two of us went to our favorite club and got very drunk. For some reason or another, I started loudly accusing Eddie of being jealous of me and of wanting to sabotage my drive for success. This really pissed him off because, in his mind, he would always have my back through thick and thin. Of course, I didn't shut up about it, and we decided to go out to the parking lot and settle it with our fists. But once we got out there we realized how stupidly we were behaving. We started hugging and crying and telling each other we were best friends. It was the closest we ever got to coming to blows outside of the gym. Right there we agreed never to fight each other for less than $1 million a piece.

In the end, our friendly rivalry paid big dividends. After a million sparring rounds, a hundred "fuck you"s, seventeen verbal explosions, and ten crying fits, we can look back and know we pushed each other to the highest levels of success. We both had long careers in the UFC, and Eddie's is still in progress.

I am also mostly responsible for Eddie's famous nickname, "Short Fuse." It must have been in about 2001 that Eddie decided to have a huge party at his house in southeast Portland. Friends from all over had converged on the place, including a guy we called Ry-Dog. Ry-Dog had some real gangster friends, who showed up when the party was in full swing. One of these gangsters was packing heat and decided it would be badass if he started firing his pistol into the sky in Eddie's front yard. On seeing this, Eddie had a fit. I watched as the skin around his neck turned red, and the redness climbed up his neck and filled his face. He looked like a human firecracker that was about to explode! Eddie immediately threw down his beer can, stomped across the lawn, and knocked the gangster out with one punch while the thug was still squeezing the trigger. Everyone cheered and we went back to drinking.

Well, several hours later, one of those dudes made the ill-advised decision to pass out on Eddie's couch. It was never a good idea to do that in my presence because I was an infamous "spritzer." (Jason "Strange Brew" Thacker learned this the hard way on television during the first season of *TUF*.) I whipped my dick out and pissed on the dude's cheek, my urine splattering on Eddie's nice couch. Again, the human firecracker went on display. Eddie stormed over to me and started screaming, the crimson climbing his neck as if his head were a cherry bomb. The only way I was able to calm him down was to convince him that I hadn't pissed on the guy, but instead had squirted a bottle of water.

Eddie had a fight a couple of weeks later. Unbeknownst to him, I conspired with the announcer to make his new nickname public. "Short Fuse" was born.

Both Eddie and I have UFC legend Chael Sonnen to thank for kick-starting our careers. In 2001, Chael had founded the FCFF—the Full Contact Fighting Federation. Many people know Chael from his famous rivalry with Anderson Silva and his later career in broadcasting. But few know that he was a trailblazer in the American northwest when it came to MMA. When he attempted to produce the first FCFF event, the state of Oregon filed a temporary injunction. But Chael and his lawyer persuaded the county court to overrule it, and successfully put on the show. Between that time and the official sanctioning of MMA in Oregon in 2004, Chael had to face the state in court several times.

Eddie's first fight took place on the FCFF 2 card, an event that operated according to "Class B Pankration" rules. This allowed for punches to the body, but only open-hand smacks to the face. All fighters were required to wear shin pads as well. To some of you youngsters, pankration style slapping might sound a little pussy-ish. That's not exactly true. MMA powerhouses like Bas Rutten could put a shitload of knockout juice into an open-handed strike. And that's what Eddie did in his first fight. Early in the match he side-stepped an attack from his opponent and whipped out the butt of his hand, smashing it into the guy's beak. Not only did Eddie knock the guy out, the dude's nose looked like somebody shoved a quarter-stick of dynamite up it.

My first appearance was at FCFF 4, and it was a big fucking deal for me. I told all of my friends and family about it. I thought I was such a big shot that I even broke up with Michelle! I had bigger fish to fry! I knew I was going to be a superstar, and I needed to find a model girlfriend who was at least an eleven. Don't get me wrong, Michelle was a beautiful girl but, like most human beings, was a little too normal for me. Beyond that, I raised a lot of eyebrows by refusing drink for almost a week prior to the fight. I wanted to be in the best shape ever. I went a whole five days without touching the sauce, which was virtually unprecedented for me at the time.

My first fight was at 205 pounds. I was a bit of a chubber back then. After I left the army, I spent so much time drinking, snorting, and taking pills that my physique and fitness level bottomed out. When I first walked into Team Quest, I was a 230-pound doughboy. Follis says to this day that, upon first meeting me, he never would have thought that I had a real future in fighting. But, what I lacked in physical prowess and natural athleticism, I made up for with extreme tenacity and heart. The fight was at the Roseland Theater in Portland. And, when I arrived before my fight, there was a line down the fucking street. I'm pretty sure they sold the place out. A lot of my friends were there, excited to see me either kick ass or get shellacked. Most importantly, Sam and Kim were there to support me, as usual.

My mom, on the other hand, was a no-show at my first fight, as usual. She had never come to any of my high school wrestling matches, so I didn't expect anything more from her. Well, actually, she came to my school one time when I had a wrestling match. It was for the district tournament my senior year, and she brought my grandmother. I won my fight and earned a medal my grandmother hung around my neck during the closing ceremony. However, my mom stayed out in the hallway the whole time, occasionally ducking outside for a cigarette. She didn't realize that maybe I wanted her to witness my biggest success in my high school career.

My mom really didn't encourage me at all while I was growing up. It's not that she was a heartless bitch; it's just that she didn't know any better and she was caught up in her own problems and her own vices. She didn't care if I did my homework. I can't recall her ever asking about it, really. Fuck, she didn't even worry whether I made it to school every day. The commute from our place in Felony Flats to high school was over an hour each way. Many times I had to beg the city bus driver to let me ride for free because my mom forgot to give me, or didn't have, a dollar for bus fare. As pathetic as it sounds, I even collected aluminum cans from time to time so I could be sure I had bus money for my commute to high school.

So, as you can imagine, when I started my amateur career, I had something to prove. Even now I still have something to prove. I didn't want to be a deadbeat like most of the other people in my family. Sadly, except for my one uncle, I don't think anyone else in my nuclear or extended family graduated from high school. I wanted to prove to myself I wasn't just taking up space on this planet—space that might be put to better use.

The Roseland Theater was set up so that the cage was surrounded by rows and rows of chairs. Higher up, a balcony overlooked the cage. And the venue had a very dark vibe. Most of the lights were off except for a bright spotlight that illuminated the cage. It seriously reminded me of the *Kumite* tournament at the end of the movie *Bloodsport*. But instead of a slick, muscle-bound Belgian karate expert fighting to honor his dead Japanese master, there was me—a pudgy dumbass with bleach-blond hair and oversized white surf shorts fighting out of the desperate need for just a small sense of pride.

When I walked out from backstage for my fight, the place was jam-packed. People were rowdy as fuck, drinking and puffing cigarettes. A heavy nicotine fog hung over the cage. Can you imagine trying to compete at a high level in any sport when you're breathing air like that? It was kind of nuts. My opponent was a local guy named Justin. And, as I recall, back in high school he was one of the better Greco-Roman wrestlers in the whole state. So, yeah, this guy had some cred, and I was more than a little scared.

I was so amped up I hardly remember the blow-by-blow of the fight. But I do remember that it was very scrappy and unrefined. I barely knew what the fuck I was doing out there with my haymaker pankration slaps and wild attacks. I finally got Justin on his back and moved into mount. I didn't know what to do, so I kept slapping and slapping. When none of it did much damage I even bopped him on the forehead with the butt of my hand. I think the audience laughed at that move. But finally, I got hold of his arm and twisted it into a keylock and cranked. Justin tapped! I jumped up like I had just won the Olympics and started bellowing into the crowd. The place went wild! After all, everyone was drunk as shit . . . so why not.

I felt like the big man on campus. The local paper interviewed me on camera after the fight.

"Great fight!" said the reporter, holding a microphone in front of my face. "From the sounds of it, this could be the start of great career. Randy Couture says you're the next big prospect for the UFC."

I was dumbfounded and so full of emotions that I looked and sounded like a buffoon.

"Really?!" I replied. "Cool!"

I still have a video of that first fight. And, let me tell you, despite everything, I have intense pride when I watch it. My technique in the cage was garbage. I was flailing around like a goofball. But, on the other hand, I took a chance—a big chance. I put myself out in front of a bunch of people. And, if I had lost, it could have been a personal disaster for me. But I won.

To this day, I show the video of that fight to a lot of the athletes I coach. They get a kick out of seeing the Crippler back when he was a young buck with little more than a single-leg takedown and a dream.

"See where everybody starts?" I ask my young fighters. "Everyone sucks when they start. What matters is that you refuse to give up. Less than four years later I faced Anderson Silva in a title eliminator fight in the UFC. Can you fucking believe that? Where you start, as it turns out, doesn't always matter. It's not the cards you are dealt, but how you play them."

Justin Terherst fought one more time a year later, losing via TKO. In 2007, while I was traveling the world, performing in front of millions of fans and rubbing elbows with the rich and famous, Justin died of cancer. Life is fucked up like that, isn't it?

Rest in peace, Justin. And thank you for being part of my journey.

# CHAPTER 4
## *TUF 1*

In late 2004 I traveled to Las Vegas to begin what would be over two months of filming for the first ever season of a reality show called *The Ultimate Fighter*. To fans, it became known by the abbreviation *TUF*. The premise of the show was ground-breaking: take sixteen MMA combatants with varying levels of experience, stuff them all into a single house, and observe them as they compete for a six-figure contract with the UFC. The basic format of the show had previously worked well on hit television shows such as *Big Brother*, *Survivor*, and *The Real World*. Like them, *TUF 1* would feature a cast of intriguing, often nutty, confrontational narcissists who would mix together like oil and water. But, what made this version of that theme special was that all of the contestants were aggressive young men who made a living—or aspired to make a living—by beating the shit out of other young men. And so disagreements and differences that might have simply resulted in a melodramatic shouting match on a more typical reality show were amplified by the smoldering potential for physical violence between the participants in *TUF*.

You can tell from the casting that the producers of that first season of *TUF* had a very good idea of what they needed to do in order to generating ratings. They must have looked at my brand of reckless, hillbilly mayhem as a potential gold mine. But I wasn't the only sparkplug they were able to recruit. There was the quirky

Albuquerque native Diego Sanchez, who referred to himself as a "Zen Master," and the mad hatter Forrest Griffin, who had previously worked as a police officer in Georgia. There was Nate Quarry, who grew up as a member of the Jehovah's Witnesses before redirecting his focus toward martial arts. And there was "The American Psycho" Stephan Bonnar, a smooth-talking Indiana boy who was oddly charming and disturbing and threatening all at once. There was the collegiate wrestling champion Josh Koscheck with his tightly curled blond hair, who would go on to become a very divisive figure in the UFC's welterweight division. And then there was Jason Thacker, the inexperienced bumpkin from Canada who just didn't quite belong.

When we walked into the *TUF* house for the first time I pretty much went straight to the kitchen. There wasn't much to get excited about as far as food goes, but the place was absolutely stocked to the hilt with booze. I wasted no time in digging into that, and, by about eight o'clock on that first night, I was wasted. TV viewers of this first episode may have assumed that I was trying to prove something—that I was trying to show off my hard-partying skills. But that's just not the case. That's just how I lived. I got drunk most nights of the week without giving it a second thought. The only difference here was that the alcohol was free and unlimited.

I felt out of place from the start. A few of the guys were pretty straight-edged, and I had less in common with them socially than I do with most nuns. They didn't react particularly well to my obnoxious drinking and to my even more obnoxious, and incessant, trash talking. Mike Swick got the brunt of it that first night. He and I had fought previously at *WEC 9*. I knocked him out in the second round. It was the only loss of his career to that point and, obviously, a sore subject. Somehow we all started talking about it and, though I tried to make it sound like it was no big deal, I did a hell of a job rubbing salt in his wound. We had barely been there half a day and we were already threatening to step out into the backyard and beat each other's asses.

Some guys talk trash to build their own confidence. Others do it to get into their opponent's head, to gain an edge in a competition. I talked trash because it was like my first language. Don't believe me? When I was born, right after I emerged from the birth canal, I told the doctor his tie made him look retarded. I joke. But, in all seriousness, I had been talking crazy shit with and to my friends for as long as I could remember. It had essentially become an art form. Growing up, my best buds and I were skater punks. We spent endless hours ripping around town, entertaining ourselves by coming up with different ways of making fun of each other.

The biggest target in the *TUF* house was Jason Thacker, and I was by no means the only one giving him a hard time. He was an MMA enthusiast, but not a skilled fighter on the level of the rest of the guys in the house. He trained pretty much on his own out of an abandoned truck stop on his family's property in wooded Whonnock, British Columbia. In fact, although Thacker had competed in Thai boxing, he had virtually zero mixed martial arts experience prior to the show. He had been armed with a heavy bag and an active imagination but little else.

I'm sure plenty of people won't believe this, but I don't purposely seek out the weak link when I am looking to sling some insults. I am an equal-opportunity asshole. I spread my shit talking around the *TUF* house like butter on a big piece of toast. The problem was that Thacker was probably the only guy who couldn't defend himself against it. He was socially backward. And I say that with the full knowledge that I was backward in many ways too! Had the *TUF* cameras taken a tour of my ramshackle childhood homes, the viewing audience would have realized how much Jason and I actually had in common. But Jason clearly had little experience with American punks who had chips on their shoulders before he agreed to take part in a reality show that would make fifteen of them his roommates. He dressed and talked in exactly the way that you would expect a guy who grew up in a disregarded part of the Canadian wilderness to dress and talk. And that's precisely why the producers of *The Ultimate Fighter* cast the poor bastard. They didn't think that Thacker was a good fighter, or that he had a chance for greatness. They viewed him as an unsuspecting redneck who would make for good TV. He was a sacrifice to the ratings gods. As shitty as I was to Thacker, I wasn't the one who knowingly threw him to the wolves.

I gave Thacker the nickname "Strange Brew" because he reminded me of that comedy about two goofy Canadian brothers who work at a brewery in Ontario. Unfortunately for Jason, we also used that nickname to refer to the funky country smell that wafted from his clothes. And, even more unfortunately, to this day he is probably better known by that nickname than by his actual name. Now, I've never been accused of smelling like a spring day at all times, but it was Thacker's special odor that got him into trouble on the first night of filming. As we were settling in for bed, Diego Sanchez pulled out a can of air freshener and demanded Jason go take a shower. As soon as Jason left the room, I jumped out of my bunk and, drunk as a skunk, pissed—or "spritzed" as I like to say—on the poor kid's bed. I rubbed it into his sheets and then climbed back up into my bed. Clean and tuckered out, Thacker returned from his shower and passed out in his soiled bed. All of this aired in episode one of the television show. I, deservedly, came off looking like a careless bully who preyed on a poor, innocent guy.

Yes, I am a bully. I bullied people for a living for eleven years. But, again, I was always an equal-opportunity bully. My decision to piss on Thacker's bed had nothing to do with the fact that he was an easy target. Frankly, you would not believe how many times I have spritzed on sleeping friends and their beds. I am thirty-five years old now. But, even today, if you get drunk and pass out around my friends or me, there is a high likelihood you'll wake up glazed with a bit of urine.

The coaches for the first season of *TUF* were UFC light heavyweight champion Randy Couture and his archrival Chuck Liddell. As you may remember, Chuck was also my coach at Team Quest, a circumstance that definitely worked to my advantage during the course of filming. The first week of filming came to be known as "hell week." During that time, Randy put us through a gauntlet of physical and athletic challenges in order to evaluate our abilities. I remember those sessions beginning at 5:00 AM. The regimen was designed to break us because, again, it made for good television. Probably the toughest challenge of that week was a grueling thirty-five-minute treadmill run that took place on the very first morning. Each fighter had to run for five minutes at five miles per hour, then five minutes at six miles per hour, then seven miles per hour, then eight miles per hour, then nine, then ten. Many of the contestants gave up little more than halfway through. Josh Rafferty ended up on all fours, heaving into a bucket. In fact, there was only one fighter who finished the full challenge, and he happened to be the fighter who was piss drunk the night before. Me.

The treadmill challenge was not so much about speed and endurance as it was about the ability to push through adversity.

Dana White and the coaches watched it very closely. Everyone was shocked I was able to pull it off, not only because I was nursing a hangover but also because I didn't have the best cardio in the house to begin with. But the outcome did not surprise me. I had been training like that my whole life. In high school, in the army, as a young member of Team Quest, I would get smashed night after night and still wake up at the crack of dawn to train or run five miles. I was never the slickest or most athletic fighter in the UFC—not by a long shot—but I would argue that there were few fighters who had more will power than me. I knew it back then, too. By the way, I tore my hip flexor during that treadmill challenge, an injury that plagues me to this day.

Most of us thought the whole show would simply consist of these kinds of physical challenges and team competitions. We didn't learn that we would be subject to elimination fights every week until we had actually started filming. Some guys were definitely upset about having to get into the cage and scrap. I didn't remotely share their concerns. To have a hesitation about fighting when your sole purpose in life is to be a UFC fighter did not make any sense. As far as I was concerned, the more opportunities I had to lay hands on dudes the better. Dana White, aware of some of this grumbling, gathered us together and gave his legendary "Do you wanna be a fighter?" speech. He said, in part:

"It's not about cutting weight. It's not about living in a fucking house. It's about do you wanna be a fighter? . . . Being a fighter isn't all fucking girls and signing autographs. It's fucking hard work, but you have the opportunity to fucking make money, be famous, and do something for the sport here. That's what this is all about . . ."

That resonated with me big time. The big man was preaching to my choir.

Hell week was horrible for all of us, but Thacker had an especially hard time. He could barely walk after the workouts, and after just a couple of days was talking about leaving the show. Some guys convinced him to stay, but in the end he lasted little more than a week. Our team lost a challenge and had to send a fighter home. The choice for Randy Couture could not have been more obvious.

I continued to be me. I drank. I fucked with people. I fucked around in the house. But when it came to training, I wouldn't be outworked. Also, I tried hard, as I always do, to be a good training partner. I find satisfaction in helping my teammates master technique and in motivating others to achieve their potential. That's why it was so natural for me, later in my career, to become a coach. However, my shenanigans early on in the *TUF* house seemed to overshadow all of that. As highlighted in the second episode of the show, my team, led by Nate Quarry, decided to call me out during a session with Randy. They were fed up.

What you might find interesting is how unaware I was of how abnormal my behavior was. I truly had no idea my heavy drinking and lewd behavior were out of the norm. As I've said before, I come from a family where Natural Ice beer was served with morning pancakes. Living with fifteen other guys who viewed me as a carnival act really opened my eyes to this. After I left that house I became much more aware of how extreme my lifestyle can be.

Of course, not every moment of our lives during the six or seven weeks we filmed ultimately appeared on national television. In particular, there was the time Dana White took us out on the town in Vegas. We went to dinner and then to a Kid Rock show at The Joint, which was a music venue in the Hard Rock Casino. What the producers decided to broadcast was the fact that we all got very drunk and then came back to the house and caused a ruckus. Diego Sanchez was so drunk he blacked out and started vomiting, for example. The episode showed the before and the after, but it did not show what went on while we were partying in Vegas.

While at The Joint a couple of us—maybe Josh Koscheck, Bobby Southworth, and I—placed a bet on who could pick up a chick while we were there. I went to work immediately and soon met a loose young lady from Indiana who was standing with a friend at the bar. I told her I was a professional fighter and my friends and I were part of a reality show. That's about all it took. Soon were making out in a booth near the back of the club.

We were all over each other, causing a scene. Actually, I probably would have had sex with her right there except for the fact that, when I looked up, I saw Randy looking at me and shaking his head disappointedly. So the young lady and I decided to find a nice, quiet bathroom where we could do our dirty work. We made our way to the women's room, but one of the show producers figured out what we were up to and prevented us from entering. So we took a lap of the club and, when no one was looking, slipped into the men's room. Indiana girl snuck into a stall with me. Right there in the filth, like pigs in heat, we both dropped our underwear to our ankles and got to work. It may sound glamorous, but fucking in a bathroom stall is not all it's cracked up to be. We struggled to avoid the toilet and arrange ourselves in the only modified doggy-style position that seemed to work. Every few thrusts, her head clanged off the side of the stall. Then, all of a sudden, we heard someone chuckling. I looked up, and there was Mike Swick standing on the toilet in the stall next to us and looking down over the partition. Someone else started banging on the door. Koscheck reached under the stall and grabbed my ankles, trying to make me fall over. The door busted open and ten or twelve of the *TUF* guys were standing there hooting and pointing. At first, Indiana girl loved it—she was putting on a show. But when I started dying laughing and couldn't perform, things got awkward in a hurry. Finally, the girl got embarrassed, pulled her clothes on, and rushed out of the bathroom. I never saw her again.

That night when we got back to the *TUF* house, Bobby Southworth and I started jawing at each other about something. I can't remember what the issue was—probably just some drunken bullshit. But the argument concluded with Bobby calling me a "fatherless bastard." You might not think that is the worst insult someone could hurl. However, keep in mind I am, for all intents and purposes, a fatherless bastard. In fact, as discussed earlier in this book, I had only met my father for the first time some months earlier when I was in Vegas for the *TUF* auditions. When Bobby said that, I had a meltdown. First I threatened to kill him. Then I started sobbing like a little boy. And, you can be sure the reality TV cameramen were there for the whole thing, shooting close ups as I cried into my hands.

I was having an emotional crisis, and it was Nate Quarry who stepped up to defend me and comfort me. While tears poured down my cheeks, he spent at least an hour talking to me and reminding me of how far I had come despite the absence of my father. Once I had calmed down, I decided to sleep out in the yard rather than in the house with the likes of Bobby Southworth. Somebody brought me some blankets and a pillow. I tucked myself in and passed out.

I woke up to the sound of laughter. Southworth and Koscheck were pouring water from a garden hose onto my blanket. When

I saw their grinning faces I went into beast mode. I hardly remember this, but I learned of all the details the next day. I got up and walked to the house. I punched a decorative window on the front door, shattering it with my fist. Blood immediately started pouring from my hand. Then I went inside and smashed two bedroom doors, literally splintering them and ripping them off their hinges. I'm not sure what my goal was, but I was seeing red and was about to throw down with Southworth in the kitchen when Nate again came to the rescue. He separated us and diffused the situation.

The producers sent me to the hospital to see a doctor about my shredded hand. The skin had been gouged so deeply over my second knuckle I could see the bone moving within the socket. It was disgusting. The doctor looked at it closely and shook his head.

"There's not much I can do for that thing," he said. "You can either keep it wrapped in gauze and let it heal on its own or you can get a skin graft. I can't stitch it."

"Can I still fight?" was my first question.

He responded, "The last thing you can do with that hand is fight. If I were you, I wouldn't throw any punches for two to three months."

I thanked the doctor, left the examination room, and headed back out to the ER waiting room where one of the producers was standing by.

"What's the prognosis?" he asked as soon as I emerged.

"No big deal," I replied. "The doctor says I should just keep it wrapped in gauze and everything will be fine."

The producer was shocked to hear this, as he should have been. Lucky for me, doctor-patient confidentiality rules prevented the cameras from following me into the examination room and prevented the doctor from sharing any medical information about me. So the production team, the coaches, and Dana White were none the wiser. Had they known how serious the injury was, my stint on the show would have been over right then and there.

Randy, Chuck, Dana, and Lorenzo had a powwow and decided that the best way to put the beef between Koscheck, Southworth, and me behind us was to have Koscheck and me fight that week: loser go home. This was music to my ears. Although Koscheck was a highly decorated wrestler—a four-time NCAA Division I All-American—I knew in my heart I would destroy him if we met in the cage.

However, you can't always get what you want, said Mick Jagger. My wrestling was not on Koscheck's level. He spent two rounds dumping me on the ground and controlling me. He did almost no damage, essentially sprawling on top for the duration of each round. That's how Koscheck got the nickname "Human Blanket," which has lingered until this day. In the end, it was a unanimous decision in his favor and I was sent packing. As I walked out of the gym, Koscheck and Southworth started singing "I'm Leaving on a Jet Plane" at the top of their lungs.

There definitely was no love lost between Koscheck and me, but I wouldn't say we were mortal enemies. They edited the show to make it look a bit worse than it was. And I don't have time to hold grudges, to be honest. Not long after the show ended, I more or less forgot about the beefs I had there. Swick and I are cool, I would say. Koscheck and I are cordial. I haven't bumped into Bobby Southworth in ages, but I wouldn't have a problem with him if I did. So it's kind of funny that every day of my life someone asks me whether I still hate Koscheck, and whether I wished I had a rematch with him. There is even an online campaign that has the goal of bringing me out of retirement to have one last fight with that curly-haired bastard. Not gonna happen, folks . . . that is, unless someone coughs up a cool million bucks or two.

After I lost to Koscheck, they sent me to the "loser house," elsewhere in Vegas, which is where I was supposed to spend my days with Thacker and the other rejects until filming wrapped. Since I didn't have to worry about competing or cutting weight for fights, I let loose a bit. To avoid sounding like a broken record, I won't go into the details of what it meant for me to "let loose." But after just four or five days there, I received a surprise visit from one of the producers. He told me they were bringing me back. Nate Quarry had severely injured his ankle in training. He could not continue with the show. Allegedly, the producers gave my Team Quest pals Nate and Randy the option to choose which one of the eliminated fighters they wanted to bring back into the competition. Of course, it was a no brainer for them. The producers could have just as easily finished the show with one less fighter. But it's pretty obvious that they recognized I was a lightning rod in the house and seized the opportunity to throw me back into the mix.

Much to the dismay of Josh Koscheck (and some other fighters probably) I sauntered back into the house and picked up where I left off. But my second tour of duty was not as drama packed as my first. Soon they lined me up against Kenny Florian for another elimination bout. Kenny happened to be one of the guys in the house who I considered my friend. What's interesting about him is that he fought at 185 pounds during *The Ultimate Fighter*. Then he fought two fights in the UFC as a welterweight—170 pounds. Then KenFlo made another dozen or so appearances in the Octagon as a lightweight, weighing in at 155 pounds. And then, for the final two fights of his career, he dropped to 145 pounds and challenged but lost to Jose Aldo in a title bout. Pretty fucking amazing. That's a forty-pound range. I can't even begin to describe how difficult it must be to cut that kind of weight and massively adjust one's body mass, yet continue to perform at a world-class level. Most guys never transition between weight classes. You can surely count on two hands the number of UFC fighters who have appeared in three weight classes. And , as far as I can tell, you can count with your pinky finger the number of guys who traversed four classes while a UFC fighter, Kenny Florian being the one and only. (However, news recently broke that Diego Sanchez will drop to featherweight for his next UFC fight, joining KenFlo's special club.)

Kenny was not a very big middleweight. We trained together a fair amount during the show and, to be honest, I kind of outsized him. At first, Kenny assumed I was an asshole. But, through training, we grew to like each other and decided to help each other advance in the competition. I showed Kenny a move I had found a lot of success with: an overhand feint followed by an uppercut. We also spent a lot of time on some of the effective clinch techniques I had mastered during my time training under decorated wrestlers Matt Lindland and Randy Couture at Team Quest. I remember teaching him the proper use of an inside bicep tie, which allows for some dirty boxing and elbow strikes in close quarters against the fence.

The fight started out as expected; I was too big for Kenny. I stalked him all over the cage, unafraid of his power. I landed a lot of heavy shots, but to the kid's credit, he weathered it very well. The first round clearly went my way. The second round was not very different, although KenFlo had a bit of success with his striking. And, son of a bitch, he threw the overhand feint-uppercut combo I had taught him. It landed flush on my chin! At that moment in the fight I remember us looking at each other and laughing. But

I kept moving forward, and I think most observers would have expected me to finish Kenny in that second round, or at least win a solid unanimous decision.

Then I pressed him against the cage and looked to work him over with some dirty boxing. But, the excellent pupil that he is, Kenny locked on an inside bicep tie. *Very good, Kenny*, I remember thinking to myself. And in that moment Kenny threw a slicing elbow strike that bit into my right eyebrow. It wasn't a concussive strike, and it didn't particularly affect my momentum, but when I stepped back, blood was pouring down my face and onto the mat. As soon as we separated a bit, referee John McCarthy stepped in between us to pause the match and have the doctor look at my wound. It was nasty. There was a four-inch gash that was spewing crimson. McCarthy, that good soul, saw that the doctor was concerned and tried to use his influence to prevent a fight stoppage.

"Doc, I don't think it's that bad," he said. "I think he's fine."

But the doctor wasn't buying it. The cut was wide open and blood was flooding my eye, affecting my visibility. It was a classic fight-ending cut. The doctor waived off the bout, giving Kenny the victory via TKO. I went out to the parking lot and broke down into tears.

The next day my hand with the ripped-up knuckle started to swell. Stitch Duran had done a great job of padding it with cotton and wrapping it prior to the fight. However, at some point my knuckle became exposed, and I think I snagged it on one of Kenny's teeth. It seemed to be getting infected, so I washed it and bandaged it carefully. But the next morning I woke up and my hand looked like a fucking baseball glove. The producers decided to send me to the hospital, yet again.

The emergency room was packed when I arrived. It was mostly the Vegas geriatric syndrome—old people who had spent the whole night pulling slot machine handles and forgot to take their blood pressure medication. So I had to wait for hours and hours while the doctors dealt with cardiac crisis after cardiac crisis. My hand continued to swell and throb, and the skin all around my knuckle was bright red and puffy. Finally, at some point in the evening they examined my hand. The doctors looked at each other with concern. It was a staph infection, one of the most dangerous infections a person can get. Immediately they transferred me to an intensive care unit and hooked me up to bags of antibiotics.

After an hour or so, the swelling started to dissipate. One of the doctors came in and examined it closely.

"We're lucky we got to you when we did or we would have had to remove it," she told me flatly.

"You mean amputate my hand?" I asked.

"Yes. It was touch and go there. We had to treat you ahead of a man who was having a mild heart attack because we thought you were going to lose that hand."

That's how it seems to go in my life. I bounce from one crisis to another. Part of me wishes that the gods would take it easy on me for once. But a bigger part of me likes having these stories to tell.

The first season of *The Ultimate Fighter* was remarkable because many of the participants went on to have successful and influential careers as professional fighters. The epic brawl between Stephan Bonnar and Forrest Griffin in the April 2005 live finale of the show is considered one of the greatest MMA bouts of all time. Dana White has credited their fight as perhaps the most significant moment in the history the UFC—a moment that not only saved the organization but put a glorious spotlight on the sport in front of a nationwide audience. Griffin went on to become the UFC light heavyweight champion, albeit quite briefly. Bonnar never became champion, but remained a beloved figure and a highly regarded fighter in the organization for another seven years. Josh Koscheck climbed the ranks of the UFC's welterweight division, ultimately challenging legend Georges St-Pierre for the belt. Kenny Florian made impressive but unsuccessful title fight appearances in two different divisions, finally retiring in 2011 to become a television commentator and analyst for various UFC broadcasts. Diego Sanchez remains active in the UFC, and is widely considered one of the most exciting fighters to have graced the Octagon. He has been awarded the "Fight of the Night" bonus a record seven times.

But one man, in particular, faded into obscurity: Jason Thacker. At the *TUF 1 Finale* he had the unfortunate experience of meeting me in the Octagon. I pounded him out in one minute and thirty-five seconds. He never fought again.

For years, Thacker remained a punch line, a cautionary tale to so many young fighters who would seek fame and fortune in the unforgiving sport of MMA. After a while, though, people stopped talking about him. He disappeared off the radar. For years, no one in the MMA community heard from him or cared enough to reach out to him. Then, in early 2015, ten whole years after the filming of *TUF 1*, curiosity got the better of MMA journalist Chuck Mindenhall. He tracked down Thacker who was still living on the same rundown property in British Columbia. He was unemployed and poor and spent most of his time taking care of his aging parents and his brother who all had serious health issues. In the photos Chuck took, Thacker looks grizzled. He wears a bushy salt-and-pepper beard, and his unkempt brown hair spills down over his shoulders. Thacker resembles a rugged lumberjack or a seasoned tugboat captain much more than the wide-eyed kid we had all gotten to know a decade earlier.

Maybe changing his appearance so drastically was a purposeful decision. In March of 2015, Mindenhall published an article for MMAFighting.com, from which comes this excerpt:

> "Right over there, that's the bar where I got into a brawl after the show aired," he said, as he drives us to lunch. It's a bar called The Office, which we laugh is a perfect name for a lushing crib. *Honey, I'm afraid I'm going to be at The Office late again tonight.* It's just an icebreaker. Thacker has a sense of humor. But within five minutes of meeting him he's telling me how he took a pipe to the face at that very bar. He was jumped by a couple of guys who didn't like the way he repped his country on the show. "A lot of people wanted to fight me after that," he says. "I got into a lot of fights."
>
> That pipe accounts for the disfiguration in his nose.

Do I blame myself for the abuse Jason Thacker experienced upon returning to Canada, a laughing stock of the sport he loved so well? No, I don't. We all made our decisions before, during, and after that show. And in life, you never know. *What would have happened? What could have been?* The answers to these questions are and will always be speculation and nothing more. Jason Thacker took a stab at greatness. He took a chance on life. He put himself in a scary, risky, ruthless situation, one that almost no one in the world has experienced. And though he had his moments of doubt, he saw it through. He didn't give up. And at the end of the show, Thacker convinced Dana White to set up a fight with me—the hardest hitter in the whole house—for the April finale. He didn't have to fight. He could have returned to Canada weeks earlier, his head held high, and left it all behind. But, you heard me right, *Jason Thacker asked to fight me.* And Dana didn't agree to the idea immediately. After witnessing what had transpired during the *TUF* filming, he was concerned for Thacker's welfare. But the kid begged for it—for one last chance at redemption even though the odds were stacked against him like a mountain against a stream. Few people have the opportunity in life to demonstrate such boldness, such bravery.

Maybe Thacker would have been better off had he never heard of *The Ultimate Fighter*. Maybe he would have been worse off. But I will tell you this: in a house full of sixteen of the toughest dudes in the world, Strange Brew had the biggest balls. And for that, I offer the man nothing but my undying respect.

After our final day of filming, Dana took all of us out for one more raucous night of celebration. We went to Cheetah's gentleman's club in Vegas. Uncle Dana handed out nice little stacks of cash to each of us, and we spent them like it was going out of style. A fitting ending to a long stretch of mayhem.

I was the last one standing that night. In the morning, with the sun already in the sky, I took a limo back to the *TUF* house to collect some things that I had left behind. When I arrived, several of the production crewpersons were striking the set. They were removing the multitude of cameras and microphones that had been mounted to the walls and hidden throughout the house. Wires were sticking out everywhere—in the kitchen, in the living room, in the bathrooms. It reminded me of that Jim Carrey movie *The Truman Show*, in which every moment of his character's life is documented and broadcast to the world. For a few minutes, in the silence of the mostly empty house, I looked around and took it all in: the empty beer bottles, the broken doors, the bloodstained kitchen floor. Something in that moment made me realize fully how wild and surreal it had all been. The men who had occupied this house had done something special and unprecedented. Maybe it wouldn't change the world. But lives had changed in those nine weeks. *Hell, on second thought, maybe it would change the world.* A big fat smile spread across my face.

# CHAPTER 5
# ESCAPE TO HAWAII

I woke up in a cold sweat. The Hawaiian Airlines stewardess was gently shaking me by my shoulder.

"We're preparing for arrival, sir. Please return your seat to its upright and locked position," she said sweetly and patiently. Barely realizing where I was or what was happening, I complied with her instructions, then wiped a dribble of saliva off of my chin. To my right sat an elderly couple holding hands. They smiled at me.

"Hello," I rasped.

My voice was like a box of sand. This was partly due to the copious amounts of booze and marijuana I had consumed at my going-away party the night before. But mostly it was because of the way I had lost my fight to a guy named Jason MacDonald six months earlier.

Hearing my voice, the old woman gave me a sympathetic look.

"You make a lot of noise while you sleep," she commented with a chuckle.

"Sorry," I whispered back. I tend to wake up in the middle of the night and shout and scream in a semiconscious state. I had probably given the poor old lady a few scares. God knows what these innocent old-timers were thinking, having to sit next to a weird dude with a red mohawk, a bruised face, and a sludgy cocktail of recreational drugs still running through his veins.

The window to my left provided me with an amazing view of the shimmering Pacific Ocean. It was illuminated in all of its glory by the mid-morning sun that followed the plane on its westward journey from Portland, Oregon. In a matter of minutes I would be touching down at Honolulu International Airport. I couldn't have been more relieved at the prospect of a change of scenery. It was May 2007 and the previous twelve months of my life had been an absolute shit show.

"But, Chris," you may ask, "hasn't your whole life been a shit show?" Good point, counselor, but read on.

As I deplaned, I was greeted by the same stewardess who had awakened me. She was a beautiful and fresh-faced Pacific Islander.

"Aloha," she greeted sweetly. I bowed my head and she looped a flowery lei around my neck. "Are you going to be the UFC champion someday?" she asked.

I was shocked that a gentle and proper young lady knew anything about who I was or what I did for a living.

"Do you like fighting?" I asked in reply.

"Of course I like fighting, Mr. Crippler," she said with a wink. "I am Hawaiian." And as I looked into her bright eyes, I knew, then and there, that I had finally made a smart life decision.

I smiled to myself and headed off into the terminal. Suddenly, the stewardess shouted after me, "I hope this summer brings you happiness and love!" I had almost forgotten: summer was about to begin. That was a refreshing thought.

*Love*, the stewardess had said. Love—and all of the shit it brings with it—was, in fact, the reason I was migrating to Honolulu. As much as I was looking forward to new experiences, new friends, and new opportunities, I was simultaneously making a great escape. OK, I admit it. I was running away—away from a girl named Lisa.

I had met Lisa three years earlier, in 2004. I knew a guy named Charlie who used to put on fight shows in various parts of Washington State. I appeared on a couple of his cards, and once, in a town called Lynnwood, after knocking the shit out of a dude named Boyd Ballard (and ending his career . . . sorry Boyd), I laid eyes on Lisa. The fight took less than two minutes, and I was riding high when I got backstage. My team and friends were hugging me and giving me high-fives when I saw her and froze. She was sexy and challenging and exactly what I was looking for in a girl. But at first she barely gave me the time of day.

I walked up to Lisa and said, "Hey, I'm Chris. I think you look really nice today."

She literally laughed in my face, then turned away and walked down the hallway. What a bitch! I was smitten.

Charlie was not just a promoter, he owned an MMA gym in Everett, Washington, which was where Lisa lived and trained. Charlie, as it turned out, was Lisa's coach, and I realized immediately that he was my only hope for getting my foot in the door with her. At the same time, my friend and trainer Dennis Davis had started going after an untouchable married girl named Rachel, who happened to be a close friend of Lisa. We started competing to see who could achieve mission impossible first. So, over the next several months, I took every opportunity to get Lisa's attention. I even took a few unplanned detours up to Everett. But Lisa was stubborn and showed no interest. It pissed me off!

Finally, in August came *UFC 49: Unfinished Business*, which featured as the main event the third meeting of my Team Quest coach Randy Couture and "The Phenom" Vitor Belfort. It was one of the biggest fights of the year, so I flew down to Las Vegas with a few buddies including Dennis Davis. We weren't especially wealthy dudes, so the four of us booked just a single hotel room.

The night of the fights Dennis and I were heading to our seats in the MGM Grand Garden Arena when, lo and behold, there stood Lisa and Rachel looking incredibly hot. I made eye contact with Lisa then walked up to her and said, "See? You can't avoid me forever!"

This made Lisa smile, and I knew I finally had a chance. We convinced Rachel and Lisa to meet us at a club after the event. We told them that we had a special hookup and could skip the line to get in.

I did have a hookup, an old buddy of my brother. But, to be honest, I hadn't exactly lined anything up for that night. Luckily when the four of us got to the club, the dude was standing out front and let us in, as promised. It worked like a charm. My game with Lisa was spot on. We spent the night talking and flirting. And toward the end of the night, we started kissing. I was on cloud nine.

I couldn't wait to get Lisa naked. However, we had a bit of a problem: I was sharing my room with three other dudes and she, too, was sharing a room with Rachel. And, when I inquired at the front desk, I learned there wasn't a single room available. The entire hotel was booked up.

So we headed up and down the strip, trying to find a place to crash. Several hotels, even some shitty ones, turned me away due to no availability. Finally we ended up at the Monte Carlo, where we walked around holding hands and fucking around for a while until I came up with a great idea. By this time, it was 6:00 AM. As we stepped through the lobby, I noticed a young man in an army uniform standing in the checkout line. I walked up to him.

"Hey buddy, do you have a second? I asked.

"What's up?" he replied suspiciously.

I took the candid approach. "I'll be honest with you. I'm about to hook up with this amazing girl, but both of us have friends staying in our rooms. Is there any way that I can pay you for your hotel key so that we can have a place to ourselves for a few hours?"

He gave me a mistrusting look.

"I promise we won't fuck up the room," I continued. "And we'll check out by noon. I'm an army guy myself. No problem."

"Well . . ." he hesitated.

"How much do you want? Just name it."

I was ready to fork over two hundred bucks if I had to.

"How about fifty?" he suggested.

Without a moment's hesitation I paid the guy off, grabbed his key, and led Lisa up to our new room. Luckily there were two beds, one of which had gone unused by the Army dude. Lisa and I got it on, and it was even better than I had hoped.

We spent another three full days in Vegas. We hung out and drank by the pool during the day and got fucked up and went wild at night. I kept skipping my flight and calling in sick to work. At that time I was a coach and trainer at Team Quest in Portland. Matt Lindland had to threaten to fire me before I finally dragged myself to the airport and headed home.

This began the most fucked up, out-of-control relationship I have ever had in my life. I started visiting Everett frequently to see Lisa. However, she insisted we hide the fact that we were dating because my reputation preceded me up there. I had slept with several girls who ran in Charlie's circle and Lisa was not comfortable admitting that she had taken my bait. So we pretended I was simply coming up to train under Charlie. And, each day when we went to the gym, I would drop Lisa off, then wait twenty minutes before returning and entering the gym myself.

Our relationship got hot and heavy in a hurry. I began commuting up to Lisa's hood every Friday to spend the weekend with her. We partied with her friends a lot, and had more sex than I had ever had in my life. And every Monday morning at around three I would hop in my car and put the petal to the metal back to Portland so I could teach a six o'clock grappling class at Team Quest. This craziness went on for about a year.

During this time, I got hit with my first DUI arrest. It was Easter in Portland, one of the rare weekends that Lisa had commuted down to see me rather than the other way around. We had spent the day with Sam and Kim drinking White Russians. At about 11:00 PM I decided I needed some cocaine. So, like a jackass, I hopped in the car and head out. Within about four blocks a cop pulled me over. The field sobriety test was short and sweet. I think I stumbled about three times while trying to walk the line. I pleaded for some Easter leniency, but the cop was having none of it. I spent the rest of the night in the clink.

When it came time for sentencing, I caught a break. I was given the option to participate in the DUI diversion program. Under this kind of probation program I could avoid jail time and expunge the offense from my record if I paid the necessary fees and participated in a drug and alcohol assessment program. Once a week I had to sit in on a long, boring class about using and abusing, and then take a piss test. Unfortunately, it wasn't long before I tested positive for cocaine. The administrator of the program called me up and gave me the news, instructing me to come in to discuss committing myself to an in-patient rehab program. I lied and said I'd be there.

Of course, at that time in my life, there was no fucking way I'd check myself into rehab. I didn't even think I had a problem. Rehab, as they say, was for quitters. So, even though I knew it meant a guaranteed stretch in the big house, I went MIA from the diversion program and, for about two years, didn't give it another thought.

I definitely was not on my best behavior during the few years I spent with Lisa. But at least I made some worthwhile new acquaintances, including Steven Nickell. He was a friend of Lisa's first, and the way the two of us met was pretty damn unusual. It happened on a night when Lisa and I were having one of our many emotional shouting matches. She called her friends, including Steven, to come over and pick her up. When they arrived I was sloppy drunk and worked up into a frenzy. While Lisa's girlfriend helped her pack some things and load them into the car, Steven was given the delicate job of trying to pacify me.

I don't exactly remember all of this, but Steven does a good job of retelling the story. Apparently, in my highly intoxicated state, I decided to make him a special plate of tuna mac and cheese. It wasn't quite award-winning cuisine. As I paced the room and began ranting and raving about Lisa and many other unrelated things, Steven politely nibbled at his cheesy fish plate. Then, I suddenly unleashed an axe kick on the coffee table, shattering it with shards of glass exploding everywhere. The only part of the table that remained intact was Steven's little corner where his mac and cheese was sitting. Apparently, I barely acknowledged the fact that I had destroyed an expensive piece of furniture and nearly maimed the both of us. I continued pacing and ranting, and he resumed eating his special meal. Much to Lisa's dismay, I'm sure, Steven and I have been close friends every since.

What's unique about Steven is that, more than anyone else in my life, he is an insatiable party animal. I thought I was in a league of my own when it came to drinking and doing drugs until I met this guy. It's a running joke that our lives are at stake any time we get together for a night or two. The kind of shit we have fallen into in the midst of a bender is the stuff of legend (or the stuff of nightmares, you might say).

Once, during this era, a friend of ours had a big party in Portland. At some point, just after midnight, Steven and I decided to head down to the corner gas station to pick up some cigarettes or chew or something like that. After we paid for our stuff and were heading back, we heard a commotion coming from around the side of store. We took a look and saw three dudes absolutely stomping another semiconscious guy who was in the fetal position on the ground. The guy was bleeding all over, and I really thought they were about to kill him. So I intervened. I jumped in the middle of it and shoved the three guys away.

"What the fuck are you doing, assholes?!" I yelled at them.

And, of course, one of them replied, "You want a piece of this?" Then he stepped forward, puffing his chest and getting up in my face.

To be honest, I really didn't want a piece of it. I wanted to go back to the party and do some lines of coke. This occurred during the early part of my career in the UFC. I knew that I could have destroyed any of these punks with the flick of a fist. But I also knew that would probably land me in the can, and I didn't need that kind of negative information sliding across Dana White's desk. Nonetheless, soon these three guys were looking at me like a pack of junkyard dogs eyeing a T-bone steak. My options were quickly becoming very limited. I raised my hands and backed up slowly.

"I don't want to fight you guys," I told them. "I think that dude's had enough. Why don't we all just walk away and leave it be."

The leader of the crew stepped toward me aggressively. "We're not going to leave it be, bitch," he growled.

I shook my head and kind of chuckled to myself. It appeared that this was going to go down whether I liked it or not, and this dumb fuck did not have the faintest notion of what he was wading into. Steven watched on with anticipation, ready to jump in if I needed him.

"Let me just say for the record that you do not want to do this."

"Oh, I definitely want to do it," was the dumb fuck's reply.

"Um . . . no you don't. But have it your way."

There was no diffusing the situation. The guy lunged at me with a sloppy punch. I ducked it, slapped a Muay Thai clinch around his neck and pulled his face downward, hard. At the same time, I drove my knee upward, a very basic but effective strike that most students learn in their first month of kickboxing class. However, I had probably practiced that particular move ten thousand times in my career. My knee found the dude's nose, which crunched on impact like a stale fortune cookie. He went face down to the asphalt, blood spraying from his beak.

I turned to the second guy who had a look of shock on his face. At the same time Steven, never one to back down from a fight, jumped into the melee and tangled with the third guy, a much larger man. In about ten seconds I had flattened the second punk with my left hand. I left him on the ground and rushed over to drag the big dude off of Steven. Seeing what I had done to his cronies, the big dude wisely decided to back off. The whole dust up had taken place in less than thirty seconds. The victim, who Steven and I had protected, had crawled away from the brawl. He was leaning against the gas station wall holding his head.

The big dude helped his battered friends off of the ground. We exchanged some more choice words, but it was clear they didn't want another serving of the beating that had just been dished out. Then we heard sirens approaching. Obviously, the storeowner had called the cops. The three punks hurried back to their nearby Pontiac and jumped in, ready to make a getaway. But, at that point, my blood was rushing through my veins, and I felt that these bitches hadn't learned the full lesson yet.

So, before they could take off, I jumped into the back seat of their car.

You should have seen the look on their faces when I then said, "I'm not done with you pussies. Let's go finish this."

They started yelling at me to get out of their car. But I wasn't going anywhere. And neither was Steven, who soon slid in beside me.

"Drive down the street. I want to finish beating the fuck out of you," I instructed the big dude who was behind the wheel.

The police sirens grew louder and the three dickheads started freaking out. The more hysterical they became, the louder I laughed and taunted them. The big dude realized that he had two choices: either stay parked in that lot and wait for the cops to come arrest him, or drive off with Steven and me in the back seat and maybe get his face bashed in. It was an unenviable catch-22 situation. He chose the latter option.

The big dude floored it, and we all burned rubber away from the gas station, a car full of belligerent drunkards cursing at each other. Unfortunately for them, the getaway wasn't nearly as successful as those punks had hoped. We had barely made it out of the parking lot before an approaching squad car was immediately on our tail with its lights spinning and its siren blaring.

"Uh oh. Now you're in trouble, dumb fucks!" I announced with a big smile on my face.

They started having a meltdown. One of them wanted to make a run for it, but the big dude thought better of it and pulled the car over to the side. A policeman's voice came over the loudspeaker telling the driver to throw the keys out of the window and the rest of us to put our hands up. It was at that point that Steven realized he had a sizable baggie of coke in his pocket. He gave me a nudge and showed it to me. I whispered to him that he should shove it in between the seat cushions, and he did.

A bunch of other cops appeared on the scene, and in short order we were all cuffed and thrown into the backs of separate squad cars. An ambulance had arrived on the scene as well. I could make out some paramedics kneeling over the beating victim who was still sitting against the wall of the gas station. The cops started questioning each of us one by one. When my turn came, I matter-of-factly explained what happened. The cop, an older man with a mustache, nodded and took notes, not saying much in return. Then he walked away.

I figured I would soon be enjoying another stretch of time behind bars. I didn't really expect the police to buy my story, albeit true. And, even if they did, they'd probably look at my rap sheet and book me for good measure regardless. On top of that, there was the bag of yayo that Steven had done a shitty job of hiding. I'm sure the cops had already come across it during their search of the car.

After about a half hour, the mustached policeman returned to my car and told me to get out. He turned me around and another cop unlocked my handcuffs.

"Your story checks out, Chris," the older cop said. "We talked to the storeowner. He says that fella would have been beaten to death if you didn't intervene."

I was dumbfounded. I really didn't know what to say. This was not the outcome I was expecting.

"And we just talked to the paramedics. They're on the way to the hospital with that kid. They think he has a cracked skull. So, to be frank, you're a hero tonight, Chris. You might have actually saved that kid's life."

With that, the cops sent Steven and me on our way. It was fucking unbelievable! We were beside ourselves with shock at how everything had gone down. Yeah, it sucked that we lost a good bag of coke, but now we were walking back to a party when we could just as easily have been rolling our way to the jailhouse. What a night! We were ecstatic.

When we got back to the house, little had changed. Some guys were playing beer pong. The girls were dancing up a sweat in the living room. A couple was shamelessly making out in the corner. Steven and I looked at each other and laughed. We had just been through one of the most insane experiences of our lives, and nobody had even realized that we were gone.

Time went on like this, and, at some point, Lisa decided she wanted a boob job. I liked her how she was, petite and small-chested. But she had started working as a stripper and I think seeing the other girls with their artificial augmentation gave her a case of boob envy. I couldn't talk her out of it. So, after I knocked out Jorge Rivera at *UFC Fight Night 3*, I gave Lisa the money for the operation. Originally she wanted a B-cup, but the doctor told her that if she didn't go big enough she'd be back in a few months for another enlargement. They did the surgery at a hospital in Seattle, and I drove up to spend a week or two with her while she recuperated.

But the procedure didn't turn out well. Lisa started experiencing excessive pain and redness around the incision, which was healing slowly. I took her back to the doctor, where we learned the bad news that she had a staph infection and the implant would have to be removed. They undid her stitches and pulled out the silicon bag.

It was a painful experience for Lisa, but she wasn't particularly devastated at first because after a few weeks of healing and antibiotics they inserted a new implant. Yet a few days later, we were back at the doctor. The skin was damaged and a new infection was spreading. Apparently the doctor had fucked up by trying to insert the second implant through the incision where they had cut out the staph infection rather than through the original incision where they had inserted the first bag. The implant had to come out yet again, and this threw Lisa into a tailspin.

She was single-breasted for about four months while they treated her mangled chest and waited for the most recent damage to heal fully. There was heavy scarring. She was forced to stop dancing. Lisa began popping painkillers like jelly beans and fell into a depression. I moved up to Everett to take care of her. It was a shitty time. Lisa and I were in the doctor's office every week for a few months. Lisa told her parents she was working at Victoria's Secret. And, to make ends meet, I took a side job at 24 Hour Fitness. Let me tell you, working at 24 Hour Fitness when you are a recognizable UFC fighter is an experience that requires a lot of pride swallowing. I'd come home late every night and guzzle two forties of malt liquor just to cope with the misery of the whole situation.

I contacted a lawyer who assured me that what had transpired was cut-and-dry malpractice and that we should take legal action immediately. But Lisa was out of her mind. She was irritable and extremely emotional and she did not have it in her to even contemplate getting involved in a lawsuit. So we let it drop and waved good-bye to what would have been a couple hundred thousand dollars in settlement. And, let me tell you, we could have used that money.

At this time Lisa was very dependent on me emotionally and financially, so I decided to make my relocation to Everett permanent. I borrowed a little money from my mom and bought a small house for Lisa and me. I figured that a little domestic stability would do the both of us good. But, fuck, I was wrong. When our relationship first began, things were good. Lisa seemed to care about me. She would show it and we seemed, for all intents and purposes, to be in love. Yet as time went on, our relationship became increasingly volatile. And with the surgery complications and all, the whole dynamic took a turn for the worse. Also, it seemed that the success that I was encountering was actually detrimental to our relationship. As I progressed in my career, I believe Lisa may have felt left behind. It seemed that a wedge had been driven into the space between us and, where there was once care and tolerance, there was now angst and hurt. It was the opposite of what I needed in that time of my life. I felt like there was nothing I could do to appease her. We were sucked into a whirlpool of negativity and the effects were far-reaching. My fight career began a downhill slide.

In mid-2006 I was riding a five-fight winning streak in the UFC that began with my shellacking of Jason Thacker at *The Ultimate Fighter Finale* event in April of 2005. I then plowed my way through Patrick Côté (split decision), Edwin Dewees (submission by armbar), Jorge Rivera (TKO punches), and Luigi Fioravanti (unanimous decision). This was a time when getting your hand raised five times in a row really meant something. I was in spitting distance of a middleweight title shot. Rich Franklin had been champion for a whole year at this point, and I began to have visions of dethroning him with a barrage of punches.

My instincts were right. UFC matchmaker Joe Silva gave me a call after the April 2007 Fioravanti fight and told me I was in a very good position in the company. He had an interesting opportunity for me—a fight with a highly regarded Brazilian Muay Thai fighter.

"He's never fought in the UFC before," Joe explained casually.

"Never fought in the UFC? Where has he fought?"

"In Brazil and Japan mostly."

Listen, Joe," I said, "I have my eye on the prize here. Rich Franklin has the belt I want. Why would I take a fight with a nobody?"

I was justifiably resistant. From where I stood, I didn't see how fighting a guy who was making his promotional debut would lead me to the belt. And for a moment Joe was silent while he thought about how to reply to my concern. Then he came out with it.

"Chris," he said. "This guy is good. Beating him is a big deal. He is very. Fucking. Good."

"I have to think this one over."

"Well, think quick," warned Joe. "I need an answer by tomorrow."

"What's his name, by the way?" I asked.

"His name's Silva," Joe replied. "Anderson Silva."

As we hung up, my heart started to race a little bit. Was it really possible that some unknown dude who had been dancing around Japan for the last four years would stand a chance against me, the hero of *TUF 1*, the heaviest hitter at 185 pounds, the Crippler? I immediately called my head coach Matt Hume and give him the news.

To my surprise, Matt was opposed to the idea from the outset. I hardly knew a damn thing about Anderson. Matt laid it out for me.

"Anderson Silva might be the best striker in the world," Matt explained. "I know he's never fought in the UFC. But they've recruited him hard, and there's a reason he's making his first appearance against a top guy like you. They think this guy could be a champion, and they don't want to waste any time grooming him from the bottom up."

"Fuck . . ." was all I could say in response. I wasn't scared, but it definitely seemed like a tricky situation.

"We haven't yet trained you for a world title fight, Chris. If you fight this guy, you're going to have to train like a champion, which means bringing in big names to spar with you, and means at least three months of hard work. We just don't have the time."

He paused and the conversation went quiet for a moment.

"I'm just going to come out and say it," Matt continued. "Do *not* take this fight."

For the first time in my career I was starting to look at fighting as a business. And business decisions involve risk and reward evaluations. I had worked hard for years to put together the track record that I then boasted. And my head coach seemed to be telling me that, unless I prepared properly, I would run the risk of throwing it all in the garbage. Additionally, the way that Matt was talking, it almost seemed as if Joe Silva was trying to dupe me into a bad move. In retrospect, I don't think that was the case. But for the moment, I was paranoid.

I waited a while to call Joe back. I needed to put my game face on. Dealing with the UFC matchmaker was never easy. He's like a little Napoleon. Every time he offers a fight, you, as a fighter, want to have more of a say in what happens and how you get compensated. Unfortunately, Joe and Dana White have the good cop/bad cop routine down pat. First, Joe makes negotiating as difficult as possible. Then, when the deal seems close to falling apart, Dana steps in with some smooth talk.

I called Joe back.

"Joe," I began hesitantly, "we don't think this is the right fight for me. Who else do you have?"

Unfortunately, he wasn't going to budge.

"Chris, you are taking this fight. Plain and simple. Let's talk numbers."

Well, you know how I am about being told what to do. I didn't react very well to Joe's commanding attitude. It turned into a bit of a dustup. We went back and forth and had some words, and before long Dana stepped in.

Fighting for the UFC is weird in that way. Technically, we fighters are employed as independent contractors by the promotion. And, in most cases in the world, independent contractors do what needs to be done and have very little to say about how their employer operates. However, stepping into the cage is not exactly the same as crunching a spreadsheet for a client. So there's this unique dance that Joe and Dana and the Fertitta brothers, co-owners of the UFC, have to perform. At the end of the day, they have most of the power, but not quite all of it. You can tell they just want to put a foot down and take a dictatorial position in the same way a big time CEO of a bank might make a top-down order. But, at the same time, they realize that every appearance in the Octagon is a career risk and a majorly emotional experience for a fighter. To maintain a reasonable morale and a productive culture, the big guys have to cede some control to us little guys. Also, as in most sports, everything that Dana decides is ultimately scrutinized six ways to Sunday in the media. The

UFC bosses realize that you can squeeze the fighters on pay sometimes, and you can decree certain codes of behavior, and you can occasionally set unreasonable expectations, but if you completely strip the fighters of a sense that they have at least one finger on the steering wheel, you'll be facing a rebellion. Dana and his partners are incredibly skilled at toeing that line.

My phone rang. Dana was on the other end.

"Leben!" he announced cheerily. "What's going on?"

"Dude, Joe's trying to sell me some weird shit," was my reply.

"It's not weird shit, Chris. It's the opportunity of a lifetime."

And with that, Dana went on to pitch the fight as if it was the best thing since sliced bread. It would be a tough fight, but there is no doubt that I could beat Anderson. Help the UFC out on this one and they'd cut me some slack on the next one. A tough guy like me shouldn't be afraid of a big challenge, etc., etc., etc.

"Well, as long as it's not a step backward . . ." I said, starting to cave.

"Definitely not," Dana replied. "Where are we at on the numbers?"

We spent the next ten minutes coming to terms on my paycheck for the fight. Ultimately, I think I got him to bump up only five thousand dollars from where negotiations between Joe and I stalled.

"Are we good?" Dana asked. It's a line he uses so much he might want to look into trademarking it.

"You know me," I told him coolly. "I'm ready to knock down anyone you stand up in front of me."

"That's why you're my guy."

Unfortunately as I geared up for Anderson Silva, my problems with Lisa were throwing all kinds of wrenches into my clockwork. My martial arts practice at this time did not serve my ambitions well. Matt Hume did his best to prepare me for the six weeks leading up to the fight. We watched a lot of footage of Anderson, and came up with what would have been the ideal game plan. "Don't chase him," Matt instructed me over and over. "Circle hard and let him come to you."

But I was distracted by incessant emotional crises with Lisa. Hell, I spent twice as much time wrestling with her issues as I spent wrestling with my training partners. It definitely wasn't my best training camp, and I knew it. But I didn't lose lots of sleep over it; there wasn't a man on the planet who was impervious to my left cross. I had only lost two fights in my life, both by decision. I had never been submitted and, of course, I had never and *would never* (or so I thought) be knocked out.

I recently rewatched some of the interviews the UFC filmed of me prior to my fight with Anderson Silva. My confidence seems to have been sky high. I thought that no matter what he had done overseas, this guy wouldn't compare to some of the guys I had already tangoed with in my career. My eye was on the real prize—Rich Franklin and his sparkling gold belt. Here is some of what I said in the UFC promotional video that preceded my fight with Anderson:

> When I get in there and I'm in his face and pressing the action . . . I'm roughnecking him. I'm throwing him around. I'm punching him. He's punching me. I'm eating his shots and just blasting him back in the face. He's not gonna be able to handle it. He's gonna go, "What is this guy? This guy's a dump truck. He just keeps going!"
>
> After he gets in there with me and I knock him out, he may want to go back to Japan or somewhere where the competition's a little easier. . . . In the midst of me getting on the inside, getting through his punches, looking to take him down, he's gonna leave his chin hanging out there and I'm gonna break his jaw.

The night before the fight, Dana White called me on the phone and told me he was coming up to my hotel room with a present. I was excited because, as most people know, Dana is one wealthy motherfucker. He's been known to give presents that include fancy sports cars. hell, he's reportedly tipped casino waitresses $10,000. And, when Dana came into my room he seemed happier than usual.

"Leben," he announced to me and my team, "I've actually got two presents for you. First of all, if you beat Anderson Silva, I want you to grab the mic and call out Rich Franklin. The title shot is yours for the taking."

We all cheered, and I told Dana I would do just that.

Then he said, "The second present is a special one. It's been in my car for two months, waiting for this moment."

Dana then pulled out a small box. I opened it, and inside was a steel belt buckle with the following engraving on the front:

LOVER BY DAY

FIGHTER BY NIGHT

DRUNKARD BY CHOICE

"As soon as I saw it, I thought of you." Dana laughed, and I offered a good-natured chuckle. But inside I felt pretty shitty. Dana had become a friend and somewhat of a father figure to me at that point. I had worked my ass off and exceeded the expectations that he initially had for me. He had given one of my UFC fighter friends a $10,000 Rolex. That's what I had expected. Instead, he gave me a five-dollar trinket that I would never use.

I felt expendable. And maybe that's why they gave me the Silva fight in the first place—because I was an acceptable sacrifice to the MMA gods.

In the hours leading up to the fight, Matt Hume must have repeated his advice a hundred times: *Don't chase him. Circle hard.*

*Let him come to you.* And that's exactly what I was going to do—
that is, until I actually got in the cage. Moments before the start
of the fight, as I looked across the tarp at Anderson, I thought to
myself, *I'm going to march forward and knock this motherfucker out.*
Yeah, that's the kind of attitude I usually take toward fighting and
life. But this time it was stupid. This time I should have known
better. Yet I gave in to the temptation to go for the kill. And part
of it, I think, was due to the fact that I wanted to show Dana and
the UFC I was worth more than they realized.

As soon as the fight began I started chasing after Anderson. As
Matt Hume had feared, the Brazilian started connecting with virtually
every strike he threw—jabs, left-right combos. His footwork was
amazing and his hands were lightning fast. I couldn't land anything
and my head had quickly become Anderson's speed bag. About
twenty seconds in, I knew I was in trouble. But I pressed forward.
He landed a head kick and a heavy three-punch combination that
sent me somersaulting backward to the mat. Right then, I knew I
was done. Anderson jumped on me and started punching. I thought
to myself, *I can stay down here on the ground and the referee will save
me by ending the fight. Or, I can stand up and let Anderson have a clean
kill.* I opted for the latter because Anderson deserved a real finish.
He was better than me and had bested me. I struggled to my feet
and Anderson greeted me with a brutal, point-blank knee to the
center of my forehead. That was all she wrote. Good night.

It was one of the more lopsided knockouts in recent UFC
history, and I was on the ugly end of it. Never again would I come
that close to a title shot.

A few of you may not know who Anderson "The Spider" Silva
is. If that's the case, it means you know very little about the sport of
MMA. And that's actually a good thing! In writing this book, I was
hoping to reach far beyond the hardcore fighting fan base. So, then,

now that you know what the guy did to me, let me take a moment to tell you about Anderson Silva—the man widely regarded as the greatest martial artist to ever step into the Octagon. After our fight, Anderson went on to viciously terminate Rich Franklin's 497-day reign as middleweight champion with a barrage of knee strikes to the head. Anderson retained the belt for the next six-and-a-half years: 2,457 days. To this day, he is the longest reigning champion in the history of the sport. During his championship era, Anderson not only defended his title fourteen consecutive times, he made his opponents look like amateurs, often leaving them sprawled out in the middle of the canvas. He finished Rich Franklin twice via knee strikes; he choked out the great Dan Henderson; he made former light heavyweight champion Forrest Griffin look like a buffoon; he knocked out Vitor Belfort with a legendary front kick to the face, he TKO'd the un-TKO-able Stefan Bonnar; and, most memorably, he finished my friend Chael Sonnen (Anderson's arch-nemesis) twice. In 2013 Anderson finally succumbed to the very dangerous American wrestler, Chris Weidman.

Anderson had a flamboyant style in the cage, mercilessly toying with his opponents until they stepped into his trap. He waited for his foe to become frustrated and then to lunge. And only then would Anderson capitalize with a whirlwind of strikes. The Spider's brilliance was undeniable. He became the most celebrated hero in the history of the sport. When he was in the cage, it wasn't just about fighting—it was about putting on a virtuoso performance. It was as if his goal in each appearance was not just to win, but to demonstrate a next-level display of martial artistry that had never before been witnessed on this planet. And he achieved this goal repeatedly.

Often, when the topic of my fight with Anderson Silva arises, people point out that I should not focus on my loss but rather focus on the tremendous honor it was to step into the Octagon with the Bruce Lee, the Michael Jordan, the Muhammed Ali of MMA. But, let me tell you something: yes, I am proud to have shared the stage with the greatest fighter of my generation. However, there is no honor in getting mercilessly bludgeoned by another human being. There is no honor in suffering from memory lapses for a full week after someone nearly crushes your skull with his bare limbs. I would have preferred any other damn outcome in the world.

Anderson isn't the only fighter who wanted to send a message to the world every time he stepped into the cage. I had my own such message. Every time I fought, I wanted to show the world that it doesn't matter where you were born or how you were raised. With perseverance and heart you can stand among the best in the world. That's right . . . the best in the fucking world. When I was young, it was almost as if the whole world was escorting me toward a dead end. But I refused to let that happen. And, every time I threw a punch, I wanted to show everybody I could win on my own terms. I didn't just want to wrestle my way to decision victories; I wanted to knock motherfuckers out. Because every knockout was like an exorcism of the demons that plagued me during my childhood. Every time my fat fist connected with a chin, it crushed a portion of the pain that I felt in my soul.

You can't take anything away from the Spider. He really was and is as great as people think—the greatest ever. And I actually like the guy. But fuck you, Anderson! If it were up to me I would have beat your face in and sent you packing into the footnotes of the UFC history books!

Bruised and battered, I returned home to my nightmare domestic situation. Losing to Anderson Silva definitely did not earn me much pity from Lisa. In fact, things got worse. Our relationship at this time was like a never-ending train wreck, interspersed with moments when we were too drunk or high to tangle. Lisa was not just emotionally and verbally abusive, she was physically abusive. She actually beat me. Some people might think it is ridiculous that one of the toughest guys in the world would take beatings from a one-hundred-pound girl. But, what was I supposed to do? Hit her back? No fucking way. So she punched me, and slapped me, and smacked me with household objects with impunity. And a big part of me—the part that hates who I am—felt like I deserved it.

Luckily, my stock was still high with UFC spectators and, just a week or two after the Anderson debacle, Joe Silva offered me a fight against streaking middleweight Jorge Santiago. Jorge had actually won his UFC debut via KO on the same night that I lost to Anderson. They put us on the books for *UFC Fight Night 6*, a mere seven weeks later. I immersed myself in training camp, grateful that I had another distraction from my life with Lisa. Day after day the grappling mat was my refuge.

My camp went pretty well and it showed on August 17 when I put Jorge to sleep with a left hook and some vicious haymakers to the side of his head while he was face down on the mat. The Crippler was back in a big way! I strutted around the cage and did my famous pose, pointing at the camera with my right index finger while cocking my left fist near my chin. The crowd loved it. The UFC loved it. I loved it. As I flew back to Oregon, I was already feeling that my previous loss was just a bump in the road. As long as I was able to let my knuckles do the talking, greatness was not out of the picture.

Not many days after I got back to Everett, my friends and I got together at Turner's—a local bar and grill that attracted belligerent drunks. As usual, we were housing drinks and making a ruckus, but it wasn't anything out of the ordinary at this dive. Nonetheless, around midnight the 6'6", 338-pound Samoan bouncer approached our table and pointed at me. (I remember his exact weight because it would later appear on the police report.)

"You've gotta go," he said.

"Bro, what the fuck are you talking about?" I replied. I'm sure that I had done something offensive or obnoxious, but at the time I wasn't aware of having done a damn thing wrong.

"I'm giving you thirty seconds to get up and leave."

"Or what, you fat fuck?" I stood up and shouted in his face. I was the last guy that would be intimidated by the size of my enemy.

"You don't want to find out," he replied without batting an eye. "I don't care how tough you think you are."

My blood began to boil. "I will beat the shit out of you!" I yelled.

Lisa interjected. "Shut up, Chris! Just do what he says and leave. Why do you have to cause trouble?"

"Are you fucking kidding me?" I replied.

She crossed her arms and huffed. I looked over to my friend Jason to see how he was reacting.

"Fuck it, Chris," he said. "This place sucks anyway. It's not worth your time."

So the two of us got up and left. I mean-mugged the gigantic Samoan on my way out. We walked down the street a ways and popped into some other shithole of a bar. We were worked up and steaming, so we decided to start downing shots of tequila. Hanging with Jason was often an adventure. He too was a professional fighter, of Hawaiian origin. In fact, due to how much he liked a tussle, his nickname became "Hawaiian Punch." By

2:00 AM Jason and I were wasted. We headed back up the street toward Turner's to find Lisa and then head home.

As we approached, we saw the Samoan bouncer standing out front with two other Samoans who were equally massive. If I remember correctly, they were all brothers. Jason got fire his eyes.

"I'm going to go smack that big fucker in the face," he said.

"No," I replied. "I'm the one he had a problem with. I should do the honors."

So I walked over to the bouncers, who happened to be looking in the other direction. I remember it in slow motion, like in a movie when one man has the unexpected opportunity to exact his revenge on another man who had previously shamed him. I reached up and tapped the monstrous islander on his shoulder. He turned around and when we made eye contact I jacked him as hard as I could in the mouth. He crumpled to the ground like a big sack of Samoan sweet potatoes.

The other bouncers jumped into action, ready to attack. Instantly I turned to run because I knew that if I didn't escape I was going to get fucking murdered. One of the giants grabbed me by the collar of my shirt and I literally exploded through it like the goddamn incredible hulk. Shirtless, I high-tailed it down the street alongside Jason. Our heavyset pursuers gave up the chase after about half a block. A few familiar local gangster-types were cruising the area and witnessed the commotion. They yelled for us to get into their Cadillac. We jumped in and sped off down the street.

Nothing like a street fight to whet your appetite. The gangster dudes had an extra shirt for me, and we all decided to go to Denny's for some late-night chow. We squeezed into a booth and ordered a shitload of food. Jason and I were still plowed and started making a scene. I threw my pancakes one-by-one like

Frisbees across the restaurant. An older man came over and told us that he was calling the cops. He was at Turner's when I attacked the bouncer, and he was going to make sure I got arrested. So we dropped some cash on the table and took off. The guys dropped me off at home around 3:00 AM.

I had barely walked through the front door when Lisa started going bonkers. I began shouting back. We probably woke up half the block. Lisa went off about how I was an asshole and a hillbilly psycho who belonged in jail.

Maybe she was right, but I wasn't having any of it.

"I may be a hillbilly, but I fucking support you, you crazy bitch!"

As we all know, women do not like to be called crazy. Lisa ran at me and started punching and slapping. She hit me in the face with a cutting board and I could feel my eye start to swell immediately. Then she started throwing things at me—the coffee pot, the blender, pots and pans, dishes. She smashed things on the floor and against the walls.

I came up with a clever idea. I picked up her purse, opened the front door and hurled it out onto the sidewalk. That purse was her baby. She freaked out and ran out to retrieve it. I shut and locked the door behind her. She started screaming again and began kicking the door as hard as she could.

By this time, several of the neighbors had awoken and were peering through their curtains out onto the fracas. There was little I could do, so I sat down on the couch and lit a cigarette and started watching TV as the banging and hollering continued. Within a few minutes two cop cars came to a screeching halt in front of my house.

As the officers emerged from their cruiser, Lisa started screeching at them, telling them I was a psycho and they should arrest me. She kept kicking the door. The cops told Lisa to calm down or they would arrest her. Finally she shut up and they put her in the back of the squad car for safe holding. I unlocked the front door and two of the cops entered.

"Officers," I said. "That girl was beating me and destroying my property. I want you to take her to jail." I was pissed and didn't want to pussyfoot around it.

"Now hold on just a minute, sir," the tall one said. "We'd prefer not to put anyone in jail tonight."

"Yeah right," I responded. "Every other time I talk to a cop I go to jail. You guys don't put hot chicks in jail."

He asked me my name, and I told him. His name was Officer Davis and his short, stocky partner was Officer Sanchez.

"Well, you are going to have to do something with her," I continued. "She's not fucking staying here tonight."

The two cops looked at each other and Sanchez spoke up.

"How long has Lisa been living here with you, Chris?"

"About six months."

"See, that's the thing," he continued. "There are tenant's rights laws here in Washington. We can't just throw someone out on the street if they are a legitimate resident."

I almost lost my shit.

"Are you motherfucking kidding me? Look at my fucking eye!" By this time I could feel it puffing up like a goddamn strawberry donut. "That bitch is crazy and she beats me! And, you know what? This is *my* goddamn house! I bought it. I paid for it. I own it and I'm not going to spend another night with her!"

I paused for a second, unsure if the cops were even listening to what I was saying.

"I want to press charges. Take her to jail," I demanded emphatically.

Third from the left.

Back row, third from the left.

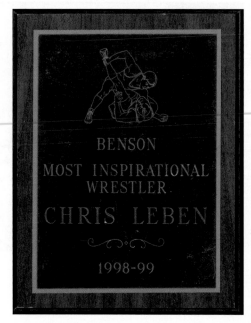

# UNITED STATES ARMY

# CERTIFICATE OF ENLISTMENT

## THIS IS TO CERTIFY THAT

PRIVATE CHRISTIAN C LEBEN

### HAS ENLISTED FOR SERVICE IN THE UNITED STATES ARMY

As a new member of the Army, you have demonstrated keen foresight by accepting the Army's challenge. You can be justly proud of your decision to enlist in the Army for service to your nation. The people of the United States are deeply grateful to you for your personal commitment to national defense.

7 DECEMBER 1998

**DATE**

MARK G. McCAULEY, LTC, AG, Commanding

USAREC Fm 589, Rev I Apr 85 (Previous editions are obsolete)

Ed Herman and Chris Leben.

Chris Leben and coach Robert Follis.

Robert Follis, Ed Herman, Chris Leben, Nate Quarry, and teammates.

Chris Leben, Stefan Bonnar, and Ed Herman.

Chris Leben is declared the winner over Jason Thacker.

Chris locks in an arm bar.

Otto Olson looks for the takedown against Chris.

Otto locks in a guillotine choke.

Chris passes out while in Otto's chokehold.

Chris regains consciousness and engages Otto on his feet.

Chris is overcome with emotion after his KO victory.

Sanchez continued. "That's not going to happen. I see that you have a black eye, but come on, Chris. That woman is a third of your size. If I were her, I would claim that I felt physically threatened and was defending myself."

My blood started to boil.

"The best thing for everyone would be for you to find another place to stay tonight."

I started to literally jump up and down in protest, but the fuzz didn't see it my way. They told me to sit down and shut up immediately. Sobering up, I complied.

"We're going to have to write up a report on this, Chris," said Davis. He began scribbling onto a clipboard. "What do you do for a living?"

"Actually, I fight for the UFC," I replied.

The two cops froze and looked at each other. This wasn't a good sign. Sanchez nodded at Davis then turned away and pulled out his radio. Davis eyed me suspiciously.

"It looks like we have our suspect from the bar fight at Turner's earlier tonight," Sanchez said into the radio.

Some static, followed by a chirp, then "Roger that," came the reply from the radio. "Standby, please."

"Give me a minute, guys," said Sanchez before stepping outside to finish his radio conversation.

I closed my eyes and shook my head. I had actually almost forgotten that I had cold-cocked a gigantic Samoan just a few hours earlier. This was going downhill fast.

Davis noticed my reaction. "Not your best night, huh Chris?"

"Definitely not," I replied and put my head in my hands.

To make a long story short, Sanchez returned in about twenty minutes with an update. "Here's the deal, Chris," he said. "You're a lucky son-of-a-bitch . . . a very lucky son-of-a-bitch. We know about what went down at Turner's and you probably should be locked up. The guy you hit is apparently in bad shape, but he decided not to go to the hospital. The people at Turner's have already discussed it and they are not going to press charges. So, like I said, it's your lucky fucking night."

"I don't feel that lucky," I replied.

"Well sleep on it, then. We're going to write you up on disorderly conduct, but we're not going to take you in. The bar says that you can't enter the premises for one month."

I laughed to myself. Everyone at that fucking bar, except for the big boy with the fat lip and his cronies, knew me and loved me. And a fight breaking out at Turner's was about as unusual as a fight breaking out during a hockey game. Plus, when you applied for a position as a bouncer there, getting lit up by a drunk bastard from time to time should have been listed near the top of the job description. When that portly prick kicked me out for no good reason he should have known something like this would go down. Moreover, he had about 130 pounds on me and I only touched him once. As far as I'm concerned, under those circumstances, what I did is about as much of a criminal offense as patting the cocktail girl's ass at a strip club. But maybe I'm old school.

They brought Lisa back in and she went straight to sleep. The cops finished up with me around 6:00 AM. As they left, they showed a little bit of sympathy and told me that I probably had nothing to worry about. If I didn't hear anything in the next month or two then I didn't have to worry about criminal charges related to the brawl. I collapsed in a heap on the couch. I was glad not to be sleeping on a jailhouse cot. Hangovers behind bars are twice as brutal. As sleep overcame me, I told myself that the whole thing was going to blow over. There was nothing to worry about.

Things finally unraveled with Lisa a few months later. We had yet another outrageous row in the middle of the night. She broke things. I punched holes in the wall. The cops made another visit. Lisa decided to call her father and have him pick her up and take her home for a few days. This was high-level toxicity, and if Lisa and I didn't separate we were both going to go down hard. So I packed a few bags and headed back to Portland. Matt Lindland was very connected there, and he found a great, cheap furnished apartment for me and my new roommate, an up-and-coming wrestler-turned-MMA fighter named Jake Ellenberger. (You may be noticing that MMA was a very small universe back in the day.)

I started training at Team Quest again, but things were not going well for me. I was a fucking emotional wreck and severely depressed. As much as I hated Lisa, there was a strange part of me that needed her. She was like a bad drug, and I was going through a nasty withdrawal. Of course, my fight game was suffering for it. I missed training days and was not seeing any improvement. Nothing was clicking. Team Quest was a great place, but I longed to be in Seattle, training again under Matt Hume. He was the best coach I ever had, the one guy who really understood me. I thought that maybe he would be able to pull me out of my funk. But. I didn't have the money or spirit to relocate yet again.

I made the best of it for as long as I could. At least living with Ellenberger was a frequent source of entertainment because we were such an odd couple. He was a very quiet and disciplined Christian kid. By contrast, now single for the first time in a few years, I was on a debaucherous rampage. I got drunk every night and often brought new friends home from the bars early in the morning. Many of these new friends were hot young stripper-type girls who liked drugs as much as I did. And usually I would bang on Jake's bedroom door when I got home, trying to entice him to join in our revelry. It was fruitless. He ignored me. Yet every once in a while Jake would wake up to use the bathroom or get a glass of water and have to weave his way past a scene of sweaty, naked intoxication. But the man was supremely focused on his fight career and his faith. He acted like he didn't even notice. I have to give the guy credit; he never sold his soul to the devil.

There was a point, however, when I was living with Jake when I tried to clean up my act. For about two weeks I stopped drinking. It was healthy, but, due to the withdrawal symptoms, a horrible experience. I couldn't sleep. I was a walking zombie. Finally I got my hands on some Ambien and took two or three one night. I passed out at about 9:00 PM.

The next morning I woke up and checked my alarm clock. It read 8:00 AM. Unbelievable! I had slept for eleven hours straight. I had probably never caught so many Zs in my whole life. I stood up, stretched, and smiled to myself. With a full night's rest behind me, it was going to be a great day. I walked out into the living room. Jake's friend Jared was staying with us for a few days and was still passed out on the couch. I went to the fridge and poured myself a glass of orange juice. Then I noticed that a bottle of Jameson was missing from the top of the refrigerator. I had purchased it about a month earlier and was saving it for a special occasion down the road. At first I didn't think too much about it. I figured I had hidden it somewhere so my depraved friends couldn't get to it.

When I went back into the living room, I spied the bottle of Jameson. It was on the coffee table, right next to slumbering Jared, and it was *completely empty*. That greedy bastard and his friends must have helped themselves to my stash. I was so pissed!

I jumped on top of Jared and started shaking him and screaming at him.

He woke up and nearly pissed his pants at the sight of me.

"Chris, what are you doing?! Stop!"

"You drank my Jameson, you fucking thief!" I started smacking him in the face.

"No! No! Calm down, dude! It wasn't me! It wasn't me!"

Jared seemed to be sincere, so I eased up.

"Then who did it?" I asked.

"It was you, you damn psycho!" he replied desperately. "Don't you remember? You fucking drank the whole thing last night!"

I was completely confused. I had no idea what he was talking about. Then Jared explained that at about midnight I woke up and emerged from my room. He said I came out and spent the next four hours watching TV and guzzling the whiskey. I didn't talk much, but he figured I just wanted to drink and be quiet. So he left me alone and fell asleep.

As Jared recounted the details of the previous night, my stomach started to churn and I belched. The unmistakable taste of a mixture of bile and whiskey crept into my mouth. Right then I knew that Jared was telling the whole truth. Ambien is known for causing people to sleepwalk. In my case, it must have caused me to sleepdrink. I didn't remember a single moment of it, but the proof was in the pudding, literally. I ran to the bathroom and spent the next hour barfing up my precious bottle of Jameson.

If I were Jake, I would hate Chris Leben for how he behaved in those days. It was beyond disgusting. There's another story (that I hesitate to tell) that will give you some insight into how bad it got. Not surprisingly, this episode involved wildman Steven Nickell. He and I and a couple of other dudes had met some disreputable women late one night and brought them back to my place. We were guzzling tequila and snorting lines until about four in the morning when, finally, and mercifully, Steven passed out. I'm not sure how long it took me to notice he was unconscious, but when I did I got pissed off that he had called it quits before me. I was having the time of my life, and I wanted my buddy to wake up and get back into the mix. Shaking and slapping him did no good. So I came up with an idea that seemed brilliant at the time. I rolled a dollar bill into a funnel shape and jammed the pointy end into one of his nostrils. Then I poured a bump of cocaine into the funnel. I figured that Steven would spring to his feet as soon as the powder hit the inside of his nose. However, that motherfucker was so dead to the world it literally had no effect.

That's probably one of the dumber things I have ever done. I was lucky I didn't put my friend in the hospital. But at the time, all I could think about was satisfying my mad cravings, or, should I say, satisfying my cravings for madness. Giving up on my mission to wake Steven, I started getting it on with one of the strippers right there on the couch next to him. Soon she and I were half naked and on the verge of doing the dirty deed. I came up with the brilliant and hilarious idea that this girl and I should have sex on top of his passed-out corpse. And that's exactly what happened. She bent over Steven, and I went to town, hooting and hollering like a nut job. Steven barely stirred, just occasionally snorting and mumbling as the girl's boobs pressed into his face. The other people in the room—the strippers and Steven's brother among them—watched on, laughing and shouting at just about the most degenerate act they had ever witnessed.

I've often thought that, if there were a hell, I would have a seat of honor in its fiery depths. But I'm quite sure that there is no hell other than the one we make here on earth. At that time of my life, my hell was warming up. Despite my attempts to distract myself with wild parties and obnoxious behavior, I grew increasingly depressed and desperate. I was completely empty inside and I could barely keep it together. I was having very dire thoughts, and I started to wonder why I even bothered with anything in the long run. I was concerned that it was going to end badly for me. Finally, after an especially bad stretch, I decided I needed to get help. I went to a psychiatrist and, between sobs, told him how bad things had gotten. He suggested we run some blood tests to make sure there were no chemical imbalances that were contributing to my depression.

Sure enough, a few days later the tests came back showing that I had an acute thyroid deficiency. The doctor explained that it was likely from all the weight cutting I had done throughout my wrestling and MMA career. It can have a horrible effect on your endocrine system. He put me on a thyroid medication, along with an antidepressant and Adderal.

Shocker, huh? Starving and dehydrating yourself to the point of collapse over and over again isn't good for your health! Who woulda thunk it! Luckily, 99.5 percent of the world does not have to experience the horrid experience of weight cutting. It truly is the worst aspect of being an MMA athlete. Many fighters have incurred serious health problems—kidney failure among them—from extreme weight cuts. A few have even died on the eve of a fight.

When I was in the UFC, I typically had to trim about thirty pounds in the ten days leading up to a fight. You heard that right. A week-and-a-half before weighing in at 185 pounds, I typically weighed 220 pounds. Those of you with little knowledge of my sport might have a hard time believing me when I say that. You might think it is physically impossible. But remember, the human body is about 60 percent water. Plus, your stomach and intestines can hold like ten or fifteen pounds of shit. Trimming 15 percent of body weight in a short period of time is par for the course for many fighters. UFC site coordinator Burt Watson, who monitors the weight cutting process for UFC fighters, once told me that there were few fighters who cut more weight than me during fight week. But I can think of at least a few examples of guys who took it to an even greater extreme. Current UFC fighter Anthony Johnson was notorious for his weight cuts. Early in his career he would literally drop from 220 pounds to 170 pounds! It almost killed him once. So then he went up in weight classes, from 170 pounds to 185 pounds. He could barely make that weight. Now he fights at 205 pounds and is one of the biggest men in that whole division.

So, with the new diagnosis I was now on a medley of drugs just to keep functioning. I would say that's not an ideal situation for a professional athlete. And it's how I entered camp for my final fight of 2006. This bout was scheduled for New Year's Eve weekend against a douchebag named Jason MacDonald, who called himself "The Athlete." I wasn't really excited for the fight, but I did want to knock this guy's block off. Besides being a tool, he had submitted my good buddy Ed Herman in October.

Yet, with all of the emotional and medical shit that was going on in my life, I was in far-from-optimal condition. The camp did not go well, and you could see it when I entered the Octagon. Some would say I looked skinny-fat for this fight. I was gassed and checking the clock before the first round even ended. Nonetheless, I think I hurt him a few times in that round and probably even won it on the scorecards. But I had little to offer in the second round. Even though MacDonald's wrestling was so-so, he put me on my back, locked in a guillotine choke and put me to sleep. I woke up with that dipshit referee Steve Mazzagatti kneeling over me. I remember trying to speak, but could barely manage a hoarse whisper. I found out later that my windpipe was partially crushed by the choke. To this day, my voice makes me sound like a seventy-year-old chain smoker. No thanks to Mazzagatti, who waited about five extra seconds after I passed out to step in and break up the chokehold.

In Spring of 2007 I put my house on the market. But, there was one little problem: Lisa refused to move out. So, every time a prospective buyer was scheduled to view the house, I would get a call from the real estate agent informing me either that the place was a pig sty due to a crazy party Lisa had thrown the previous weekend or complaining that Lisa had locked all the doors and was refusing to let the buyer in for a viewing. A few hours away in Portland and avoiding Lisa at all costs, there was little I could do other than continue to pay the damn mortgage.

At this point, if there was one thing I knew, it was that I needed a fresh start. I needed to cut the umbilical cord that Lisa had tied like a noose around my neck. And I needed to get even further away. That's when God answered my prayers. Let me rephrase that, as I am a spiritual atheist; that's when the vibrations of the universe responded favorably to the desperation I was projecting into the cosmos. A messiah called me: a messiah who goes by the name of T. J. Thompson, and who is not exactly Christ-like but a good guy nonetheless.

T. J. Thompson was the founder of a legendary Hawaii-based fight promotion called Super Brawl. Between 1996 and 2008, Super Brawl (and its successor Icon Sport) put on more than fifty MMA events, most of which were staged in Honolulu. If you were to see a list of all the future MMA stars who appeared in Super Brawl events, you would probably be shocked. Most MMA followers, even diehard fans, probably had little awareness of the promotion. Here are just a few of the notable fighters T. J.

corralled into his fight events: Mayhem Miller, Robbie Lawler, Phil Baroni, Rich Franklin, Vitor Belfort, Ben Rothwell, and Josh Barnett.

Well, around the time that my life in Oregon was careening wildly downhill, T. J. was opening the first Icon MMA gym in Hawaii. He needed a head coach and he got wind via Matt Hume that I was looking for something new. T. J. called me and barely finished making the offer before I accepted. I would fly out to Hawaii as soon as possible and T. J. would provide me lodging and $2,000 a month to run the gym. It sounded too good to be true. But in this rare case, it lived up to everything I hoped it would be.

In late May, I lost another decision to another middle-of-the-road fighter named Kalib Starnes. It was an exciting enough match, and we won the "fight-of-the-night" award, but that was no consolation. In my prime I would have walked right through that guy. Thankfully, two days later, my best friend Sam hosted my going-away party at his house in Portland. And let me tell you, it was fucking epic—the craziest party ever. It started at noon. There had to have been five hundred people there over the course of the day and night. It seemed like everybody in town showed up. We had a dozen kegs and thousands of cans of beer. There was every drug you could imagine, and people were not holding back. We set up skateboard ramps, and there were guys launching themselves on minibikes in the front yard. As the party progressed, the crowd made a circle and drunk dudes in boxing gloves started beating the shit out of each other for fun. Even the accused whiskey thief Jared got into the action. He was knocked out by a kid named Kimo. And although hundreds of people witnessed his eyes roll back, Jared hilariously insisted that he wasn't out. It was the rager to end all ragers. I could not have imagined a better send-off.

The next thing I know, it was 7:00 AM and I was snorting lines with a few of my buddies when one of them says, "Chris, we have to get you on a plane to Hawaii!"

I grabbed a duffle bag and my guitar and said good-bye to the state of Oregon.

I remember emerging from the Honolulu airport into the comforting sunlight of the aloha state feeling like I was the guy from "Shawshank Redemption" who crawled through a river of shit and came out clean on the other side. T. J. was there waiting for me in his open-top Jeep Wrangler. He laughed when he saw the state I was in.

"It's time to go to work!" T. J. shouted.

"What the fuck are you talking about?" I replied, tossing my things into the back of the Jeep.

"You've got three-hours of Brazilian jiu-jitsu to teach this morning, my friend!"

And, even though I was a hungover puddle of garbage, a ripple of excitement ran through my body. I got into the car. T. J. patted me on the back and flashed me a smile. "Buckle up, son," he said. "It's going to be a wild ride." We sped away from the airport and took scenic route 92 through Waikiki toward my new home in Niu Valley. As we rolled past the beautiful beaches on the south coast of Oahu, I gazed out onto the vast ocean and let my mind relax. I put my hands up to let the fresh Pacific breeze run through my fingers. Good things were coming. I could feel it.

# CHAPTER 6
# POTIONS

Hawaii worked for me. It was almost as if the gods designed the island and its people with the Crippler in mind. The climate seemed to feed my soul and help heal so many of the emotional wounds that I had incurred back on the mainland. There is spiritual energy in the rainforests and hills and volcanoes and oceans of Hawaii. Hawaiian people call it *mana*. They say a person can draw strength from the majestic natural environment of the islands. There really is something to this, if you ask me. Within a week of arriving, I felt as if I had been born again.

There is something special about the society as well. In my opinion, the Hawaiian people are among the most accepting and welcoming in the world. There are many who choose Hawaii as a home because it is the one place where they do not feel judged. It is the one place where they can pursue their uncommon lifestyles without having to worry the neighbors or the morality police or the *actual* police will unnecessarily interfere. In Hawaii I came into a sense of belonging I had never before experienced. My being a fighter helped because Hawaiian people tend to honor the powerful and fearless. There is a warrior culture on the islands. It dates back more than fifteen hundred years to the early settlement of the islands. Back then there were many battles between competing chieftains and their tribal *koa* warriors. These warriors were revered for their bravery. They fought in loincloths and covered themselves in tattoos to strike fear into their enemies.

As this was explained to me, my heart raced with a sense of connection to the mystic history of this tropical paradise. I began adorning my body with tattoos around the age of nineteen. Today there are very few spots on my body that are not covered in intense, colorful ink. So, obviously, the koa warrior body decoration tradition resonated with me. As I thought about myself in this warrior context, I began to develop a new purpose: to honor the Hawaiian ancestors through my fighting. And subsequently, the Hawaiian people responded to my dedication and my stubborn refusal to quit. In their eyes I was the epitome of a warrior who lived and died by the sword. Wherever I went, people knew who I was and treated me with respect. I was more of a celebrity the moment I stepped foot in Hawaii than I had been in my hometown of Portland. I used to say that my stock had split like Microsoft.

And then there were the ladies. Hawaiian women were exactly what the doctor ordered. I had always been a sucker for Asian features, which are everywhere there. On top of that, the women embody a mix of grace and free-spirited boldness I have found nowhere else in the world. The martial arts classes that I taught at Icon Fitness were filled with these goddesses. And, wouldn't you know, many of them were digging my big-man status. My success rate there was unprecedented.

However, sometimes I got attention that I didn't necessarily earn. Soon after I relocated to Hawaii, T. J. Thompson took me to a local bar. He wanted to celebrate my arrival and talk about his plans for the gym and how I fitted into the picture. Before I had even finished my first beer an attractive Hawaiian woman approached and put her arm around me.

"Hello, daddy," she purred. "Will you buy me a drink?"

She was wearing a short dress and a smile and I almost got a boner just from looking at her. At this point, I was used to working hard to get a woman's attention, not the other way around. Back on the mainland women almost never made the first move or dared approach me, unless, that is, if I was at a strip club. This place was definitely not a strip club.

"Wow," I replied in shock. "I'd love to buy you a drink, but my friend and I are talking about some important stuff. Can we talk in a little bit?"

"Sure, sweetheart," she replied, placing a soft kiss on my cheek. Then she walked away. We watched her go.

T. J. patted me on the back. "Whoa, Chris! That girl was all about it! It looks like Hawaii is the right place for you."

T. J. seemed suspiciously enthusiastic. Nonetheless, my confidence skyrocketed. And in just a few minutes an even better-looking Hawaiian woman walked up to me, her snug dress clinging to her perfect curvy body. She asked me to buy her a drink. I couldn't believe it! I looked at T. J., who raised his eyebrows and gave me a nudge with his elbow. This time I couldn't pass up the opportunity. I bought her a drink and she took a seat next to me. We started talking, and she listened intently, laughing at every other clever thing that I said. I felt like a king.

After a while, the woman excused herself to go use the bathroom. She told me she would be right back. I turned to T. J. who was talking to the attractive lady bartender.

"Holy shit!" I announced. "I think this woman actually wants to go home with me!"

T. J. and the bartender shared a knowing look and then started laughing.

"It's her job to make you feel that way," whispered the bartender, smiling broadly.

"This is a buy-me-drinky bar, buddy," T. J. said, barely able to contain his laughter. "That's how it works. You buy the lady a drink and she'll keep you company for the evening."

"You mean she's a hooker?"

"Not a hooker," replied the bartender, slightly offended. "No sex. Just a friendly companion. Make sure to tip her before you leave."

Either way, I was disappointed. There's a big difference between meeting someone who likes you for who you are and meeting someone who likes you for the twenty-dollar bill you have in your pocket. T. J. could see it in my face. He patted me on the back.

"Better to have a gorgeous Hawaiian keeping you company than not, wouldn't you say?"

And, as always, he was right. I actually spent the rest of the evening talking with my companion. I told her about what I had gone through in the past year and what I hoped would happen now that I was in Hawaii. She seemed genuinely interested in what I had to say, and she offered wise advice when I discussed my problems.

"Here in Hawaii," she said at one point, "we give our troubles away to the ocean."

The woman looked closely into my eyes as I talked, chuckled when I said something funny, and rubbed my shoulder when the conversation took a darker turn. It was probably the best therapy session I had ever had. And, as much as I wanted to fuck this gorgeous Hawaiian creature, I never crossed that line because I was so grateful to have someone show me so much care and concern. Some people ridicule these buy-me-drinky bars. I think they are the best thing since sliced bread.

Yes, Hawaii worked for me. In step with my personal life, my MMA training also improved. I established a new training camp crew. Guys like Chris West, Carl Barton, Steven Saito, Joe Gogo, and Mayhem Miller worked with me regularly in the Icon gym. I felt healthier and had some stability and consistency for the first time in a long time. Psychologically it paid off and led to positive results in the Octagon. After finding my groove in Hawaii, I won two fights in a row, earning "knockout of the night" honors for both. Those awards each came with $50,000 bonuses, so my pocketbook got healthier too. The first of those two fights is somewhat legendary in MMA circles. It was against a stocky slugger from Chicago named Terry Martin. Like Mike Tyson, Terry was a 5'8" mountain of power. At the time he sported a 16–3 record, and he had ended twelve of those fights with KOs and TKOs. That included six finishes in a row before he met me at *UFC Fight Night 11* in September of 2007.

I've pulled victory from the jaws of defeat many times in my career. But my fight with Terry Martin takes the cake. Even though Terry did not go on to be a major figure within the sport, fans and friends like to talk about this fight as much as any other. It's because the ending was so memorable.

Terry was not at all afraid of my power. In fact, he was a good bit stronger than me. His punches were like sledgehammers, and in the first two rounds he hurt me several times. Though I have brawler instincts, I was forced to fight a technical fight, using well-timed inside leg kicks, Muay Thai clinches and knees, and flurries of punches to counter his brutal attacks. Even my wrestling was ineffective against Terry. He stalked me around the cage, throwing leather and daring me to trade him punch-for-punch. I had a point deducted in the first round for grabbing the cage when Terry tried to slam me, so, at the start of the third round I was pretty sure the only way I could win the fight was to knock that bruiser out. The problem was that I was exhausted. And if I couldn't hurt the guy in the first or second round when I had a lot of juice on my punches, then it was very unlikely I could hurt him when my arms felt like wet noodles.

With about a minute left in the third and final round, Terry caught me with a left hook. I staggered. Then he landed a straight right hand that threw me back against the cage as if I had been smashed by an iron wrecking ball. My brain was scrambled and I could barely tell what was going on. All I knew was that there was a blurry, hefty black dude standing in front of me and that he was about to take my head off. I waded forward, wobbling as though I were knee deep in surf. Terry hit me with another right, a left, and another left hook that were as hard as any punches I had been hit with in my career. The lights were going out in my head. It happened in slow motion. I kept stumbling forward for an eternity, slow-marching to my death. But somehow in the midst of this I was able to wind up and throw a massive left-handed haymaker. It landed with a thud on his chin—on that perfect spot of the human head that reacts like a "power off" switch if you touch it just right. Terry's eyes rolled up and he dropped straight backward to the mat. I dove forward and landed one more huge arcing left hand to his temple before referee Herb Dean dove in to end the fight.

When I stood up, I literally had no idea what happened. The crowd was going crazy. Dana White was standing and applauding excitedly just outside of the cage. It took a good five seconds before my head cleared and I realized I had knocked Terry out. Joe Silva hurried over with a big smile on his face and congratulated me. But I was hurt so fucking badly that I nearly started crying right there in the cage.

My success against Terry Martin and my follow-up knockout of Alessio Sakara in March of 2008 once again had me on the move in the UFC's middleweight lineup. The next bout that the promotion set up for me was against a British kickboxing star who was in the midst of a meteoric rise in the sport of MMA. It was Michael "The Count" Bisping. Prior to our meeting he had only lost once in eighteen outings, a split decision to future light heavyweight champion Rashad Evans. Bisping then dropped to middleweight, cruising through two fights before getting his date with me.

We were first scheduled to meet in June of 2008 in England. However, a phone call from my lawyer changed all of that. I had an outstanding arrest warrant in Oregon, and there was no way I was going to be granted a travel visa. Remember when I got that DUI and then bailed on the diversion program after testing positive for coke? Well, that wasn't such a smart move after all. My Bisping fight wouldn't happen unless I appeared before a judge in Portland. Just a few days after agreeing to the fight, I hopped on a plane and headed home to face the music.

Because it was a no-bail warrant, I had to spend several days in jail before I could get a hearing. Nothing much exciting happened during that time, so I'll spare you the boring details. When I finally got my chance in court I was, as usual, hoping for more leniency than I would ultimately be granted. The judge didn't give a shit about how important my upcoming fight was. He sentenced me to thirty days in the slammer, less the time I had already served. That meant I wouldn't see daylight until just a week or two before my scheduled date with Bisping. There was no doubt about it; the fight was off.

Jail sucks. However, the inmates at the Clackamas County Jail in Portland were pretty good to me. I wasn't a pedophile or anything like that, and my cage-fighting cred earned me some friends and admirers among the population. One day a group of us were hanging out, when one of the guys—a little Puerto Rican dude—asked me to show him how a rear-naked choke works. I was happy to oblige. I told him that I would demonstrate on him but that he should tap if it got too tight. I wrapped my arms around the Puerto Rican dude's neck, explaining proper technique to the twenty other guys who were watching on. As I continued to talk, the guy did not tap. I remember being impressed by how tough he was. Most people would have passed out after just a few seconds. Of course, when I released my grip, the guy dropped straight to the floor—out cold. The other inmates started absolutely freaking out, laughing and yelling and shoving each other. The Puerto Rican guy was unconscious, snoring and shuddering. With all of the commotion, I was sure that a group of correctional officers were going to come running to find an incapacitated perp at my feet. I kept trying to get everyone to calm the fuck down, but they were having a field day. Luckily the little guy woke up about a minute later and we all had a good laugh. No harm done. The was the beginning and the ending of my inmate coaching career.

Fortunately, upon my release from jail I learned that my fight with Bisping would be rescheduled to October 18, 2008, in Birmingham, England—the Count's home turf. It was the first of two times that I was the headliner on a pay-per-view event in the UFC. It was a big stage and a big deal. Things picked up where they left off in Hawaii. It did not take long for me to get back into the swing of things. My training camp was very solid, and I felt that, if I could continue with this level of consistency, there were few men in the world who could stop me.

Then I did something stupid . . . something very stupid.

Shortly after returning from my stint in jail, I was talking to a bodybuilder friend of mine. I told him that I still felt like my body wasn't where I wanted it to be, and that I wanted to get leaner. He recommended I try a steroid called Winstrol. When I expressed my concerns about getting popped for performance enhancing drugs (PEDs), he told me not to worry. A four-week course would get me where I wanted to be, and then it would be completely out of my system within a month of when I stopped taking it. I would have two months of clean training between cycling off of the Winstrol and fighting Bisping. Furthermore, the fight was in England, outside of the NSAC jurisdiction, and the UFC had very rarely taken on the burden of overseas drug testing when there was no athletic commission in place to handle it. *No problem*, I told myself. I took the Winstrol for a month and then forgot about it.

I flew to England two weeks prior to the fight so as to avoid jetlag and get some final training in. While I was there, T. J. called me and told me he had decided to close Icon Fitness. It was bleeding money and he couldn't float it anymore. Fuck. I didn't need the stress of knowing that I would be out of a job when I got back to Hawaii. I was making decent money in the UFC, but nothing that I could really build a nest egg out of. Also, I loved coaching. The thought of folding up shop and waving good-bye to all of the young fighters I was working with saddened me. I did my best to put that concern out of my head as I made final preparations.

*UFC 89* arrived. The National Indoor Arena in Birmingham was rowdy as fuck. The Brits loved their man Bisping. But at that time, my popularity was soaring, too. I got a loud welcome as I walked to the cage.

Some people talk shit about Bisping's lack of punching power, and, yeah, he's not the heaviest hitter in the world. But The Count has fantastic footwork and excellent boxing. And he's a tough dude. No one had yet come close to stopping him. I expected our fight to be a stand-up war. My game plan was to stalk him down and force him to trade in the pocket. If one of us was going to land a lights-out hook, it would be me.

I felt calmer than normal in the first round of the fight. I came out and stuck to my strategy and took the fight to Bisping. I'm pretty sure I stung him a couple of times in that frame, but his counterstriking was on point, and he bloodied up my nose. The second round was similar. I charged forward and Bisping circled and sniped at me. I came to realize that my only hope was to get deep within his reach and land a bomb. So I took chances and decided to eat a few punches if it meant putting my hands on him. But he frustrated me. As time ticked down on the round he split my cheek open below my right eye. I was pissed!

I gave it everything I had in the third in final round and landed the only takedown of the fight. But I wasn't able to do much damage and Bisping got back to his feet. I continued to move forward, and he continued to use his crafty movement to avoid damage and land well-timed jabs and straights. Enough of this counterstriking! I had to get that motherfucker to engage. Finally I just put my hands behind my back and marched forward with my chin out. I wanted to get him to make just one mistake so I could whip out a left hook and put him to sleep. He threw a slow kick toward my face and I headbutted it angrily. The crowd loved my brazen moves. They even started chanting my name. But the Count was too smart for that. He didn't take the bait. Time ran out and he was awarded a unanimous decision by the judges.

I wasn't ashamed of my performance. Bisping was a top-ten middleweight at the time, and we had put on a good show as headliners for that event. But I started to feel pretty dejected as I flew back to Hawaii. What was I going to do with myself now that Icon was closing down? Luckily a couple of my teammates were on the flight with me. During the voyage we came up with the idea that I should find a way to open my own gym on the island. By the time we landed in Honolulu, I had a rough business plan and a name for the gym that I would open: Chris Leben's Ultimate Fight School.

I spent a week recovering from the fight and relaxing. I talked to some influential friends on the island, and it started to appear that my goal of opening an MMA gym was, in fact, feasible. I was excited and optimistic.

Then Dana White called.

His number appeared on my caller ID and I got butterflies. If Dana was calling me out of the blue, it was either a great thing or a horrible thing. I answered the phone. To the best of my recollection, the conversation went something like this:

"Dana! What's up, man?!"

He didn't have time for small talk. "Listen, Chris," he said. "You tested positive for steroids after the Bisping fight."

The phone went silent as I ran through all of the scenarios in my head. Had I taken a steroid during my training camp? No. In the past month had someone given me a supplement that might have contained steroids? No. Could it have been the Winstrol that I took four months earlier? That was supposed to be long gone from my system. But, by process of elimination, I realized the Winstrol was the only possibility. I had gotten my information about the drug from my bodybuilder friend who had provided it. I never took the time to research the details on my own. That was my downfall.

This was not a good moment in my life—a drug violation coming just a few months after I got out of jail. I thought about bullshitting Dana, but I figured I was fucked either way. Might as well go down like a man.

"Yeah," I replied. "I took some stuff. I thought it would have been out of my system long before the fight, but I guess I was wrong. I fucked up."

Dana paused, and I awaited his wrath. But he was surprisingly calm and somewhat sympathetic.

"Well, Chris, that sucks. But I have to say that you are the first fighter we confronted like this who admitted the truth. So you have that going for you."

"No point in dragging out the inevitable, I guess," was my response.

"Exactly," said Dana. Then he thought for a moment. "OK. Just stay quiet about this for now. We need time at our end to figure out how to address this. Just don't say anything to anybody. Understand?"

Was Dana suggesting that we sweep this under the rug? Holy shit, I thought, maybe the gods are smiling down on me.

"I understand completely," I replied.

My fantasy that Dana would save my ass didn't last too long. Two weeks later, on November 3, 2008, the report of my failed PED test appeared all across the MMA press. I was suspended for nine months and fined one-third of my substantial *UFC 89* payday.

I talked to Bisping after that all went down, and, to be honest, he wasn't too pissed. He told me that, regardless of the PED test failure, he thought I was a good fighter. However, in recent months, he's made headlines by vehemently speaking out against PED users. As I said, Bisping started off his career by going 17–1. But after beating me, his record has been a mediocre 10–6, with four of those losses coming against fighters who were revealed to have used steroids or other PEDs. I guess I can't blame him for becoming a bit cynical.

Although I had once tried synthetic testosterone prior to my fight career, the first time I took a PED with hope of a result was prior to the filming of the first season of *The Ultimate Fighter* in late 2006. After I was selected to appear on the show, I had about three months to get into shipshape. First of all, I was still skinny-fat, and I didn't want to look like a doughboy in front of millions of people. Secondly, I knew this was my big break. Winning the *TUF* competition would secure me a spot on the big stage for at least two fights.

The UFC wasn't known for its drug testing at the time, and since participation in *TUF* wasn't really sanctioned by the NSAC, I figured I had nothing to worry about. So I ordered some synthetic testosterone online and got my hands on some trenbolone through a hookup I knew in Portland. Trenbolone is a steroid that was originally used on livestock. But it was adopted by bodybuilders because it helps build mass fast. I took both chemicals a couple of times until about a month prior to the start of filming. It was then that I received an unexpected phone call from the UFC. They informed me that, in just a few days, the UFC would be flying all of the contestants into Las Vegas early for PED tests.

Holy shit. This was a DEFCON 5 situation. My piss would probably light up every indicator in the drug testing book. I pulled every string I could pull in the hopes of finding some way to mask my steroid use. Finally, I found a supplement shop where they were selling some heavy-duty drink that, when consumed, was supposed to make you pee clean for three hours. The guy at the shop told me this was my best option. So I plopped down fifty dollars and took it to go.

Nate Quarry flew down with me from Oregon to Vegas. We landed around 1:00 PM, and our urine tests were scheduled for 2:30 PM. So, as soon as we landed, I grabbed my luggage that contained the masking agent. I told Nate I had to shit, then ran off to the airport bathroom. I shut myself inside a stall and pulled out the thirty-two-ounce bottle. I opened it and peered inside. I almost wretched just from the stench of it. The fluid looked like a gray industrial sludge, and it smelled like rotten eggs. Desperate times called for desperate measures. *Here goes nothing*, I told myself, throwing my head back and guzzling the horrible concoction. It took every ounce of will power not to stick a finger down my throat and unload that goop into the toilet.

I immediately started to feel ill. My stomach blew up like a balloon, my face turned red, and I started to sweat profusely. I emerged from the bathroom and found Nate, who gave me a strange look.

"Dude, are you OK?" he asked.

"Yeah," I replied. "That was just a rough one. I was holding it in for the whole flight. That's all."

Nate shook his head and we headed to the pickup location where a UFC van awaited us.

We got the results of our tests the next day. Unbelievably, I had pissed clean. That bottle of disgusting shit had actually worked as advertised. But not everyone was so lucky. Josh Burkman (currently a top-notch welterweight in the UFC) was slated to compete in the 205-pound division of that season. But he was turned away after his test results showed evidence of steroids in his system. He later admitted to taking Winstrol, and, like me, said that he was surprised by the pre-filming PED test.

PEDs have been a hot-button issue over the last five years in the sport of mixed martial arts. There is a tangled web of perspectives that an athlete or an observer can take. I've spent a lot of time thinking about where PEDs fit into the big picture, and my position has definitely evolved over time. To help you understand this, I must first offer some background.

I love Chael Sonnen. I consider him a mentor, a trailblazer, a legend, and a friend. At the time I was writing this book (in late 2014 and early 2015), he was at the center of the PED use debate in the sport of MMA. Did Chael *use* more drugs than anybody else? No. Did he get *caught* more times than anybody else? No. Did his use of prohibited substances result in an unfair advantage? No one can say for sure. Then why is his use of these substances more heavily scrutinized than most other instances in the world of mixed martial arts? Well, there are a lot of variables to that equation.

Chael is a fellow Oregonian. He grew up not far from me, in West Linn, a southern suburb of Portland. He is a renowned wrestler, whose accolades began piling up in high school. He was an All-American member of the University of Oregon wrestling team and a two-time PAC-10 runner-up. After college, Chael began training to become an MMA fighter. He appeared in his first professional fight in May 1997 in a local promotion called BFV (Battle of Fort Vancouver), then proceeded to go 13–7 in his next twenty fights over nine years before finally making a debut in the UFC. He was submitted by Babalu Sobral at *UFC 55* in April 2006, then took a decision over Trevor Prangley, then was armbarred by Jeremy Horn at *UFC 60*. The UFC deciders had seen enough. They cut the twenty-nine-year-old Chael, whose record now stood at fifteen wins and ten losses. For most fighters, that would be a nail in the career coffin. It would not have been reasonable to expect another shot at the UFC, and a mediocre record like that wouldn't even earn a guy a headlining spot on a regional card. In fact, five events later, Chael was only the co-main event on a Portland fight card whose headlining bout featured

Gerald "The Finishing Machine" Strebendt and Will Shutt. (I don't expect you to have heard of either of them.)

In February of 2009 Sonnen beat the odds and earned a return trip to the UFC. Unfortunately, his first test was against Brazilian grappling phenom Demian Maia. In the first round, Maia threw Chael onto his head, mounted him, and finished him with a brutal triangle choke. It was arguably one of the more spectacular submission finishes in promotional history. This loss did not bode well for Sonnen's second act in the UFC. Again, most fighters would have flamed out at this point. But did I mention that Chael Sonnen is no ordinary fighter?

Lo-and-behold things changed. And they changed in a fucking hurry. Over the next twelve months Sonnen won three tough UFC fights by decision—against Dan Miller, Yushin Okami, and Nate Marquardt. Then he started talking shit. And talking shit, and talking shit, and talking shit. His target? The champion, Anderson Silva, of course. And it worked, goddamnit. Silva-Sonnen I was booked for *UFC 117* in Oakland, California.

Maybe today, in an exceptionally crowded and competitive middleweight division, such a turn of fortune would not be possible. But back then, in spring of 2010, something was rotten in the middleweight division. Anderson Silva was champion and had defended his belt nine straight times since fall of 2006, when he first dismantled the previous champion, Rich Franklin (right after beating me). But the Spider's dominance did not resonate with the fans. Simply put, most people didn't enjoy his fights. He either destroyed his opponent in an apparent mismatch (Forrest Griffin, James Irvin, and . . . um . . . er . . . me), or he put on the most boring fight of the night. In three of his title defenses prior to his date with Chael, Anderson was actually booed by the crowd in the middle of the fight.

After the Demian Maia fight, in which Anderson spent twenty-five minutes toying with the challenger and eventually won via a ho-hum decision, the MMA world had had it up to here. Even UFC president Dana White was disgusted.

"I don't think I've ever been more embarrassed in the ten years of being in this business," White told reporter Ariel Helwani. "It was the most horrible thing I have ever seen. . . . It's the first time that I've ever walked out of the main event and given the belt to the guy's manager and told him to put it on him."

A changing of the guard was in the offing, and Chael Sonnen had stepped up to lead the middleweight revolt. He was relentlessly aggressive and confident with his rhetoric in the weeks leading up to the fight. It was the birth of true showmanship in the UFC, and Chael was the daddy. Uber-promoter Dana White seized the opportunity, and the UFC gave Sonnen every opportunity to run his brilliant mouth on camera.

What was particularly interesting about this was that, as much as Chael had the MMA world transfixed, few people really believed he stood a chance against Anderson. Sure, Chael was an exceptional wrestler, but look how Anderson obliterated other world-class grapplers like Dan Henderson and Demian Maia. When the day of *UFC 117* arrived, Anderson Silva was a more than four-to-one favorite over the cocky Oregonian challenger.

But, as they say, even if the odds are long, they should put on the fight anyway. The bell rang to start the fight, and, unbelievably, Chael Sonnen spent four-and-a-half rounds absolutely dominating and destroying Anderson Silva. For the majority of the fight, Chael was on top, delivering a lopsided whooping. It appeared that, not only was Anderson going to lose the fight, he was going to be absolutely shamed. Going into the final round, the judges had the fight scored 40–36, 40–35, and 40–34. This was easily one of the most lopsided championship fights in the history of the UFC.

Unfortunately for Chael, title fights are twenty-five minutes long, not twenty-three minutes. Because, it was with about two minutes left in the final round that Anderson, on his back and defending Chael's never-ending ground-and-pound onslaught, slapped on a triangle choke/armbar combination. Chael desperately attempted to yank himself out of the champion's clutches, but to no avail. Unable to breathe and with his arm being wrenched backwards, Chael tapped and the fight was over. Anderson had pulled victory from the jaws of defeat. Or, should I say, Chael had pulled defeat from the jaws of victory. Had Chael run away from Anderson for the entirety of the last round he would have left the cage as champion. But in fucking MMA, that's the way the cookie crumbles.

The UFC had flown me to Boston to participate in a *UFC 117* promotion at a popular sports bar. My job was to just sit there and chat with fans and watch the fight. But I don't think I have ever been so animated in my life. When Chael submitted, I threw a chair across the room and almost caused a melee.

Pretty nuts, huh? Well, this is where the story gets even more controversial. A week later, it was announced that Chael had failed his post-fight drug test. His urine sample showed a testosterone-to-epitestosterone (T/E) ratio of 16.9:1. The T/E ratio is one of the primary indicators of whether an athlete has utilized a PED, such as a steroid, synthetic testosterone, or human growth hormone. A typical healthy man has a T/E ratio of 1:1. The Nevada State Athletic Commission (NSAC)—which is the leading governing body of combat sports in the United States—allows for a ratio of up to 4:1.

So, what happened then? The UFC released the news. A few members of the media were outraged. But the majority of MMA fandom raised their eyebrows, groaned, and moved on. After all, Chael had lost the fight, so the belt was still around the appropriate waist, right? In his defense, Chael provided evidence that he was being treated for hypogonadism, a condition that affects the ability of the human body to produce testosterone. But when all was said and done, the NSAC fined Chael $2,500 and suspended him for a year.

Chael returned in 2011 and overwhelmed middleweight standout Brian Stann. He then won a close decision against perpetual contender Michael Bisping, and, before you knew it, the Sonnen-Silva rematch was set. Considering the controversial outcome of their first contest, which was multiplied by Chael's relentless verbal assaults in every possible media outlet, the second matchup was exponentially more hotly anticipated. In fact, to date, it is one of the top-ten top-selling pay-per-view events in the history of MMA.

The fight world quickly forgot about Chael's failed drug test and embraced his juicy rivalry with the Brazilian middleweight king. But, interestingly, in the twenty-three months between their fights, Chael went from respected challenger to despised cretin, while Anderson evolved into the most celebrated champion in the history of the sport. How'd it happen? To be honest, I can't fucking explain it. In that time period, Anderson threw a front kick that KO'd the great Vitor Belfort and delivered a brilliant beatdown of the red hot and rising Yushin Okami. But displays of such mastery hadn't stopped people from booing, even hating Anderson in the past. Maybe people just started to focus on the artistry of his combat rather than his various shortcomings. I don't know, and I think the guy that can explain or predict exactly what the MMA community wants or doesn't want from its fighters is worth his weight in gold.

Whatever the reason, Chael became the greatest villain in the history of combat sports. And, always the genius showman, he embraced it. He dubbed himself "The American Gangster" and basically told anyone who didn't like him or how he behaved to go fuck themselves. He drove the Brazilian fans nuts, insulting their culture and people. He hilariously claimed that the fighting Nogueria brothers once tried to feed a carrot to a bus. In another interview, Chael said, "You tell Anderson Silva that I'm coming over and I'm kicking down his backdoor and patting his little lady on the ass. And I'm telling her to make me a steak, medium-rare just how I like it." With every button Chael pushed, and every fan he irked, his pocketbook got fatter. Some observers speculate that he took home more than a million dollars from Sonnen-Silva II.

The fight, of course, couldn't possibly live up to the hype, but it was a memorable one. Sonnen took Silva to the ground within the first five seconds of the first round, and he did his best to rough up the champ for the remainder of the period. But, in the second round, Anderson came out with a fresh swagger. As Chael stalked forward and shot for takedown after takedown, Anderson connected with sharp, accurate strikes. Frustrated, Chael tried to land a spinning back fist. Anderson displayed his legendary head movement, ducking under the strike like a matador, and Chael went tumbling to the floor. Anderson stepped forward and threw a brutal knee to challenger's chest. He then piled on with a barrage of accurate, powerful right hands. The referee stepped in, and the roof of the MGM Grand was almost blown off by the eruption of the audience, led by a huge contingent of rowdy Brazilians.

That fight, or at least the run up to it, was certainly the pinnacle of Chael's career. He fought in the UFC three more times, impressively submitting Shogun Rua, but getting beat handily by both Jon Jones and Rashad Evans. He was given a regular spot broadcasting UFC events for FOX. The UFC, the fans, the media, they all began to love and respect Chael as they had never done in the past. Here was a guy who put his money where his mouth was—a guy who, without hesitation, dared step up to the most dangerous man in the sport. Chael was responsible for creating the most intriguing, exciting, and lucrative rivalry in the history of the UFC. Hell, even the Brazilians started to warm up to him.

Then, after filming a much-watched series of *The Ultimate Fighter* opposite "The Axe Murderer" Wanderlei Silva, Chael again got popped. He was reportedly caught with four illegal substances in his system: anastrozole, clomiphene, HGH, EPO (none of which, it should be noted, are anabolic steroids). For many fans and observers, the incident confirmed what they had suspected all along: Chael made it to the top of the UFC mountain because he was taking drugs to boost his testosterone. I wholeheartedly disagree with this perspective, by the way. I've seen Chael train many times, and I would argue that he is one of the most naturally talented, hardest-working athletes in the world. In my book, he deserved every success. Nonetheless, the fans and media abandoned him in droves. Fox sacked him, and Chael retired from the sport.

OK. That story was a bit longer than I had planned for it to be. And many people already are familiar with it. But, I took the time to tell this tale with some detail in order to set up the following question: would it have been better for Chael Sonnen to have never taken PEDs?

Let's assume, for argument's sake, that Chael's PED use contributed in a real way to his success. Considering his medical condition and what happened to his career, to his life, and to the sport as a whole, I think the answer is not as clear as many people would like it to be. Not only did Chael get to live his dream, travel the world, soak up the limelight, and help build the sport he loved, he amassed millions of dollars in the process. When you tally up what he earned from fight purses, from bonuses, from sponsorships, from his stint as a *TUF* coach, and from his role as a broadcaster, it's conceivable that Chael netted more than $5 million between 2010 and 2014. That's a shitload of money in the MMA world. By comparison, I brought home around half a million over ten fights in that same time period.

What would have happened had Chael never used PEDs? Well, maybe he would have retired in his early thirties with not much to show for it. Maybe he would have gone back into real estate. Maybe he would have done just as well in his MMA career and risen to the same heights. It's very possible that the PEDs were not the key ingredient in the Chael Sonnen recipe for success. After all there's a lot more—I mean *a lot more*—to the sport than strength and endurance.

In terms of the sport, had Chael Sonnen not developed into one of the better fighters in history, perhaps the expansion of the UFC would have stalled. Perhaps no one would have properly filled the role of Anderson Silva's nemesis. Maybe many fans would have turned their back on the sport, irritated by a champion who didn't deliver the goods that they wanted.

What did Chael Sonnen lose? Well, his reputation, certainly, was severely tarnished. But, guess what: he never would have had a reputation worth tarnishing in the first place had he not ascended to the top of the mountain. Anyway, unsurprisingly, as of early 2015 Chael was back in the broadcasting game, hired as an MMA analyst by ESPN. The guy can talk about the game better than anyone in the world, and he has the career to back it up.

In short, I don't judge Chael for a fucking second. I don't discount a single thing that he achieved. The man is still a hero in my book. And, as a PED user myself, to question any of it, of course, would be the pot calling the kettle black.

On the other hand, many people who engage in the PED debate are, I think, lacking a fundamental understanding of what it means to be a professional combatant. What MMA in its current form can be best compared to is a warrior contest called "pankration," which emerged in ancient Greece something like three to four thousand years ago. Pankration, like MMA, was a form of total hand-to-hand combat. It involved boxing and wrestling techniques along with leg strikes and joint locks. The fight was terminated by the judge, or ended when the losing fighter submitted, was knocked out, or died. The origin of pankration preceded Roman gladiator fighting, which differed in that it allowed weapons. But the premise was more or less the same for both: glory for the winner; shame, injury, or *death* for the loser.

There was a famous fighter ("pankratiast") named Arrhichion who won the 55th Olympiad in 568 BC despite dying during the contest! He was choked by his opponent, but, right before passing from asphyxiation, he snapped his opponent's big toe in half (or so the story goes). The opponent submitted from the pain. The judge raised Arrchichion's arm to declare him the winner, only then discovering that he was holding the arm of a corpse.

Now imagine a young pankratiast from the Greek highlands whose only hope for success and prosperity was to compete in this deadly sport. His alternative would be to live a goatherder's life—a monotonous eternity of drudgery and poverty. And maybe this poor young man has a wife and an infant child who depend on him for food and shelter. Well, one day, a medicine man offers the pankratiast a special potion that will help him train harder, prepare more frequently, and recover from injuries more readily than he has in the past.

"Take this," suggests the medicine man, "and you'll be less likely to die."

Would you fault the guy if he took the potion? Would you decry him as a fraud and a cheater? Would you publicly shame him and call for his banishment from all pankration events? Would you demand that he give up his dream and return to goatherding? Maybe. Maybe not. But keep that analogy in mind when you judge an MMA fighter who has used testosterone or a steroid.

Friends, I don't want your pity. That's the last thing I want. But I do want to emphasize how complicated this issue is, because there is a huge difference between sitting in a La-Z-Boy, screaming at the UFC pay-per-view on your flat screen and actually stepping into a fucking cage to face off against a person who might cripple or kill you.

Think about that Greek goatherder's situation and compare it to mine. I am convinced that if professional MMA did not exist, I would have been an aimless druggie alcoholic working as a pipefitter. Or, more likely, I would have died of an overdose years ago. And, even after earning the opportunity to have a professional MMA career, I had to face a morbid dilemma every time I stepped into the cage: either I won the fight, or I risked being sent back to where I came from to fade into oblivion.

I'm being as literal as I can be. If I had been a failure at MMA, I would probably not be alive. And that's an especially risky proposition because of how fucking easy it is to be a failure at MMA. First of all, every time you fight, your career could be over, either due to injury or due to the fact that you lost so bad that you get cut from your promotion. And bad shit can happen no matter how long and hard you train. A half-second of distraction and you get knocked out. One wrong step or kick or jump and you might break your ankle or tear a hamstring. These aren't the kind of mishaps that keep baseball players awake at night. Second of all, unlike most other professional sports, only a small proportion of MMA athletes earn a comfortable living. Even in the UFC, there are plenty of guys who make only $10,000 per fight and only appear on one or two cards a year! So, truly, you have to either have plenty of family money, big-time sponsors, or a lucrative side job, or you have to be a top-tier fighter if you want to generate a respectable wage.

Every time I stepped in to the Octagon, I thought to myself, *If I don't win, I may not be able to fight again. If I don't win, I may not be able to put food on the table for my wife and me. If I don't win, then I will end up in a ditch just like everyone expected in the first place.* And, everywhere I turned there was a medicine man saying, *Chris, if you take this potion, you'll be much more likely to survive.*

As I have said, my position on all of this has evolved over time. But early on in my career, when I was certain that a large majority of my competitors were using steroids or testosterone, I believed that if taking something allowed you to vastly increase your income, keep your job, and provide for your family, then fuck the ethics. I succumbed to the fear of disaster and the desire to be the best. I took the goddamn potion.

In retrospect, was I right to take PEDs? No. But should I or other violators be burned at the stake for our indiscretions?

I don't think so. There should be punishments and sanctions for fighters who break the rules. And yes, the UFC and other promotions should do what they can to even the playing field. But the life of a fighter is so goddamn complex, so volatile, so brutal that vilifying a guy who gets clipped once doesn't make a lot of sense to me.

Some call MMA "the hurt game." I always liked that nickname for the sport, because it reminded me of what I put on the line every time I fought. Hell, just a few days before I put these words on the page, a fighter in Azerbaijan named Ramin Zeynalov died in the cage as the result of a fight-ending punch to the head. It knocked him out and caused a brain hemorrhage. He never woke up again. Ramin was twenty-seven years old. I am sure that some of my dickhead readers will think, *Oh, that's no surprise. Azerbaijan is a backwards country anyway and this guy was probably some inexperienced dumb fuck.* Well, first of all, the guy had a black belt in Tae-Kwon-Do and won a silver medal in a national kickboxing tournament. And you know what? This accident has nothing to do with the country he was in or how naïve he may have been. The man died from something that happens to American fighters every goddamn day, something that your opponent wants to deliver to you more than anything else—a hard punch in the face.

Mark my words—in the next ten years a fighter will die on television in a major promotional event and the shit is going to hit the fan. Am I saying that people are stupid to choose the path of an MMA fighter? No. They are no more stupid than race car drivers, boxers, football players, or high school cheerleaders who are all *more* likely to die from their chosen sport. I am just saying that an MMA death on television might finally make fans realize what is at stake and bite their fucking tongues when they get the urge to judge these athletes for their mistakes.

Or maybe they won't.

During the peak of my career, I would estimate that 75 percent of world-class MMA fighters were taking PEDs or were between cycles. Actually, the only guy I can really vouch for as a completely clean UFC fighter is Eddie Herman. That statistic may blow your hair back. And it may be wrong. But do you think my sport is that much different from baseball and competitive cycling, where, according to various insiders, PED use is par for the course?

What should the UFC and the athletic commissions do about PEDs? I'm glad that those decisions aren't my burden to bear. But I do know that professional sports leagues and promotions like the UFC need to do what they need to do to protect their athletes while still making money, advancing the sport, and preserving the fanbase. One could make the claim that there was a period—maybe from the time of the Zuffa purchase of the organization in 2000 until 2012—when fighters with a little extra testosterone might have been exactly what the UFC needed. During that time, the organization and athletic commissions were relatively lax with their testing and not too severe with their punishment of violators. The level of competition and performance abilities of the fighters skyrocketed. Guys who seemed like ferocious champions in the early years of this millennium—Royce Gracie, Matt Hughes, Frank Shamrock, Tim Sylvia among them—were shoved to the back of the fast-moving herd.

To be clear, I am not saying that the UFC encouraged PED use, or even tacitly approved of it. But it didn't necessarily hurt the organization during this time. In that twelve-year span, the UFC grew from a debt-ridden and struggling enterprise into a billion-dollar powerhouse business. But, even more importantly, the sport found a spot on the international stage and developed a meaningful and devoted following. I would argue that modern UFC fans are as passionate as those of any other sport in the world. How did Dana White feel about PEDs during this period of exponential growth? Undoubtedly, he did not like it when fighters got caught and publicly exposed for PED use. Incidents like that create a PR nightmare that threatens the sport. But, in regards to responsible, behind-the-scenes PED use, I don't think Dana held a black-and-white position. I think, as it should have been, PED use was probably a very complicated issue for him that required not just a cost-benefit analysis but also constant contemplation about how his actions and statements about steroids and testosterone replacement therapy (TRT) might affect the careers and livelihoods of the men who performed for him.

Fuck, when I was in the UFC, drug testing was more of an IQ test than a chemical one. For the most part, fighters were only tested immediately after the fight. So, if you cycled your drug intake properly—which is not rocket science—you could easily enjoy the vast benefits of using TRT or steroids during training camp while pissing clean after the fight. That is, you could use the drugs when you needed them, in order to practice harder and for longer, and then stop in time for them to clear your system. I knew dozens of guys who did it. It was easy. Only idiots (like me) or lazy dicks fucked that up. So, I think that my idea of a 75 percent user rate is not crazy. This is supported by the fact that between December 2013, when regular out-of-competition testing was instituted by the UFC, and February of 2014, five of sixteen fighters who were randomly tested for PEDs failed. That's 31 percent. Throw in the likelihood that some of those tested were users who had cycled off, were in-between usages, or were using substances that were not detected by the tests. Let's be fair and double that number up to sixty percent. Go back a few years to the mid-2000s when the testing was not nearly as stringent, and you can understand where I came up with my calculation of fighters who have used PEDs.

I also have some inside knowledge about TRT use in the sport of MMA. Let's just say I have a friend—we'll call him Billy—who used it during training camp leading up to a few of his fights. Billy wasn't really looking for a performance enhancer so much as a performance stabilizer. Late in his career, his body was a mess. The bumps and bruises were adding up. He became very inconsistent in the gym and struggled to put together worthwhile training camps. So, Billy said *fuck it* and began a standard dosage of TRT that never put him over the allowable limit.

It's kind of funny how TRT works. Any doctor can prescribe it but *only if you demonstrate a need for it.* That means you have to show abnormally low testosterone levels in your blood. In this way, it's kind of a self-perpetuating cycle. When you come off TRT you have to use a post-cycle agent, like HCG, to revive your testicular production. If you don't do that, your testosterone level drops significantly. When that happens, you can go to your doctor and get a blood test. Now, while he can't prescribe TRT if your levels are normal, he can prescribe as much as he deems necessary as soon as you show a deficiency. So, for an athlete like Billy, there's actually an incentive to drive your testosterone levels down prior to medical examinations.

It was very easy to maintain the supply that Billy wanted. He didn't have to use special doctors or shady prescription hawks. His doctors were regular people, and he told them upfront about the fact that he was a professional athlete who had to be very careful about the testosterone levels he showed. Maybe they didn't like it, but they were bound by patient-doctor confidentiality. Nonetheless, they all insisted that Billy sign a waiver stating that he would not blame them for a PED test failure and that they were not condoning his use of TRT as a performance-enhancing program but as a medical necessity.

Some of you might be thinking that this is disgusting and that it gives fighters like Billy an unfair advantage over other fighters who are trying to succeed in a clean way. I hear you. But the thing is that life is a big, smelly, putrid parade of unfair advantages. Some people are born with genes that make them beautiful and smart. Other people are born into old-money families with net worths of billions of dollars. In my sport, most guys have to work side jobs in addition to their job as a professional athlete. Do you realize how fucked up that is? Imagine if Lebron James had to work forty hours a week selling insurance so he could afford to be a basketball player. Do you think he would be as great as he is?

UFC hall-of-famer B. J. Penn is the man. He's a quintessential Hawaiian fighter, and, like me, he wants to stand and trade. I've trained with his brother Reagan. B. J. grew into one of the most successful and popular MMA fighters in history, winning both the lightweight and welterweight belts. He is a big reason why the UFC was so popular in the 2000s. But B. J. gets a lot of shit because he comes from a wealthy family. Some say he is a spoiled rich kid (which I disagree with). However, the question becomes, Would B. J. Penn have been one of the greatest ever if he was born into a lower-class family and had to work menial jobs to pay for his Brazilian jiu-jitsu classes? I don't know what the answer to that is, but I will say that having money is a huge fucking advantage—an advantage that is probably as unfair and as impactful on one's success in fighting as injecting testosterone every once in a while. Did anyone ever argue that B. J. Penn should have given back all of his family money and start over? Of course not.

Another example is Jon "Bones" Jones. That motherfucker has probably the most extraordinary set of chromosomes in the history of the sporting world! Not only is his reach a staggering eight-five inches—compared to most of his competitors who have seventy-six- to seventy-eight-inch reaches—but he is freakishly athletic and was able to master high-level techniques that most people take a lifetime to learn. It's not fair, man! He has an absolutely unfair advantage, and, as a result, he has dominated some of the greatest fighters in the history of the sport: Shogun Rua, Chael Sonnen, Lyoto Machida, Rampage Jackson, and Glover Teixeira to name a few.

Here's my point. No matter where you go or what you do, whether you are an MMA fighter or a real estate agent or a screenwriter, you are going to discover that certain people have unfair advantages. They have money, or supermodel looks, or superhuman strength, or their fathers are well connected, or they have a genetic mutation that allows them to calculate numbers faster than someone else. Does that mean these people should not be allowed to compete? Does that mean these people are scum? Because that's how the world looks at fighters who use PEDs.

The American public puts people on pedestals who artificially modify themselves all the fucking time. Pam Anderson got a boob job and became America's dream woman for a decade. More recently, Olympic hero Bruce Jenner underwent a sexual transition to become a woman, and he was hailed as a hero. The cosmetics and plastic surgery businesses generate billions of dollars a year helping people look younger and feel better about themselves. And you better believe these kinds of modifications

matter as much as it does to most people. Some argue it should matter even more than that. It's fucking complex.

Again, I am the last one who can judge Anderson Silva or Chael Sonnen or any other athlete or human being for that matter. Anyway, good for those two guys. For a period of time, they ruled the fight world. PEDs or no PEDs, they showed the rest of us what was possible.

# CHAPTER 7
# DOWNS AND UPS

I should mention here that, although I claim to have escaped to Hawaii and to have left my troubles 2,600 miles behind in Washington, I actually did not cut Lisa out of my life completely until years later. A couple of months before the Bisping fight, I reconnected with Lisa and asked her to move to Hawaii to live with me.

"The girl from the codependent abusive relationship that previously nearly ruined your life?!" my reader asks in shock.

"Yes, that one." I reply.

"You are a complete and utter dumb fuck," says my reader.

"I know."

I wasn't in the best mindset after I tested positive for steroids. In the few weeks prior to the report, I had made a lot of progress toward opening my Ultimate Fight School in Oahu. I had lined up some investors and some pretty badass sponsors, who were going to provide much of the equipment. But, when the PED news came out, they dumped me like a satchel full of cow pies. It cost me a lot of money.

I was kind of lost at sea spiritually, and, like a good addict, I went back to the drug I knew best. In this case, that drug was Lisa—the woman who had already once ripped my balls off and shoved them deep up my ass.

At some point I drunk dialed her and told her how much I missed her and how sorry I was that things didn't work out between us. The next thing you know, she appeared at Honolulu Airport. We decided to move forward with opening the gym despite the setbacks, and soon found a great location near the University of Hawaii. And, to top things off, we rented a little cottage to share that was within walking distance of the gym. We were snug as a bug in a rug.

I scraped together all the money I needed to set up the fight school, but I didn't really know what the fuck I was doing. I had never started a business before, so I let Lisa deal with the lawyer and handle most of the necessary startup paperwork. Once we got going, she ran the front desk while I focused on building out the gym and finding the best coaches I could get my hands on to join my team. Things actually started to come together nicely, and in a short period of time, we had a sizable membership. So, in addition to preparing for my occasional UFC fights, I was now the head coach of my very own MMA training center. It was a fighter's dream situation.

If only it could have been that simple.

As you would expect, my relationship with Lisa picked up right where it left off. We got drunk a lot and did our fair share of drugs. We were constantly at each other's throats and had blowout fights almost every week. I wasn't faultless in the least, but I remember thinking to myself over and over that I would have done almost anything for us to experience a little bit of peace and happiness. On the other side of the equation, Lisa was very hard on me. Often, she flat out treated me like shit. In retrospect, I think that she had a neurotic need to tightly control our relationship and she felt that crushing my confidence was the best way to achieve her goal. The result was a toxic and unstable relationship that was like spiritual quicksand; every time I made an effort to improve my life, I got dragged down deeper. Sometimes I bit back when she insulted me, or belittled me. But after a while I got into the habit of bending over and taking it. Why? Because that's the way I deserved to be treated, or so I thought. I felt that a hillbilly from the sticks of Oregon couldn't do much better and I should be grateful for the bitter table scraps the gods were offering me.

Soon things became intolerable. I tried to break up with Lisa, but she simply wouldn't accept it. She wouldn't move out of the apartment, and she staged public meltdowns every time I tried to push her away. She bought red paint and painted *Fuck you, motherfucker!* all over the walls of our house. Numerous times she attacked me physically, and we started getting domestic disturbance visits from the police.

Once, in the middle of the night, Lisa got upset about something and, yet again, started smashing a bunch of my stuff. I can't remember what started the episode or exactly what she was destroying, but the only way I could prevent her from obliterating the entire cottage was to grab hold of her and wrap my arms around her until she calmed down. This did not have the effect that I had hoped it would. She bit me as hard as she could and twisted herself out of my grasp. She ran to the phone and called 911 and started screaming at the dispatcher about how I was attacking her.

Well, as a UFC fighter and well-known brawler, I didn't expect to get the benefit of the doubt when the cops showed up to address her claims of domestic abuse, no matter how popular I was on the island. So I ran out the front door and down the street about half a block. I found a hiding spot in some bushes and waited for the situation to resolve itself. As I crouched there in the dirt I had flashbacks to the other time I hid from the cops in the bushes, at the Civil War football game when I was busted for going AWOL.

Sure enough, a few minutes later, a police car with its lights on came speeding down our street and stopped in front of the cottage. From my position I could see two policemen go into the house, and I could hear Lisa shouting and crying. At some point it seemed they were able to calm her down. And about an hour later the cops left. I never heard from the cops about the incident, and, when I returned to the cottage the next day, Lisa did not even bring it up.

Yep, believe it or not, my situation with Lisa in Hawaii was turning out to be even worse than the situation back in Washington. As our relationship fell apart, Lisa began doing shit that was disruptive to my business. She had the phone service at the gym turned off. Then she cancelled the credit card service contract so I couldn't sign up new members. With time, as the end drew near, Lisa's tactics evolved to become more personal. She tried to get my coaches and members to quit and go to other gyms. She posted libelous shit about me on the Internet. And she tried to interfere with some of my most important personal relationships. What's really disturbing is that I don't believe she loved me any more than I loved her at this point. I don't think she wanted to draw me back into her life, and I don't think she saw a future for us. It seemed to me that, to punish me properly for leaving her, Lisa wanted to fucking bleed me dry.

During this time Lisa even insisted that she was a partner in the gym, and that she would only walk away if I paid her a lot of money. Obviously she was crazy. As dumb as I was to bring her back into my life, there was no way I was going to make her a partner in the gym. So I went to my friend Brandon Ito—a lawyer on the island—and asked him for help. He told me to bring over all the paperwork that I had signed in the creation of the gym.

Unfortunately, after a brief review of the documents, he gave me the bad news.

"Chris," he said. "I hate to say it, but Lisa is right. These documents indicate that she has a fifty percent ownership in the Ultimate Fight School."

"Are you fucking kidding me?!" I yelled. "There's no way. We never even discussed that."

He read me a section of the operating agreement. It said in plain words that "for services rendered" Lisa was given half of the ownership. When we were setting up the gym I didn't take the time to read the legal documents I was signing, due to both my laziness and my illiteracy. I would never have consciously agreed to giving Lisa a piece of the ownership. But the provision made it into the agreement and, like a lamb to the slaughter, I signed off on it.

"You're not in a good situation," Brandon said with a frown.

As I left his office I felt like I was going to shit my pants with anger.

I decided to leave town for a while and just get away from the situation. I would be fighting again in August in my hometown of Portland against a tough All-American wrestler named Jake Rosholt. That was just about four months away. So I flew to Seattle and began training with Matt Hume at AMC. But the bad news kept coming. While I was there, Lisa went on a major spending spree. Of course, she was the one who created our bank accounts when we got started, and, of course, she made herself a co-signer on all of them. So now, with me out of town, she took a bunch of money and bought herself a new Toyota Tacoma and rented herself an expensive apartment. I started to worry that soon we wouldn't have enough cash to keep the gym afloat.

I had to deal with the shit storm that had erupted. So after little more than a month in Seattle, I returned to Hawaii for a few days to take care of the business. The good news was that Lisa had moved out of the cottage. The bad news was that she wasn't done tormenting me.

A few days after I arrived back home I got a phone call from Matt Hume. "Chris," he said. "I got a phone call from your girlfriend. She said that you're doing drugs again."

"What are you talking about, Matt?"

"She said that you are getting messed up day and night and that you are a danger to yourself and to other people. This is disturbing, Chris."

This was not good. I was in the middle of a training camp and my coach seemed like he was about to tell me to take a hike.

"Matt, of course I'm doing drugs and drinking. You know me. You've always known me. It's what I do. But I'm not doing anything worse than I have ever done before and this stuff about being a danger to other people is absolutely untrue. You have to believe me."

Matt hesitated for a moment, and I thought I had gotten through to him. Then he said, "Chris, I don't know what the truth is anymore. But I do know that you have some issues in Hawaii that you need to figure out. And I also know that I can't be part of it. I'm not going to enable you, and I'm not going to put my reputation at risk."

I couldn't argue with the man. If I were in his position I would have done the same fucking thing. We agreed that I would make other arrangements for my training camp and that I would only get back in touch with Matt once everything had blown over.

Next, Lisa called my best friend Sam and told him that I was having serious drug problems and that my gym manager Steven

Saito needed to talk to him to set up an intervention. Sam, concerned for my welfare, agreed right away. Lisa followed that with a call to Steven Saito with a similar yet vague message: *Sam is concerned about Chris and wants to speak with you.* So Steven then called Sam, and Sam poured his heart out, detailing my history of drug abuse and alcohol problems. What Sam did not know, however, was that Steven was completely in the dark about all of this. Steven had no idea that I struggled with these issues, and he might never have worked for me had he known. Steven promptly called me and quit the gym. It was a disaster.

For a long time I blamed Sam for what went down. I thought that he was trying to cut me off at the knees. Our relationship suffered badly. It was more than a year later before I learned and accepted the truth: Lisa had orchestrated the whole thing.

I was up shit's creek. As much as I hated to admit it, Lisa had won the war. I threw in the towel and scheduled another meeting with Brandon Ito. I told him that I was willing to pay Lisa off to get her out of my life. Brandon agreed to take care of the negotiations. Unfortunately, the best we could do was arrive at a cash settlement that would wipe out my savings. We agreed that it was a small price to pay compared to the hell I would endure if we didn't end it right then. I wrote a check on the spot.

There, more or less, ended the Lisa saga. In the coming year or two she popped up on the radar once or twice, but without causing major destruction. Unfortunately, all of the damage was done. I was in financial ruins and thought seriously about shutting down the fight school. My life, once again, was headed for the toilet.

That's when a girl named Kaleena came to the rescue. Well, now that I think about it, actually, she's the one who broke my heart and drove me back to Lisa in the first place. So maybe

Kaleena didn't exactly rescue me since she kind of threw me to the wolves in the first place. Let me explain.

I had first met Kaleena back in 2007 at Dave & Buster's arcade restaurant in Honolulu. Before you start ripping on me for being a total dweeb and hanging out at a bar that features ski ball and whack-a-mole, let me just say that this place was off the hook on Wednesday nights. They had a killer rooftop deck and lots of people went there to get their swerve on . . . fuck it. You're right. I am a dweeb.

Anyhow, I was there at Dave & Buster's one night with my friend, former UFC fighter Kendall Grove. Kendall is a Maui native and a UFC veteran who beat good ol' Eddie Herman in the *TUF 3 Finale* back in 2006. I also happened to be trying to hook up with Kendall's sister at the time. A group of us were hanging out and getting drunk as usual when this stunning islander with a flower in her hair approached me.

"You're one of those fighters, aren't you?" Kaleena asked with a fair amount of sass.

"Yes, I am one of those fighters. Do you like fighters?"

"I like some fighters. But I saw you on that UFC reality show and I couldn't stand you. So I guess I don't like all fighters."

That made me laugh and spit out my drink. Kaleena gave me some hardcore shit right off the bat, which is a great way to find a place in my heart. We spent the rest of the night talking and laughing and downing beers and shots. Then, when it got late I came up with a clever move. I gave Kendall my car keys and told him to go ahead and drive it home. Then I told Kaleena that I didn't have a car and would need a ride back to my place. She needed a little convincing, but ultimately obliged.

Kaleena slept over at my place, and we were inseparable for the next two weeks. It was awesome. We just totally clicked. We spent hours on end, just the two of us. And when we needed a social atmosphere, we'd go out together and meet up with some friends. Shockingly, she liked to party almost as much as I did. This girl seemed flawless to me. I was in love and I started professing my emotions almost immediately. I was convinced that we were going to be together forever. I told her that. . . repeatedly.

Then, just two weeks after we met, Kaleena called me up and broke up with me. She didn't offer much of an explanation, other than to say that I was "too much for her." Me? Too much? Unbelievable. (That was sarcasm.) It was traumatic. And you know how I am with my emotions. Not good. I hated myself. I obsessed over our breakup, thinking endlessly about what I did wrong and what I should have done instead. And, of course, I went on a bender. When the dust cleared I found myself over the edge—into the depths of another relationship with Lisa.

So, as I mentioned, yes, Kaleena later saved me; but first, she ripped my heart out!

Well, fast-forward two years to 2009. I had just settled up with Lisa and kicked her to the curb. The horizon wasn't looking too bright. I was at the gym and my phone started ringing. Holy shit it was Kaleena. Of course, I had saved her phone number this whole time, just in case. Lisa had even noticed Kaleena's number in my phone once or twice (Lisa would dig through my address book as she saw fit) and I had to make up some bullshit about how Kaleena was a cleaning lady for the gym.

As the phone continued to ring, I froze up like a pussy. It had been a long time since we last talked, but the pain lingered. I was also afraid that maybe Kaleena had sat on her phone and wasn't calling me on purpose. I'd answer the phone like an idiot and she'd say "whoops! I didn't mean to call you." My brain ran through all of the possible negative outcomes that could result from me accepting the phone call. I let it go to voicemail.

I immediately started cursing myself for being so sackless. Then I started to have fantasies about us reconnecting and falling in love again. Had I just missed out on the opportunity of a lifetime? She was the girl of my dreams after all. Should I call her back? If so, what should I say? I felt like a nervous schoolboy. Then my phone started ringing again. This time it was my friend Brad Ito, the brother of lawyer Brandon Ito. I answered.

"Dude!" he said. "Why didn't you answer your phone?!"

"What are you talking about? What's going on?"

"I'm sitting here with Kaleena and she wants to talk to you! I'm putting her on!"

Before I could protest, he handed the phone over to Kaleena.

"Hello, Chriiiiis," she said, dragging out the pronunciation of my name mischievously.

I could never forget that voice—a Hawaiian accent that was part sassy and part sweet like a pineapple with Jack Daniel's poured on top. Kaleena went on to tell me how sorry she was for ending things the way she had ended them two years ago. Although I still find it hard to believe, she said it wasn't so much the fact that I was over the top in professing my love for her, but rather that she had been intimidated by my fame, and that, as a mellow Hawaiian girl, it was a challenge for her to be with someone who was the center of so much attention. I accepted her apology and she accepted my apology for being an overall dipshit, thank God.

Kaleena invited me to meet up with her and Brad later, which, of course, I agreed to do. They were at some local bar. She looked as beautiful as ever, and I knew I'd have to work hard to keep her if I was able to successfully woo her again. We spent the whole night next to each other, catching up on each other's lives. She mentioned she was looking for a job.

"That's funny," I said. "We happen to be hiring a desk girl this week. Come in tomorrow and you can interview for the position."

Of course the job was Kaleena's as soon as she mentioned she was looking. But I figured it would be more professional—and more entertaining—if I made her jump through a couple of hoops to get it. The next morning, when I arrived at the gym I fired the front desk girl. Don't feel bad for her. She was a friend of Lisa's who Lisa had hired to do the administrative and receptionist job that Lisa had agreed to do in the first place! Then Kaleena came in, looking like a cute little tree sprite, and my friend Bastian and I grilled her for about forty-five minutes, asking her all kinds of stupid shit like, "Do you know how to use Microsoft Word?" and "Can you answer the phone and type at the same time?" Half of the questions offended her, I'm sure. Nonetheless, when we finished the ridiculous interview we offered Kaleena the position and she accepted.

Life suddenly got good again. Kaleena and I were not hooking up immediately, but it was awesome to see her at the front desk every day. Typically she wore an outfit that consisted of a bikini top, tight camouflage shorts, and a bandana. Occasionally, if she was severely hung over, she would take a nap under the front desk. I didn't care, of course. She could have told prospective members to eat shit and die and I wouldn't have even considered firing her. I played it cool and bided my time for about two weeks until her first payday. When I gave her the paycheck, I invited her to go out for drinks with my little half-sister and me. She agreed.

To make a long story short, Kaleena stayed over at my place that night and she never left. For the next four years, until we relocated to San Diego, we were virtually inseparable. We slept together, woke up together, worked together, and partied together. And, somehow, we never got sick of each other. The icing on the cake was that after that first paycheck I never had to pay her again!

But things didn't always come up roses for us. I was kind of out of control in those first months after we reconnected. I travelled back to Portland to train with Team Quest and coach Robert Follis for the last month before the Rosholt fight. Having been dumped by Matt Hume and beaten down by the Lisa debacle, I was in bad shape physically and emotionally. My training camp sucked, and I was drinking like a fish. I was literally blacking out drunk every night. To make matters worse, things with Kaleena were rocky. She was at the end of her rope with my wild lifestyle and erratic behavior. Finally, three weeks before the fight, she called me and told me that she couldn't take it anymore. She wanted to break up.

This, of course, threw me into a death spiral. I spent the next three days lying in the corner of the back room of my mom's house covered in a pile of blankets, drinking whiskey and scarfing down OxyContin to numb my brain. One weird side note: one of the blankets I had buried myself under was a blanket I remember having when I was about five years old. It was light blue and covered in ducks. When I was a scared or sad little boy, I would cover myself in it and pull it up tightly to my chin. More than twenty years later, this ratty old blanket was still taking up space in my mom's house. And, quite appropriately, it was what I turned to for comfort when my life was falling apart.

I was extremely depressed and was even cutting myself, slicing my arms and legs. This is something I had started doing back in Hawaii, but the habit got much worse during this stint in Oregon. I don't know how or why it began, but I think I did it to punish myself—to mark myself in a way that would remind me of all the times I had screwed things up. My memory is a bit hazy, but I would say that I was probably suicidal at this point. Even my mom, who wasn't fazed by much, started to get scared. She called Nate Quarry and asked him to come help. Other than Eddie Herman, Nate's the one other fighter who was there by my side during the first five or six years of my career.

I was in a stupor when Nate showed up. He dragged me out of the back room and shoved me into the rear seat of his car. He drove me to his house and helped me into the bed in his spare room. He called a doctor over, who checked me out and made sure I hadn't done too much damage. And, within the next day or two Nate got me back to the gym.

Nate also insisted that I immediately join an AA program. I agreed, and in addition to my twice-daily practices, I started going to meetings twice a day. Unbelievably, within two weeks Nate helped me recover and get into fair enough shape to make an appearance in the Octagon. Mind you, I wasn't close to peak condition. However, it was a miracle compared to the disgusting puddle of a man that I had been just fourteen days earlier.

I've said it many times, and I'll say it now for the world to hear: not only did Nate Quarry save my fight career, he saved my life. I very well may have died there in the back of my mom's shitty house under that grimy children's blanket had someone not intervened. Thank you, Nate.

Fight night arrived. *UFC 102.* August 29, 2009, at the Rose Garden in Portland. Jake Rosholt and I were the third fight on a main card that featured a heavyweight championship between Antonio "Big Nog" Nogueira and Randy Couture. The good news was that this was Portland: my hometown, my backyard, my stomping grounds. All of my friends were going to be there.

The crowd was sure to favor me in a big way. But the bad news weighed heavier. Though mostly recovered from my depressive episode, the weight cut had been a nightmare. It felt like all of the chemicals in my body were off balance, and I thought my whole system was going to shut down in the final hours leading up to show time. On top of that, as I warmed up for my bout, Kaleena was missing in action. We had reconciled after Nate Quarry's intervention, and I flew her to Portland to be with me for a few days leading up to the fight. That night she was supposed to arrive with Brad. But shortly before game time I headed to my hotel room to see Kaleena, and only Nate was there. He told me that Brad and she went shopping for some strange reason. I called both of them, but neither answered their phones.

I was upset. Kaleena knew that all of my fights were important to me. But this one—on my home turf after one of the worst months of my life—was an especially critical moment in my journey. This was strange and not like Kaleena. Despite our ups and downs, she was the last person who would bail on me in a pinch. I was concerned that something was seriously wrong, but Nate insisted I not worry. So I did my best to focus my chi and get ready to step into the cage.

As you would expect, the Rosholt fight was not my best performance. I felt like a disgusting mess and I looked even worse. The first round was decent, but I was definitely hesitant and not feeling myself. We traded a lot of leg kicks, and, to be honest, Rosholt hit me with some heavy ones. He also bloodied up my nose. Then, in the middle of the round, he attacked with a knee strike, which I caught and turned into a takedown. We were against the cage, and I was on top, but I wasn't able to do much damage. Rosholt got back to his feet and, by that time, I was already winded and checking the clock. I wanted to put this guy to sleep, so I started chasing him and winging heavy left hooks. No luck. The round ended.

The second round was better for me, despite the fact that I was fading fast. He caught me early on with a hard right-left combo (that, I later learned, broke my eye socket), but I retaliated with an overhand left that sent him tumbling to the center of the mat. I jumped on top and unloaded as much ground-and-pound as I could. Again, I didn't do much damage, so referee Yves Lavigne stood us up. Then came my best strike of the night. I threw a left kick to the head, which Rosholt partially blocked, and then I delivered a booming straight left to his chin. His head bounced against the cage, and I would have expected him to crumple. But, props to Rosholt, he stayed upright. I ended the round throwing haymakers with both hands. Alas, I couldn't finish the guy.

I rewatched the fight later, and had to laugh at some of the commentary from Joe Rogan and Mike Goldberg between the second and third rounds. You can go back and check this out yourself if you have access to the video. During the break, the camera zoomed in on my left shin to reveal a series of scabbed-over incisions. These were from two weeks before when I was a zombie in my mom's back room, cutting myself with a kitchen knife. By fight time the wounds had pretty much healed, but the scabs were obvious evidence of self-inflicted harm.

Noticing the camera focused on my shin, Joe Rogan says, "Look at that. That's nasty."

To which Mike Goldberg replies, "That's what's called 'checking a kick.'"

I have a feeling that Rogan might have known what was up, but poor Goldie seemed to believe that series of wounds was actually Muay Thai related. In fact, that might be the first time in pay-per-view history that a spotlight was placed on self-injury related to mental illness. In retrospect, that moment was pretty fucked up.

By the third round, I had nothing left. Rosholt took me to the ground with ease and maneuvered an arm-triangle choke. As Yves Lavigne watched on closely, I—as always—refused to even consider submitting by tap out. I lost consciousness. Yves stepped in to end the fight, and as Rosholt stood up to celebrate, I went into convulsions.

Less than a minute later I woke up. It took a bit for me to realize where I was and what happened. I left the cage dejected, a loser in front of my hometown crowd. And, as mentioned, I had a broken orbital bone. I made the dumb mistake of trying to blow the snot and blood out of my nose, causing the area around my right eye to swell up like a goddamn balloon. In fact, it made my eyeball bulge out so much that I felt the need to keep pressure on it with my left hand because I thought it was going to pop loose.

Kaleena and Brad were backstage to greet me, thank God. They had made it back in time to watch my fight. Had they not been there when I finished, I probably would have gone back to the hotel, gurgled some OxyContin and chased it with a fifth of vodka.

Kaleena did not look well. She hugged me and comforted me a bit before telling me what was really going on. And it wasn't good. Kaleena and Brad had been drinking heavily earlier in the day. Don't ask me why. Unfortunately, Kaleena was on some pretty heavy cold medicine and antibiotics at the same time. Apparently, she had a severe reaction to the combination of chemicals and passed out. Her breathing got shallow, and Nate and Brad couldn't wake her up so they called an ambulance. Thus the real reason that Kaleena wasn't in attendance before my fight started was that she was in the emergency room getting her stomach pumped. What a fucking debacle. I'm glad Nate didn't tell me the truth before my fight. I know I would have ditched the Rose Garden to go be at Kaleena's side. If that had happened, I think the UFC would have had no choice but to terminate my contract.

Normally, after a UFC fight, I would hit the bars with my friends, get shitfaced, and either celebrate my win or drink away the sting of my defeat. But after the Rosholt fight I was in no mood for that. I was clinging to the hope that I would get my life back on track, and to the hope that Kaleena and I would work things out for the long run. Hell, we had both almost died in the past two weeks! It was time for some serious soul searching. Kaleena and I decided to head straight to an AA meeting.

My AA sponsor Bastian was with us as well. He had some experience with groups in the Portland area. He made a couple of phone calls before learning that there was a meeting in progress a couple of miles away, and if we hurried we could make it. Kaleena, Bastian, and I left the Rose Garden and began looking for a taxi. But, post-fight, it was madness. Everywhere, I bumped into people I knew and fans who recognized me. I guess it was hard to keep a low profile with my swollen face and crazy red-purple hair. It seemed like every person I passed wanted to stop me for a hug or a pose. It was one of the only times in my life that I had to tell fans that I didn't have time for autographs and photo ops.

After a half-hour of fighting our way through the crowd and searching, there was no taxi to be found.

"I have an idea," Bastian announced.

Nearby, a female police officer was leaning against her car, watching the crowd. We approached her and Bastian did the talking.

"Excuse me," he said. "I'm hoping you can help us out."

"What do you need?" she replied.

"Well, my friend here needs to get to an AA meeting right away. He's really struggling with some issues right now, and if he doesn't make it to this meeting then he'll be in serious risk of relapsing."

Bastian paused as the cop looked at him curiously.

"We can't find a taxi, and I'm hoping that you'll give my friends a ride to the meeting. It's not far away."

The cop raised her eyebrows. I was sure she was going to tell us to take a hike. But then she looked at me and saw the fucked up condition I was in. Her face softened.

"Get in," she said.

It was one of the very few positive interactions I've ever had with a police officer. Her name was Patty, and I'm sure that she had no idea who I was. It took her ten minutes to drive us to the meeting, and she was nice as could be. Maybe she had someone in her life who was struggling with the same kind of shit. There was sympathy in her voice.

By the time we got there, the meeting was over.

So we headed over to a nearby park, and, under the moonlight and the stars, the three of us had our own mini AA meeting. We talked about the challenges that we faced and the futures that we hoped for until, exhausted and at peace, we decided to go home and sleep.

After the Rosholt fight my life stabilized a bit. I was still drinking and occasionally doing drugs, but nothing heavy like the shit I did during my darkest days. By my standards (and probably *only* my standards), I was clean. It may not surprise you that I then entered the most successful stretch of my UFC career.

I held my camps for the next four fights at my own gym in Hawaii. And, during this time, I worked with a core stable of coaches and training partners: Robert Follis, Nate Quarry, Chris West, Greg Thompson, and Burton Richardson, among them. In January of 2010, I beat a Brazilian guy named Jay Silva 30–27 on all of the scorecards, it was a solid decision, but nothing to write home about. This Silva wasn't a primetime fighter. Beating him didn't prove much.

So for my next fight I asked for a tough up-and-comer named Aaron Simpson. He was undefeated in eight fights, ending six of them by KO or TKO, and was a highly regarded All-American wrestler out of Arizona State. Aaron had three wins in the UFC over the span of about eight months, including an injury TKO over my boy Eddie Herman. The fight was stopped when Eddie's knee blew out. I figured that if I handled this kid, I would be right back on the path to the top and I would get some vengeance at the same time. UFC matchmaker Joe Silva obliged and scheduled our scrap for the main card of the *TUF 11 Finale* in June of 2010.

When the fight began I was surprised by how hard Simpson came at me. Not only was he looking to clinch and take me down, but he was willing—unlike most mortals (hehe)—to trade punches with me. And a couple of his straight right hands landed flush. But I ate them like cornflakes. After all, my head is harder than most fire hydrants. To Simpson's credit, he scored two high-crotch takedowns that made me look silly. His wrestling was on point. I spent a good portion of that round getting flopped on my back, defending his ground-and-pound, and then climbing back to my feet.

But the second round was a whole different story. For some reason, Aaron got it in his head that he should stand back and exchange with me on the feet rather than work the clinch game that had paid off for him in the first round. And, early in this round, I realized that he was losing steam. I knew I could march forward. And that I did. I happily took one or two shots to the head in order to get inside his range and turn the fight into a brawl. With about one minute left I landed a very hard straight left hand that made him dance. I then stalked him across the cage and unloaded a combination that dropped him to his knees. I immediately started throwing bombs to the left side of his head. Miraculously, Simpson got back to his feet. I rewarded his effort by landing a punishing right-left combination right on the button. He stumbled and staggered all the way across the cage before flopping on his face. Then referee Josh Rosenthal mercifully ended the fight.

I had brutally TKO'd a very tough dude. Dana gave me the knockout-of-the-night bonus for that performance. Finally the momentum was shifting in my favor. And it felt great.

Kaleena and I flew back to Oahu early the next morning. On the way we talked about how we looked forward to a relaxing couple of months before I had to start another hardcore training camp. I had busted my ass in preparation for the Simpson fight and, to be honest, my body was paying for it.

That night we ordered a pizza and watched a stupid movie before calling it an early night. The next morning I woke up to the sound of my ringing telephone. Normally, I would have rejected the call and resumed my snooze, but I happened to glance at the caller ID. It was matchmaker Joe Silva. Generally, he doesn't call unless he has a big fight to offer. And the fact that he was disturbing me at 8:00 AM probably meant that he had a whale of a proposal.

I answered the phone with a gravely voice. "Joe, I hope you're calling me with something exciting!"

"Don't I always?" he replied. "Sorry to wake you up, but this one is kind of urgent."

"Well, tell me what's going on then."

"How banged up are you from the Simpson fight?"

I thought about it for a second and realized that, number one, except for a bloody lip, I was in pretty good condition, and, number two, even if I was banged up, it was probably a good idea to tell Joe Silva I was ready to fight. You never know what kind of gold he's selling.

"I'm pretty damn good, Joe. Almost good as new," was my reply.

"Good enough to fight again in two weekends?"

"Two weekends?!"

"Yep. Wanderlei pulled out of the Akiyama fight due to injury and we need someone to step in. Considering your performance on Saturday night and considering how much the fans love you, we figured that a Crippler–Sexyama showdown would be just what the doctor ordered."

I put Joe on hold. I turned to Kaleena and told her that he wanted me back in Vegas on July 3.

"That's fucking nuts, Chris," Kaleena said, shaking her head at the idea of me making a two-week turnaround. "But it's your body and your career, so you do what you think makes sense."

I told Joe that I needed to talk to my team and that I'd get back to him in a few hours. The proposed fight was with Yoshihiro Akiyama, a Japanese judoka and MMA great who, at this point, had become an A-list celebrity in Japan. He had appeared in both the Dream promotion and the Hero's promotion in Asia, where he won the light heavyweight title via an armbar of the brutal Dutch striker Melvin Manhoef. They nicknamed Yoshihiro "Sexyama" due to his good looks and his extreme popularity with the ladies. This was bolstered by the fact that he had married a famous Japanese fashion model.

Akiyama had made his UFC debut about a year earlier, defeating Alan Belcher in the *UFC 100* fight-of-the-night. The promotion knew they had an international star in the making, so they lined him up against Brazilian slugger and fan favorite (and one of my idols at the time) Wanderlei "The Axe Murderer" Silva. Wanderlei had first rose to fame as long-running middleweight champion in the Pride MMA promotion in Japan. By that time he had beat major names including Dan Henderson, Kazushi Sakuraba, Ricardo Arona, and Rampage Jackson. Now the UFC was asking me to fill in for him. As I contemplated the opportunity, I thought for a moment that taking Wanderlei's spot against Akiyama was kind of like stepping in as a designated hitter for Babe Ruth.

After hanging up with Joe Silva I called my coach Burton Richardson. He agreed that I didn't take too much damage in the Simpson fight and that, since I was in great condition, I probably had a very good chance of knocking off Akiyama. If that happened, I would steal the Japanese star's thunder and make it my own. The decision was made. But, on the advice of Nate Quarry, I didn't call Joe back immediately. Nate thought the UFC was in a desperate situation. Why else would they be asking a fighter to go twice in fourteen days? He said if I held out, I'd see more dollars.

Nate was right. I didn't answer Joe Silva's texts or phone calls for about three and a half hours. When I finally did pick up his call, I told him that I wasn't feeling great about the compensation, given the short notice. He offered me a nice little bump in pay, and I told him I'd see him in Vegas for fight week. As it turns out, two UFC fights in the span of just fourteen days was a record, at least for the modern-day, post-tournament-style UFC. It stood for over four years until that dirty bastard Chas Skelly notched a thirteen-day turnaround in September of 2014. (Just kidding, Chas. You're not a dirty bastard, as far as I know.)

Because it represented a huge comeback from major adversity, my win over Aaron Simpson was probably the UFC win of which I am most proud. However, the Akiyama win was not far behind because it was such an epic back-and-forth battle.

Against Akiyama, I started off by attacking with leg kicks, and several landed with heavy thuds on the Japanese star's thighs. But then we began trading with our fists, catching each other with some hard punches. Akiyama missed with a spinning back fist, but, soon after, when I attacked, he employed some of his world-famous judo on me and dropped me onto my back. My coaches and I had planned for this. Our idea was to be as active as possible on the ground. I immediately pulled a very high guard—my legs wrapped up around his chest—and then I transitioned for an armbar submission. I almost locked it in! But in making that move, I left myself open to an armbar attempt by Akiyama! He switched into a mounted triangle and started prying my arm in a direction I didn't want him to pry it. I defended and twisted in to a better position. It was probably the highest level ground fighting of my career. The crowd was really into it. Finally I escaped his submission attempt and returned to my feet where we engaged in more fisticuffs. As the seconds ticked down, Akiyama again caught me with a judo trip and threw me to the ground. That's where the round ended.

That first frame was a high-paced and dynamic contest. The MGM Grand Garden Arena was rocking with appreciation during the break. And, even though I had probably lost the first five minutes of the fight, I knew that Akiyama and I were putting on a hell of a show. I was ready for more.

The second round was when the shit went off the hook. We immediately started slugging, bouncing coconuts off of each other's faces. I caught him with a straight left. He responded with a spinning back fist to my jaw. I followed up with a superman punch and a hard left hook. And then we went to the mattresses, as the Godfather would say. It became an all-out slug fest. I threw everything but the kitchen sink at him, and he responded in kind. We hurt and wobbled each other. In fact, he landed a left hook to my chin that put me into zombie mode. For a few seconds I was out on my feet. My eyes crossed and I could hardly feel my legs. I couldn't even clearly make out my target. I just thought, *keep moving forward . . . keep attacking . . . keep throwing punches and hopefully you'll connect.* And that's what I did, clubbing away and hurting Akiyama almost as badly. The mayhem only slowed down momentarily, when Akiyama executed another judo toss. But I got right back to my feet and the fireworks continued. We spent the final minute of the round standing in front of each other and winging punches like a couple of invigorated old drunks. It was madness!

At the sound of the bell, the crowd went absolutely ape shit. I was eating it up. As I headed back to my corner I waved my arms up and down, calling for even more noise. Akiyama had almost knocked me out in that second round. By the time I got to my corner, I was fully recovered, but I wasn't sure whether I had inflicted much damage on my opponent. I knew that I had turned it into a brawl and found his face with my fists at least a few times, but the last three minutes of it were a blur. Then, as the cut man began working on my cheek, one of my cornermen told me that Akiyama tumbled off his stool. Yep, I must have landed some good ones! I started laughing.

The third round began with Akiyama and I smiling broadly at each other. His left eye was as swollen as my right cheek. We both knew that this fight was an instant classic. We met in the center of the cage and tapped both hands to show respect. Then we reloaded and got to work.

We started off a little slower in the third round, and I could tell Akiyama was still a little wobbly. We boxed for a few seconds before I landed a very hard head kick—probably the hardest head kick I ever landed in my career. But he just absorbed it, that stubborn Japanese bastard! Then he caught my next kick and again tripped me to the ground. As Akiyama started to work from the top, I decided to try and do as much damage as I could from the bottom. I began throwing hammer fists and elbows against the sides of Akiyama's skull as he rained down punches on my face. Once I even hit him with both fists on both sides of the head at the same time, something called a lobster punch! Flat on my back, I couldn't get much juice on these strikes, but I could tell they were hurting him. If I kept going they might just cause enough damage that he would do something stupid or desperate and give me the opportunity to attack.

We continued to batter each other. Then, with about forty seconds left, Akiyama started to lose steam and focus. He allowed himself to get too low in my guard, his head resting just below my chest. This was the moment. I threw my right foot over and hooked it with my left knee, trapping Akiyama's head and right arm in a triangle choke. He did everything he could to pull backward and release himself from the grip. But my legs were latched on tight. And while he struggled desperately, knowing that it only takes moments to lose consciousness in this position, I beat his reddening face with both hands. Finally, I pulled on the back of his head to put even more pressure on his neck and constrict blood flow to his brain. That is the key to finishing the triangle choke. It worked as advertised.

With twenty-four seconds left in one of the wildest fights in UFC history, Akiyama submitted by tapping on my arm. The referee dove in to break it up. I had won.

The MGM Grand nearly ripped at its seams as I stood up and left Akiyama lying there in a heap. I looked over and saw broadcasters Joe Rogan and Mike Goldberg shouting into their microphones and pointing at me. I took a position in the center of the cage and spread my arms wide. I gazed up toward the bright lights of the stadium. The roar of the audience, the applause, the cheers, the screams, the emotion—it all poured over me and through me like a raging, spiritual river. I felt, if just for a moment, as though I, Chris Leben, the worthless, junkie piece of shit from the piss side of nowhere, were a god.

# CHAPTER 8
# THE OXYCONTIN AFFAIR

There is a narcotic painkiller named OxyContin that was first approved by the FDA in 1995. It is manufactured by a company called Purdue Pharma, which is headquartered in Stamford, Connecticut, not far from New York City. The drug comes in pill form and slowly releases a chemical called oxycodone, which is a derivative of opium. Drugs of this family are called opioids. They are sought by users—both medical and recreational—because they generate a sense of a euphoria, or, you might say, a glorious high. There is another opioid that you are probably more familiar with: heroin. In fact, from what I understand, the oxycodone and heroin molecules are very similar. In my opinion, the difference between a heroin addict and an Oxy addict is that the heroin addict can't get what he needs from the local family physician, unless that physician does deals on the black market in his spare time.

Like heroin, Oxy is very fucking addictive. According to some studies, approximately one-quarter of users would qualify as addicts. And, like heroin, Oxy is dangerous if not ingested as prescribed. In 2010 alone, 16,651 people died of pharmaceutical opioid overdoses. By comparison, in the ten years from 2003 to 2012, only around 4,425 members of the US armed forces were killed while participating in the war in Iraq. My writer came across this quote in a 2011 article in *Fortune* magazine:

When it was introduced in the late '90s, OxyContin was touted as nearly addiction-proof—only to leave a trail of dependence and destruction. Its marketing was misleading enough that Purdue pleaded guilty in 2007 to a federal criminal count of misbranding the drug "'with intent to defraud and mislead the public,'" paid $635 million in penalties, and today remains on the corporate equivalent of probation.[1]

Despite all of this, OxyContin soldiers on. It generated $3.1 billion in revenue for Purdue Pharma in 2010. And the bodies continue to pile up.

I first started taking opioid painkillers when I started selling cars. Painkillers are like jelly beans for used car salesmen; all of those sleazy bastards are popping pills. It helps them run their mouths. Never one to shy away from a decent high, I started popping, too. It was mostly vicodin and percoset, which are cheaper and less potent than OxyContin. During the couple of years I spent hawking cars I was drunk virtually every night and high on Oxy about once every week or two. I bought as much as I could afford. Back then a hundred dollars of pills was quite a party for me. Later on, when my OxyContin addiction became a serious deal, a hundred bucks wasn't enough to get me through half the fucking day.

I also took painkillers throughout my career. First I used them for the typical aches and pains I encountered in training. But later I started using them as an alternative to booze. Drinking tended to make me fat and make my weight cuts harder. When I realized I could take a handful of pills and feel even better than how I felt after drinking a whole fifth of whiskey, I started popping opioids a lot more.

---

1   "OxyContin: Purdue Pharma's painful medicine," *Fortune*, November 9, 2011.

Pills provided an escape from some of the problems I was experiencing in my training camps. I had been working mostly with coaches Greg Thompson and Burton Richardson in my camps in 2010 and 2011. Additionally, I would fly Nate Quarry out to Hawaii to work with me. And for my fights with Jay Silva, Aaron Simpson, and Akiyama, it really paid off. Those guys forced me to work hard. They held me accountable when I fucked up or slacked off. The proof was in the pudding. But cracks started to appear in the foundation of our camp early on. First of all, Nate was pissing me off. For one of my camps, I flew him out to work with me and rented him a car, but he spent more time doing touristy shit around Hawaii than training me. He brought his daughter and would spend days swimming with the dolphins or whatever. I got angry, and I vented to Kaleena. Then she started having a major beef with Nate, and it totally stressed me out.

On top of that, Burton and Greg began having major friction, especially leading up to my *UFC 125* fight with middleweight contender Brian Stann. Their coaching styles clashed, and it seemed like they were both vying to be top dog. One would instruct me to fight in a certain way, and then, in the next minute, the other would give me completely opposite instructions. It seemed that they were micromanaging my training and fight style, and I often left the gym feeling frustrated and pissed off. A good example of this occurred during a grappling practice. Greg kept insisting that, if I was able to take my opponent's back in a standing position, I shouldn't hold the position, but rather release and return to my striking game. Then Burton started shouting something about it and the two of them erupted into an obnoxious yelling match while I continued to work on my drills. It went on so loudly and so long that I finally stopped practicing and blew up at the both of them.

"Listen, you fucks!" I shouted. "If I take his back, I'm not going to give up that fucking position! That's the dumbest thing I've ever heard."

I stomped out of the gym and didn't come back for three days. Nothing a couple of extra OxyContin couldn't fix, though.

There was also a very unusual situation that happened during that camp. Shortly after I signed off on the agreement to fight Stann, some dude named Chris showed up at my gym and told me that he wanted to train with me. He claimed to be a military guy that knew Brian Stann and had trained with him at Greg Jackson's camp in Albuquerque. Not only that, but Chris told me that he had been Jake Shields's number-one training partner for eight years. Jake Shields is a guy that's been in the fight game for over fifteen years. He's been a champion in several promotions, including the now defunct Strikeforce, and beat a whole slew of badasses such as Robbie Lawler, Demian Maia, Dan Henderson, and Carlos Condit. If this guy was one of Jake's main training partners *and* had experience sparring with Brian Stann, then he was probably worth considering as a collaborator in my camp.

So I decided to give this dude Chris a chance. I sparred with him and rolled some jiu-jitsu with him, and he was good. He seemed to have a high-level fighting pedigree. I invited Chris to join the camp. He started showing up every day and training with me. He was actually a really good teammate. In particular, we worked hard on a wrestling move called a lateral drop. It is a takedown that the team thought Stann would be especially vulnerable to, so we drilled the shit out of it—over and over and over again.

While my training camp was solid leading up to *UFC 125*, my pill intake started causing problems. I had used OxyContin in camps leading up to previous fights. The tricky part was not so much figuring out how to wean off the pills so that I wouldn't get popped in a drug test, it was figuring out how to wean off them at the exact correct pace so I wouldn't experience hardcore withdrawal symptoms. But, because I had upped my usage and was not professionally advised on how to step down my doses, things did not shape up well during fight week prior to my matchup with Stann. With just a few days to go, I started experiencing nausea, vomiting, dizziness, and diarrhea. Once again, my weight cut was very complicated.

As if this wasn't distressing enough, when I arrived in Vegas for the fight, I had a perplexing run-in with Jake Shields while walking through the MGM.

"Jake!" I shouted to him. "I've got to thank you!"

He crossed the lobby to shake my hand and chat with me.

"Why?" he asked. "What did I do?"

"Well, I prepped for a good month with your former training partner, Chris. He's an awesome grappler and wrestler."

"Chris?"

"Yeah, you're buddy, Chris . . . the military dude."

Jake game me a strange look.

"I've never had a training partner named Chris," he said slowly.

My stomach started to feel even weirder than it had been. I pulled out my phone and showed a photo of Chris and me to Jake. He shook his head.

"I hate to tell you this, but I've never seen that guy in my life."

"Holy fuck," I replied.

Obviously, something messed up was going on. Maybe Chris was just a big fan who felt that he had to bullshit his way into my camp. If that was the case then no harm, no foul. But deep down, I couldn't believe it was that simple. If you know me well, I am a big follower of conspiracy theories. My writer, especially, thinks

I believe way too many of them (and he can eat shit!). Either way, when something shady is going down, my mind tends to connect the dots in the most sinister way possible. And in this case, I immediately became convinced that this imposter Chris was not a hanger on, but a spy sent by the Stann camp to see what I was up to. After all, Brian Stann is renowned not only for his fighting prowess, but for his service as a United States Marine. Coincidentally, Chris, as I mentioned before, was also a military guy—though I don't remember which branch.

The combination of irritation with my coaches and obsessive paranoid thoughts about this spy situation seemed to enflame the symptoms of my dope sickness. All the way up to the moment I was supposed to walk out for my fight, I was a fucking mess. In fact, when Burt Watson came to get me and lead me to the cage, I was on the shitter.

Burt started bellowing, "Leben! It's time to roooollll! We rollin'!" But, he had to wait a minute because I was finishing a bout of simultaneous vomiting and diarrhea. Jesus, it sucked.

My bowel movements were the prelude to a bad night. Early in the first round, I went for the lateral drop move that my team had been so convinced would send Brian Stann to the mat. We wanted him on his back because his ground game was a notable weakness. As sick as I was, if I could get him to the ground, I knew I could win. But he defended it well—too well. I remember thinking in the middle of that first round that that fucking spy Chris had given Stann all of the details about the moves we were training. Stann just seemed way too ready for everything I threw at him. And he took no mercy on me. He brutally TKO'd me in the first round with a series of punches and knees.

Now, for the record, I am not officially accusing Brian of sending that spy and stealing my game plan. Lots of people say he is too good of a guy for that. But, when you lose that bad, it's hard not to search for explanations. I'm not the only fighter who has suspected that Jackson's MMA sent a spy into an opposing camp. Rampage Jackson accused them of the same thing leading up to his title fight with Jon Jones. And I've watched the video of my fight with Stann like five hundred times. He seemed to defend my lateral drop attempts before I even went for them. Maybe he's a takedown defense psychic.

The whole situation was an undeniably strange experience. It got even stranger a year or so later when "mystery Chris" showed up at my gym out of the blue. I shook his hand and pretended that everything was cool. When I asked him where he had disappeared to, he fed me some bullshit explanation. Then suddenly he asked me if I knew where he could score some OxyContin. Let me tell you, that's not the kind of thing you ask someone for casually, especially if you hardly know the person. I told Chris to hang on and then grabbed Steven Saito and headed into my office. We shut the door and discussed how to deal with the situation. I was freaking out. Was this guy a narc? Did the UFC put him up to this to see if I was taking drugs? How was Brian Stann involved? It just wasn't adding up. We thought about roughing him up and even considered calling the cops. In the end, I went back out and told Chris that I had no access to OxyContin or any other drug. He left shortly thereafter, and I never saw him again.

Now, there is probably some reasonable explanation for everything that went down with "mystery Chris," but the conspiracy theorist in me can't help but imagine scenarios in which Brian Stann recruited, trained, and planted a fucking sleeper cell in my camp!

That loss was definitely a setback, but I had bigger flies in my ointment and other fish to fry. Two months later the UFC proposed a fight that many fans had been clamoring for: The Crippler versus The Axe Murderer. Wanderlei Silva and I were known at the time as just about the two hardest hitting, wildest swinging brawlers in the middleweight division. Although his record was not the prettiest in the preceding few years, he was coming off of a decision win over Michael Bisping. And, moreover, he was a Brazilian national treasure, a big fan favorite, and a big draw for the UFC even after a string of losses. Hardcore fans remember Wanderlei best from his epic seven-year stretch in the Japanese Pride promotion, where he won and repeatedly defended the middleweight championship. During that run, Wanderlei was a fearsome headhunter, knocking out the likes of Kazushi Sakuraba (three times) and Rampage Jackson (twice). Rightfully so, the UFC expected my fight with Wanderlei to be a fireworks show. They scheduled it for *UFC 132*, which would take place on July 2, 2011. This was a big stage: Independence Day weekend.

In preparation for this fight, Greg Thompson actually moved in with me so as to more closely control my training and nutrition. It was a good strategy on paper, but we didn't make the best roommates. Some of Greg's idiosyncrasies started to drive me nuts. For one, he had a strange obsession with clothes and gear. I started to suspect he was ganking some of the swag I had received from sponsors, so I felt the need to hide all that shit while he was staying with me. The whole thing became an uncomfortable and distressing situation. We had enough friction that I even spent several nights in a hotel room, leaving Greg to his own devices in my house. Meanwhile, Greg and Burton's relationship continued to deteriorate. To cope, I proceeded to liberally consume both OxyContin and Percoset. However, in order to avoid another horrible withdrawal experience, I asked Kaleena and my friend

Ralph to ration my pills. This worked pretty well. I stepped down effectively in the month leading up to the fight and passed my post-fight drug test afterwards.

I brought a lot of anger with me into the cage when I faced Wanderlei. All of my training camp shit was boiling over. Also, I felt that Wanderlei was disrespecting me as we worked to promote the event. He seemed to think that I was not a worthy adversary. At weigh-ins, when we squared off, something about how he looked at me seemed to say "you're wasting my time, kid." In that moment, The Axe Murderer went from being one of my heroes to being someone whose head I wanted to rip from his shoulders.

As expected, Wanderlei got wild with his punches early in the first round. He threw a four-strike combo that he had thrown countless times before in his career: a straight left, then a straight right, then a left hook, then a right hook. This is exactly what Burton and I had prepped for endlessly. I blocked the hooks and connected with my own left hook behind Wanderlei's ear. This caused him to stumble into my clutches. He tried to grab a Thai clinch, but I sidestepped and was able to find the mark with two heavy uppercuts. He fell to his knees and I unloaded a barrage of haymakers to the side of his head. When the Axe Murderer face-planted on the mat, referee Josh Rosenthal dove in to save him.

It was honestly the only time in my career that a fight went down *precisely* as I had planned for it in camp. I knew he was going to throw that combo, and I knew exactly how I would react. It took just twenty-seven seconds for me to destroy the heralded Pride champion. In the MGM Grand Garden Arena, thousands of American hands clapped and thousands of Brazilian jaws dropped while I stomped around the perimeter of the cage, roaring triumphantly.

I had taken literally no damage in the Wanderlei fight, so I asked the UFC for another dance as soon as they could line it up. However, they didn't want to throw me back into the cage at the next availability. I think that, at this point, they recognized my brand was deserving of marquee match-ups. Well, nine days after my *UFC 132* win, Southern California–based Mark Muñoz added another notch to his impressive win streak with a decision over Demian Maia. That made it seven of his last eight for the Filipino-American star. The UFC liked the idea of pitting Muñoz's slick wrestling and ground-and-pound style up against my aggression and power. They tapped us as the headliners for *UFC 138* on November 5, 2011. It would be a return trip to Birmingham, England, for me, and also the very first, five-round, non-title fight in the history of the promotion.

Unfortunately, my drug abuse was off the rails at this point. Robert Follis came out from Portland to work with me for a week or two, compelling me to try to cut back on the Oxy. But all I was able to do was switch to Percoset and Vicodin. That's little more than the equivalent of substituting wine coolers for whiskey, and, in the end, it was a lost cause. Greg was pissing me off on a daily basis. The camp was probably the worst one of my career. Every little irritation seemed to feed my hunger for painkillers. Domestic turbulence with Kaleena, Greg and Burton's game of one-upmanship, the financial challenges of running and owning the Ultimate Fight School—all of these things gave me excuses to ramp up the frequency and amount of my doses.

At my worst, I was taking at least 180 milligrams of Oxy, and up to 300 milligrams, on a daily basis. To give you an idea of how severe my habit was, the maximum recommended daily dosage for pain-reduction purposes is 80 milligrams a day and most people take only 20 to 40 milligrams. I have heard of

replace it again with Vicodin and Percoset. But, of course, I did not feel remotely stable. To ward off severe withdrawal symptoms and pain I had to resort to taking an additional 2,400 milligrams of ibuprofen per day. And, when no one was looking, I guzzled cough syrup. It was a sad sight, I'm sure. In short, in that final week leading up to the fight, I was flailing and increasingly hopeless.

The day before weigh-ins, Kaleena arrived in England. I made her promise to bring a stash of Oxy, which, as usual, I intended to hit hard immediately after my fight. Yet, as it was, I was losing my mind. She had barely made it off the plane before I demanded some pills.

"Chris," Kaleena said, "if you do this, you are going to get busted when they drug test you."

"At this point, I don't give a fuck," I replied, throwing the pills into my mouth. And in my head, I thought to myself, *an OxyContin addict is what I am. No point in hiding the truth any longer.* To be honest, a big part of me wanted to get caught with opioids in my system, because a big part of me knew I needed help. I needed help immediately. My mind and body were so out of whack that I stayed in bed, under the covers, the entire day of my fight. I only emerged from my bedroom about two hours before I was due to appear in the cage.

As you might expect, if there's one fight in which my head was simply not in the game, it was the Muñoz fight. I could think about hardly anything other than my withdrawal symptoms and my Oxy cravings. Additionally, my relationship with Greg Thompson had completely bottomed out. He was disappointed in how camp went, and was really letting it show, openly blaming me for slacking and for what he announced was an impending defeat at the hands of the Filipino Wrecking Machine. Moreover, I was very unhappy with the weight-cutting regimen Greg had set up for me. He had bought into something called the "Dolce Diet," which was pioneered by an MMA fitness guru named Mike Dolce. I had never previously considered using that system because I could tell it wouldn't work well with my metabolism. But Greg insisted. So, in the weeks leading up to the fight, I ate a lot more calories than I was used to, consisting of foods that I was *not* used to. The day before weigh-ins, I was a good three pounds heavier than my target. As a result, the final twenty-four hours before I had to step on the scale were utter and complete torture.

Then, on the day of the fight, I learned that my team had racked up over $2,000 of incidental charges at the hotel, which were to be charged to my room. Apparently, instead of eating the breakfasts and lunches that were provided for us by the UFC, the guys had decided to enjoy every meal in the fancy hotel restaurant. Greg, unsurprisingly, was the worst offender. When the hotel made me aware of the massive bill, I was apoplectic. In fact, I was so pissed off and done with the whole situation that I considered purposely losing the fight just to spite Greg. As I like to say, you have to dance with the girl that you brought to the ball. Unfortunately, I didn't bring the prom queen to the Muñoz fight.

In the first round we took turns taking each other to the canvas. When on top, Muñoz would pour on the ground-and-pound with that vicious right hand of his. On our feet, we threw hard shots at each other, although I think I offered a fair standing game.

By the second round, I was already winded due to my withdrawal and the horrible weight cut. Muñoz repeatedly dragged me to the ground and delivered beatings. He connected with something that split my left eyebrow open. Soon, blood was filling my eye and pouring onto the mat. When I was able to get back to my feet, referee Marc Goddard separated us and paused the bout to inspect my wound. My first instinct was to let him and the cage-side doctor know I was having a hard time seeing.

Goddard said, "If you tell me that you cannot see, then I have to end the fight."

That changed my tune. "I can see," I lied.

Goddard restarted the fight, and Muñoz continued to rough me up. He controlled me on the ground, pinning me against the cage and unloading right-handed missiles. When the second round ended, I returned to my corner and informed my team I was all but blind in my left eye. I couldn't even seen what I was doing out there. They notified Goddard, who waved off the fight, giving Muñoz the TKO victory.

To this day, that's one fight I prefer not to reflect upon. I've been told that, as Muñoz was having his hand raised, and as my bloodied head hung in shame, Greg Thompson announced to the corner, "See? I knew Chris didn't have it in him. I knew he would lose." Then he walked out of the arena. I never spoke to Greg again.

I've already alluded to the fact that painkillers aren't the only narcotics I have abused. Pretty much, the only destructive chemical that hasn't bubbled through my veins is heroin. They say that the first time you shoot up heroin, your days are numbered. I've been lucky enough to avoid that dragon. On the other hand, I have snorted coke off a Playboy model's ass, and I have smoked crack underneath a bridge. Literally.

In 2006, after I knocked out Jorge Santiago and earned a knockout of the night bonus, I had some money to burn. My buddy Sam Songer came down to Vegas for that fight and agreed to spend another week with me there causing trouble. The Red Rocks Casino was nice enough to cash one of my prize money checks, allowing me to sprinkle money around town like it was my job. One night we took a limo with famous fighter Tito Ortiz and his porn star wife Jenna Jameson to the Wynn Hotel. I brought along some girl I had randomly connected with on Facebook. There was a long line at the entrance, and when we got to the front, the bouncer would only let four of us in. Being an enormous asshole, I left the poor girl out on the street. Tito, Jenna, Sam, and I went in and got a table in the champagne room at Tryst, the club there. One of my buddies from the UFC (I won't name names) gave me a handful of ecstasy, and Sam and I started rolling. The place was crawling with Playboy models. Soon a playmate named Jasmine Fiore cozied up next to me. She was a devilish blonde with a huge rack. And she loved coke. We snorted a bunch of lines at the club.

When we went back to my hotel that night, Jasmine noticed some of the Facebook girl's personal effects strewn about the room.

"Who does this belong to?" she asked.

I told her the story of the Facebook girl and how I had ditched her at the club. "I'm sure she'll show up here sooner or later," I explained.

Jasmine gathered up the girl's stuff—her shoes, her rolling luggage, her sunglasses—and tossed them out into the hallway. Then she turned to me and began to remove her clothes.

"You're a star, baby," Jasmine purred. "You're a UFC fighter and you deserve better than some random hoochie you found on the Internet. You deserve a Playmate like me."

Needless to say, my boner shot up like a bottle rocket.

We spent that night and the next three days blowing through piles of cocaine and zipping around town in her Mercedes convertible. Jasmine bought expensive Gucci and Dolce & Gabbana sunglasses for Sam and me. We ran into Coolio the rapper at the pool and spent an afternoon smoking joints with him. It was just balls-out hedonism and a fucking riot of a time. Oh, and yes, I did snort some coke off of Jasmine's ass.

Jasmine dropped us off at the airport, and that was the last I ever saw of her. However, she appeared in the news a few years later. The poor girl was found strangled to death and stuffed in a suitcase. Her fingers and teeth were removed. Her ex-husband, Ryan Jenkins, was charged with the murder, but the filth hung himself in a motel room before the cops could get their hands on him. Jasmine was a character—maybe not the sweetest girl who ever walked the planet, but a carefree wildchild who wanted to wring every last drop out of life. I cherish people like that, and I'm sad she's gone.

Of course, not all of my adventures in drug use were glamorous. There's another story that also involves Sam that I think demonstrates how dark things got for me from time to time. This took place early in my UFC career. On a random Friday night, Sam, his mom Kim, his girlfriend Zoe, and Eddie Herman joined me for some drinks downtown. Of course, I got absolutely shitfaced and coked up and started making a scene. I was yelling at people and talking shit. I could tell that Kim was getting a little bit uncomfortable. At one point, I demonstrated to Zoe how to lock in a rear-naked choke. I invited her to try it on me. Sure enough, she squeezed as hard as she could for ten or twenty seconds and put me to sleep! According to Sam, I collapsed to the floor of the bar and started snoring. All kinds of people were standing around and going wild about the fact that a girl had just choked a UFC fighter unconscious.

When I came to, some dude started asking me to take a photo with him. He wanted me to pretend to be choking him. I obliged without a second thought. Unfortunately, in my hyperactive state, I squeezed a little too hard and *actually* choked him. The guy passed out and went crashing into a table full of bottles and glasses that then smashed on the ground. (Side note: this guy later sued me for $50,000, but lost.)

Sam did not like my behavior one bit. It was one thing to allow his girlfriend to choke me. It was quite another thing to choke a stranger unconscious. He started flipping out on me.

"Chris, what the fuck?! You can't be doing this shit!"

"Oh, calm down, Sam, you little bitch. He asked me to do it," I slurred.

Sam replied, "Can't you show just the smallest amount of restraint? I bring my mom and girlfriend out to spend time with you, and you're a complete fucking mess!"

"Fuck your mom and fuck your girlfriend!" I shouted back.

Well, I guess that was the straw that broke the camel's back. Sam, Zoe, Kim, and even Eddie decided they had had enough. They grabbed taxies and headed home while I shouted obscenities after them.

Left to my own devices, I chose to go out in search of some drugs. Stumbling around downtown Portland, I encountered a bum who offered me some crack. I had never tried it, but fear of the unknown had never stopped me before. I bought a couple of hundred dollars worth off of the guy. He guided me to a dilapidated building not far away. It was some kind of halfway house or something. The guy had a tiny room that was in disgusting condition. We spent the rest of the night taking turns on his crack pipe.

When the sun came up he announced, "Time to go to work!"

"You have a job?" I replied with surprise.

"Of course I have a job, brother! I collect aluminum cans every morning. I'll have to ask you to be on your way."

I emerged into the sunlight and made my way down to the waterfront. I was sweating profusely and seemed to be on the verge of a psychotic meltdown. Healthy people were jogging up and down a nearby running path. I distinctly remember thinking to myself, *those people are in tomorrow, but I'm in yesterday.* I made my way to a hidden spot underneath a bridge and smoked my last little rock.

Most of the rest of that day is a blur. I remember running around like a hysterical tweaker. I think I tried to rent a motel room, but the place turned out to be just a diner. I got my hands on some more pills and coke and, even though I was scared and freaking out, kept feeding the beast. I called a couple of people, hoping that someone would help me, but no one was answering their phone. At least another twenty-four hours of tripping went by. Somehow, I finally ended up at Sam's house. When he opened the door, the look on his face was one of complete horror and disgust. I must have looked like I was dragged through the sewers of hell.

"Sam," I croaked. "I need help."

"I know," he replied.

Sam put me in bed and let me stay there for something like thirty hours. Then he nursed me back to health as I detoxed for a couple more days. A good guy, that Sam is.

Two weeks after the Muñoz fight, I got another uncomfortable phone call from Dana White.

"Chris, you got popped again," he said, this time pissed off. "Percoset and OxyContin."

"Dana, I tweaked my back two weeks ago and I didn't want to bail on the fight . . ."

Dana cut me off. "Don't feed me bullshit, dude! Are you addicted to these things, Chris?"

"No. No, I'm not." I replied defiantly.

Dana told me to stay tuned for more information about the drug test failure and the consequences. There would be a fine and a suspension, of course. I apologized and we hung up.

I immediately started to hate myself. First of all, I have a very guilty conscience, and lying to someone I work with makes me feel horrible. Secondly, hadn't my Oxy use right before the fight been a not-so-subtle call for help? Wasn't I at peace with the fact that I was an addict who couldn't cope with this affliction on my own? Apparently, I was not as comfortable admitting these things as I had hoped. I spent the entire day in bed, crying.

The next morning I summoned up the courage to call Dana back.

"Dana, I lied," I stammered through my tears. "I'm an addict. I know that I am. I'm addicted to painkillers and I need help."

Dana was silent for a long moment. "All right, kid," he finally responded comfortingly. "Take it easy. You'll hear from Donna later on today. She'll take care of it."

I spent the next several days conferring with Kaleena and my agent at the time, Malki Kawa. There was no doubt I needed rehab. The focus of our discussions was about whether it should be an inpatient or an outpatient program. Malki suggested that, since we had now learned I would be suspended for a full year, it made sense for me to do an inpatient program. Not only would the therapy be more intensive, it would be positive for my image both in the UFC and in the eyes of MMA fans.

By this time, Kaleena and I had become engaged. Our original plan was for a July wedding. However, her grandfather was dying. So we pushed the date six months earlier to January 8, 2012. It was a beautiful event in a *heiau*, or Hawaiian temple, near the beach in Wai'anae. The ceremony was conducted by an honorable local medicine man who Kaleena had somehow connected with. The event was very spiritual. From where we stood during the wedding, we could see dolphins swimming in Pokai Bay, and in the light breeze, Kaleena looked like a fairy goddess sent from the Hawaiian heavens.

But the specialness of the moment did little to loosen the grip of my addiction. In order to function during the ceremony and to be able to walk down the aisle without shaking, I crushed and snorted an OxyContin tablet right before I got out of the car and walked up to the heiau.

Five days later, I checked into the Canyon rehabilitation facility in Malibu, California. As I filled out some initial paperwork, providing my date of birth, I realized that I was thirty years old and not dead yet. I almost started crying right then and there because I had never expected to survive that long.

The Canyon sits in the midst of a hilly, 240-acre site in a lush green coastal area just north of Los Angeles. It is a prime example of the luxury rehab and wellness facilities that are sprinkled throughout California and the southwest United States. It is much more like an all-inclusive resort than a medical or psychiatric facility. Here's how the Canyon describes its offerings on its website:

> Spacious and elegant accommodations within a secluded natural setting create a nurturing environment for the healing process. The Canyon at Peace Park, with 120 acres of oak trees and mountaintops is recognized for its amazing natural beauty and as a center for healing and spiritual gatherings. Enjoy hikes on a number of trails with breathtaking views, spend quiet time in the meditation temple, journal in one of many gardens, enjoy a swim in a pool just steps from your room, or watch a canyon sunset; at the Canyon we encourage you to give yourself this time to be nurtured and begin healing.

Nice, huh? I imagine that there are plenty of healthy non-addicts who would be willing to fork over a pretty penny just to spend some time in a utopia like that.

But, I'm not a typical person, and I knew shortly after beginning my thirty-day stint that the Canyon was not going to be a great place for me. Within twenty-four hours of entering the facility, I began experiencing acute early-stage withdrawal. Think of it as some of the symptoms that I have already described—nausea, vomiting, diarrhea, sleeping problems, cold sweats—combined with all sorts of other intense shit like weakness, panic, muscle pain, and confusion. After five days of this I was in a very serious state and could not get out of bed.

I spoke to a doctor who explained that my condition was on the extreme end of the withdrawal spectrum. He said that chemically my brain was completely out of whack, and that, if we didn't take action, the severe symptoms could last for another month. This would be followed by several more months, if not a year, of "post-acute withdrawal syndrome," which features symptoms like low energy, insomnia, anxiety, confusion, and depression. He recommended administering a drug called Suboxone—a combination of buprenorphine and naloxone that, like the better-known methadone, is used in opioid replacement therapy. Essentially, Suboxone does two things. First, it prevents the user from experiencing a high from opiate use. Inject some heroin and you'll hardly feel a thing. Second, it almost completely alleviates withdrawal symptoms.

When I first decided on rehab, I insisted on a facility that would allow me to detox without the use of methadone or Suboxone. I was committed to beating my addiction in the most natural way possible. So, facing the fact that chemical-free recovery was impossible was, metaphorically, a very hard pill to swallow. I felt

how they were unacceptable. I told him that I wanted to switch back to the Suboxone.

He listened quietly, made a note in my medical chart, and then said, "I'm not putting you back on the Suboxone. We're going to up your dosages on the rest of the meds."

I was in shock. That sounded like the most absurd response to my concerns. In fact, it was probably the opposite of what I needed. I shouted at him, punched a hole in the wall of his office, and stormed out. A few days later, at the end of my month-long tour of duty, against the advice of the medical staff, I checked myself out of the Canyon.

When I arrived back in Hawaii, the first thing I did was find an opioid addiction treatment clinic. They issued me a new prescription for Suboxone. I returned home to Kaleena and threw out the other seven medications. I never took them again.

# CHAPTER 9
# THE END AND THE BEGINNING

*. . . two round blue pills —*
*. . . the back seat of a car —*
*. . . an illuminated red sign —*
*. . . staggering down a busy street —*
*. . . men in dark uniforms —*
*. . . a struggle —*
*. . . strapped to a gurney —*
*. . . a needle in my arm —*
*. . . sleep . . . at last.*

Once I resumed Suboxone treatment in Hawaii and committed myself to a life free from booze and drugs, things stabilized. In Spring of 2012, I began training again. Rehab had taken a spiritual and physical toll on me, yet, slowly but surely, my strength and endurance and mental fortitude returned. My attitude during this time was one of general acceptance. I decided to let my life unfurl at it own pace, and I was ready to deal with whatever came my way. My mantra was "wait and see." Kaleena and I embraced our sobriety and enjoyed an extended period of tranquility. Simply put, things were just nice. Notably, I made progress in overcoming my previously insatiable need for validation and instead found new ways to calm my spirit. I would sit on the roof of our little cottage for hours at a time, watching the sun dip below the western horizon and the blue-blackness of night spill into the sky from the east. In the distance, the ocean's pulsing waves sounded like rhythmic, healing breath of the gods. Maybe I had turned a corner on the path of life and was headed in a healthy new direction.

The Ultimate Fight School began to run into some difficulty. Especially when I was absent—at rehab, away from training camps—the place would lose momentum and memberships would dwindle. Our cash situation was ugly so I found a new location where the rent was half the price and relocated the gym. But, within a few months, a brand new UFC Gym opened about three blocks away and began poaching students. It's hard to blame those kids though; I was charging $139 a month at my modest location, while the UFC Gym offered 40,000 square feet of high-quality equipment and facilities for just $50 a month. Even some of the coaches at my school began moonlighting at the UFC Gym. It quickly became a losing battle. By the end of the year we had to shutter the business.

As the days ticked away on my one-year suspension I began speaking with the UFC again. Joe Silva told me they wanted me to get back in the Octagon, but only if I felt physically and spiritually fit to fight. I let him know that things were going well and that when my suspension expired I would be good to go. He was happy to hear it, of course. Putting the Crippler in the cage was good for business and would allow the UFC to make back some of the dough they had dropped on my stay in rehab. In summer, Joe connected with my manager, Bobby, and said they had an opponent for me: a Czech wrestler and bodybuilder named Karlos Vemola. It definitely was not a high profile match-up and, though Joe didn't come out and say it, I was pretty sure this was supposed to be a warm-up fight for me. Karlos was 2–3 in the UFC, most recently losing via rear-naked choke to Francis Carmont. Frankly, he was not on the level of Mark Muñoz or Brian Stann or Michael Bisping. Nonetheless, I wasn't in a position where I could hold out for a better opponent. The UFC had surely lost some faith in me, and my bank account was in bad shape. My bout with Vemola was scheduled for the main card of *UFC 155*, which would take place in Vegas on December 29, 2012.

About two months out from the contest, I was actually in really good shape. I was eating healthy and following a very strict strength and conditioning program called heart rate variability training. My resting pulse dropped to about forty-eight beats per minute, a sign of excellent cardiovascular health. I felt so good, and was so confident in my new sobriety, that I decided that the time was right to phase out my Suboxone use. Moreover, I did not think the UFC would allow me to fight on that drug. I didn't even want to address the issue with them for fear that their response would be to bar me from the cage. I figured I had no choice in the matter.

At the time, I was on eight milligrams of Suboxone a day. It seemed to be the perfect dose. My side effects were very minimal, and I had virtually no opiate cravings. I immediately reduced my daily intake by half, down to four milligrams. In almost no time, I started to have noticeable issues. I felt foggy and sluggish. My biorhythms started to get funky, and so my sleeping became inconsistent. However, it was manageable. I believed that coming off Suboxone was simply a matter of willpower. In other words, I just had to tough it out.

But, here's the thing about Suboxone. While it is very effective as an opiate replacement and addiction inhibitor, its users are often at least as dependent on the drug as they were on heroin or OxyContin to begin with. From what I understand, Suboxone was originally intended to serve a short-term detox function. Long-term use is dicey. There is a very high rate of recidivism, and some experts believe that a patient who begins a Suboxone program may be best off taking the drug for the rest of his life. My own doctor had extensive experience with Suboxone patients and told me that he only witnessed one person, out of many dozens, wean off of the drug successfully and permanently.

Additionally, many patients discover that the withdrawal from Suboxone is more agonizing than the withdrawal from the opiate they were originally trying to eliminate. I learned this the hard way during the writing of this book. In spring of 2015, I went up to Oregon for my half-sister's wedding. Because I was on a twelve-milligram daily dose, I should have brought at least twenty-four milligrams with me. However, when I arrived, I discovered I only had two eight-milligram pills. I took one of them on Friday and one on Saturday before the wedding. By 4:00 AM on Sunday when I headed back to the airport, I was already feeling uncomfortable. I flew back to San Diego, but headed straight to a May Ride motorcycle gathering. I did my best to hold it together, but by evening I was sweating and vomiting. A friend came and picked me up and we headed to a tattoo shop. On the drive, he gave me a handful of Vicodin, which I scarfed down in the hope of staving off further withdrawal.

I didn't get home until about noon the following day, and I was in absolutely horrible shape. I went straight to my medicine cabinet and popped twelve milligrams of Suboxone. However, something went wrong. I think either the Buprenorphine or the Naloxone contained within the Suboxone reacted with the Vicodin in my system and caused what is known as a "precipitated withdrawal." This means I went into severe withdrawal in a matter of minutes. First I had diarrhea. Then I started vomiting. Then my vomit turned bloody. Then I began seizing uncontrollably. I was in pure agony, and truly thought I was going to die. I lay on the floor of my bathroom for hours and hours until my system began to recover and I was able to drag myself to bed.

So, as you can imagine, a few weeks before my date with Karlos Vemola, when I reduced my daily dosage to just two milligrams, I began to lose control. I knew I was in bad shape, but I felt that my dependence on this drug was not only a personal failure but would cause the end of my fighting career. I fought through the misery and, one night, while out driving on the highway, I took the remainder of my Suboxone prescription and threw it out the window.

Not a day later, I started to lose my mind. The withdrawal was merciless—sweating, pain, vomiting, panic attacks, hyperventilation. I did not sleep for four days straight. Worst of all, I turned to alcohol for relief. I discovered that if I quickly guzzled two bottles of wine I would fall into a stupor for a few hours. My nearly yearlong sobriety was officially over. I was desperate for sleep, but it wouldn't come. I began to have crazy thoughts and wondered if going cold turkey would be the end of me.

I called T. J. Thompson for help. He had been sober for a good twenty years at the time, and had been a guiding voice for me as I dealt with my issues of alcohol and drug abuse. By the time he arrived at my house later that day, I was on the verge of a psychotic episode. Kaleena later told me what transpired, but I only remember intermittent blips of it. T. J. gave me two Valium pills and got me to my feet to try and walk it off. As we walked through the neighborhood, I started frothing and yelling about some guy who had repeatedly made sexual advances on Kaleena. I told T. J. we needed to go find this guy's house so that I could beat his ass. It took all he had to convince me otherwise and drag me back to my house. Having realized how severe my condition was, T. J. spoke with Kaleena, insisting that I go to the hospital immediately. She agreed. The two of them escorted me to T. J.'s car and laid me down in the back seat, where I continued to hysterically spaz out.

When we arrived at the emergency room, T. J. and Kaleena tried to guide me inside. However, I started to freak out.

"I can't be here," I shouted and slurred. "I can't go into . . . the hospital . . . I have to fight . . . next month . . ."

When they tried to grab hold of me and direct me into the emergency room, I started to thrash and scream deliriously. I broke away, shoeless and shirtless, ran off down the street in nothing but my board shorts. Kaleena hurried inside the hospital and told someone there to call the police.

I had made it three or four blocks when the first squad car arrived on the scene. It pulled over to the side of the road near the sidewalk where I was staggering along. Soon another three or four police cruisers showed up. A group of eight or ten officers began cautiously following me on foot.

"Chris, are you OK?" one of them asked me repeatedly. "Just slow down and come with us, please." I don't remember responding to him.

When the moment presented itself, the cops surrounded and bum-rushed me. I convulsed and screamed and fought back. They piled on and held me down on the ground. Finally, when I calmed down, they took hold of me—two cops to a limb—carried me over to a squad car and deposited me inside the back seat.

The next thing I knew, I was on a gurney in the emergency room. My arms and legs were secured with leather straps. As I stared up into the fluorescent lighting panels of the hospital ceiling, a nurse rolled an IV stand over. She cleaned my arm and pushed a needle into the vein on the inside of my left elbow. It was a strong sedative. In a few moments, I was unconscious.

The hospital moved me into a private room, and for the next two days they kept me sedated and in a state of semiconsciousness. To be honest, I hardly remember a thing. Apparently my personal physician, who had been managing my Suboxone treatment for the past several months, made a few visits to check on me and confer with the staff about the best course of action. I believe that a couple of my friends also came to the hospital to visit with me, but again, I can barely recall anything from my stay. Approximately seventy-two hours after the cops had dragged me into the hospital, I was stable enough to be discharged.

My doctors and I agreed that my psychotic episode made it abundantly clear that my Suboxone treatment would have to continue indefinitely, until such time as it would be safe to very slowly and gently reduce my dosage under medical supervision. This created a dilemma for me, however. The only way I would be able to fight in a few weeks would be to appeal to the UFC for a medical exemption. For half-a-second I thought about keeping my situation under wraps, but it was pretty obvious that if I got popped one more time for an illicit substance, my UFC career would be over on the spot. And there was no doubt they would be asking for some urine after the fight.

My doctor communicated with officials at the UFC who then provided him with appeal forms. I was required to explain the circumstances of my addiction to "prescription painkillers" and how Suboxone was a necessary treatment. A few days later, to my great surprise and relief, the UFC granted my exemption and cleared me to fight.

About two weeks before *UFC 155*, Karlos Vemola broke a cheekbone in training and was forced to withdraw. They replaced him with Derek Brunson, a standout from the old Strikeforce promotion and a former three-time NCAA Division II All-American wrestler. The fight was not in the least bit memorable. I had terrible ring rust, and still felt somewhat out of sorts due to the traumatic interruption of my training camp. Brunson smothered me with his wrestling for three rounds, barely inflicting any real damage. It was very Josh Koscheck-esque. The judges awarded him a unanimous decision and sent me back to the drawing boards. It was a forgettable loss to a guy who wasn't exactly the best competition I had ever faced.

About six months earlier, in mid-2012, Kaleena and I began having some serious discussions about our future. Post-rehab, it was becoming increasingly clear my days in the UFC were numbered. And, unfortunately, I had pissed away all of my career earnings, along with most of what I owed to Uncle Sam in taxes, on the gym, on drugs, and on wild, misguided spending. On top of that, Kaleena had hardly earned a single penny in the four years that we had been together. If it all came crumbling down, we would be facing some very tough circumstances. The only way forward was for the both of us to bring some money into the household.

In the previous year, the amount of money I had spent on legal fees was roughly equal to the tuition at a typical three-year law school. If you can't beat 'em, join 'em, is what I say. So I suggested to Kaleena that she become a lawyer. It took a little convincing, but Kaleena ultimately agreed to go for it. She applied to a few schools and was accepted to the Thomas Jefferson School of Law in San Diego.

A long-distance marriage spanning the Pacific Ocean didn't seem feasible, so we had to decide whether law school was worth relocating away from our beloved Hawaii. I wasn't too keen on the idea. However, San Diego was not a horrible alternative. It's close to the ocean; the climate is not that different from what I had grown to love on the islands; the surf culture is chill. And I would have the opportunity to train at Alliance MMA under the direction of highly regarded coach Eric Del Fierro. We decided to go for it. I sold my motorcycle and we made the move back to the mainland, into an apartment in Ocean Beach, San Diego.

Relocating to Southern California, I think, was more than just a physical migration; it was a spiritual transformation, and, maybe, not an ideal one. As evidenced by my ho-hum loss to Derek Brunson, it seemed that the intense fire that had once burned within me—the fire to win in style, to never quit, to make the world take notice—might have cooled off a bit. In fact, the loss didn't bother me quite so much as it would have five or six years earlier in my career. I think this is mostly because, as I mentioned, the post-rehab Crippler was less desperate for the world's approval and adoration. I had become more accepting of who I was, for better or for worse, and more accepting of the life that had been laid out before me. Now, I don't think the art classes, or the nature walks, or the group therapy sessions at the Canyons deserve the credit for moving me in this direction. I think it was the simple act of surrendering that changed the game for me. Yes, at several points in my life I had asked friends and family like Nate Quarry or Sam Songer for help in my times of need. But that had always been to get me out of a temporary jam, or to interrupt a streak of madness or self-harm. I didn't consider those episodes to be epic failures. They were moments of weakness when I needed a boost. Don't all people have those moments, if not so extreme?

But checking myself into rehab was different. In my mind it was an admission that, unless I took intense, prolonged action, my death was imminent. If you've read the previous pages of this book, you know I've been in bad shape before. And on several occasions, I had wondered when and how I would pull out of my nosedive. But in those cases, in the back of my mind I think I always believed I would pull through—that someone or something would reach down into the pit of despair and grab my hand. To some degree, I believed that I was invincible. I don't think I had ever really accepted the fact that my recklessness and drug abuse were an irreversible death march. And, even more significantly, I had never acknowledged a desire for a long life. My friend Steven recently reminded me that I said this to him once: "I am a shooting star. My job is to light up the sky for just a brief period of time and then fade to black." Handing myself over to rehab was a turning point in this regard. I wanted to live as long as possible.

Moreover, I was, for the first time, asking strangers for help. This was a big shift for me and a scary leap of faith. Psychologically, perhaps the hardest part about checking into rehab was the fact that I had to admit to these strangers—and to the MMA community—that I couldn't go it alone. Expressing that to my friends and family was never a big deal for me, but sharing my weaknesses with the world was. Part of me felt that, by opening myself up publicly, the wolves would have a prime opportunity to rip me apart. But, of course, that didn't happen. As it turned out, the world was not conspiring against me.

These epiphanies made me a more stable person, a calmer person, a person more comfortable with his station in life. But, in a sport that requires you to hold onto your angst and convert it into focused aggression, this kind of inner peace does not necessarily translate into success. Six months after losing to Brunson, I met a tough young middleweight named Andrew Craig at *UFC 162*.

It was a gritty fight, and we were pretty well matched through the first two rounds. However, in the third round, Andrew clocked me with a solid combination that sent me sprawling on the mat. He jumped on top and nearly finished the fight with a barrage of ground-and-pound. I somehow made it back to my feet and recovered, only to lose by decision. It was another uninspiring loss against a middle-of-the-pack 185-pounder.

I returned to San Diego and Alliance MMA fully aware the end was nigh. That was three losses in a row in the UFC: against Muñoz, then Brunson, then Craig. Many fighters are cut from the roster after that kind of skid. I kept training and awaited the fateful call from Dana. But, it did not come. Instead, a few months later, my manager Bobby received a call from Joe Silva offering one more fight. This one would be against a lanky and vicious kickboxer named Uriah Hall.

Uriah was not particularly well known until he participated in season seventeen of *The Ultimate Fighter*. There, in episode three, he sent Adam Cella to the hospital with a spinning hook kick that Dana White said was one of the nastiest knockouts in the history of the promotion. Uriah then lost in the *TUF 17 Finale* to a gutsy wrestler named Kelvin Gastelum, and subsequently dropped a miserable decision to John Howard. So really, although he had flashes of furious brilliance, Hall had a very rocky start to his UFC career. Moreover, Dana was very vocal about his disappointment how this kid had performed of late. Our meeting at *UFC 168* on December 28, 2013, was going to send one of us packing for good. This would not be a title eliminator; it would be a career eliminator.

The night before the fight, my wife, Bobby, Eddie Herman, and I had dinner at an Italian restaurant in Las Vegas. I was in great shape and had trained hard, as I always do. But, as we dined and talked, spiritually I did not feel right. I wasn't afraid of facing Uriah Hall the following day. I wasn't afraid of losing the fight or of the end of my career. However, I did sense that this would be the last time I made the long walk to the Octagon. Some part of me knew I would leave my fight career behind when I exited the cage the next day.

I felt an unfamiliar numbness as Bruce Buffer introduced Uriah and me prior to the start of the fight. It was as if I wasn't fully there. I felt neither anxiety nor excitement. I looked around at the cheering crowd and at the press corps seated at tables near the cage and at Dana White who watched on from a cage-side seat. And I simply did not know whether I wanted to win or lose. My presence in the Octagon seemed to have lost its meaning.

For the first four minutes of the fight, I chased after Uriah, who used his speed and athleticism to evade my winging punches. He threw the occasional sharp jab as he backpedaled, splitting both of my cheeks early in the fight. For a moment, I thought about how this approach was dangerous—that Hall was a counterstriker who would look for the right moment to catch me reaching or off-balance. *Fuck it*, I thought. *I'm not a finesse fighter. I never have been. Might as well go out in the same way that I came in: hunting for that KO.* And around and around we went, me pressing forward and throwing heaters, Uriah shuffling and evading. We must have circled the cage twenty times in that manner until, right after the ten-second warning, Uriah threw a vicious right cross. It connected cleanly on my mouth, one of the most devastating shots that I had ever taken in my career. I crumpled to the ground. He tried to finish me off, but I was saved by the bell.

I went back to my corner in a complete daze. I thought that the fight was over.

"Was I knocked out?" I asked coach Eric Del Fierro as he led me to my stool.

"No," he replied. "That was the end of the round."

I could barely tell what was going on, but, in that moment, I realized that the time had come. Maybe I could have gotten off my stool for long enough chase Uriah around the cage a bit more. But I was dazed and I couldn't see straight. It would only be a matter of time before he landed another brutal strike, maybe that famous spinning kick of his. Either way, my heart didn't have it and my head didn't have it. There was nothing left.

"I'm done," I told my corner. "I'm done . . . I'm done . . . I'm done."

Referee Steve Mazzagatti came over and, as I sat there bleeding, waved off the fight.

I was done.


This is the way a fighting career ends: not with a bang but a whimper. I wish I could say I retired on a high note. In reality, it was a prolonged decline that ended in exactly the way I had wished it wouldn't. Coming to terms with the fact that I was no longer a UFC fighter was not easy. There's something called post-Olympic stress disorder that many Olympic athletes experience. Having spent their lives devoted to their sport and devoted to the pursuit of greatness, they are faced with a deep, black abyss after the final fireworks of the closing ceremonies burst. *What do I do with myself now?* is the question that arises the next morning. The lack of purpose and direction can be terrifying.

I had post-UFC stress disorder in the weeks after my career ended. As you would expect, I went through many emotions: depression, anger, anxiety, and self-pity, interspersed with fleeting moments of optimism about what life held for me. Complicating my troubles was the fact that, after eleven years of professional prizefighting, I had not much more than two copper pennies to rub together. Yes, I had been financially irresponsible. But I also felt that the UFC deserved some blame. They hadn't compensated me appropriately for what I had contributed to both the organization and the sport as a whole.

I started drinking again, heavily, and quickly sunk into a deep emotional hole. I really needed to see a psychologist, but I didn't have the funds to pay for it. Additionally, I was suffering from severe carpal tunnel syndrome and arthritis in both of my hands, the result of years of intense grappling. I did not have health insurance to cover the surgery that I needed in order to be able to use my hands like a normal human being and pursue my plan to become a full-time MMA coach. In short, I was fucked.

In early February of 2014, my beloved dog died. It was really the final straw. I had a meltdown and, in the midst of it, tweeted the following message:

> I wish I would've drove truck last 10yrs, then at least I have insurance to see a counselor. Ufc left me broken with nothing.

At the time, all I could think about was the bowl of shit I had found myself in. It was hard to summon the glory and the greatness of the past eight years when questioning whether my devotion to the sport had been worthwhile.

Minutes after publishing my tweet, my phone started ringing. The caller ID indicated that it was Dana White. My blood pressure immediately jumped. I was fucking pissed at him. Our last conversation was six weeks earlier, right after the Uriah Hall fight. Dana had told me the UFC would help me find my footing as I transitioned into retirement. He asked me how much I owed the government. I told him that it was a lot. He said the UFC would help me figure that out as well.

I remember him telling me he'd take care of me.

A month later, at a media event for *UFC 169*, Dana took it upon himself to announce to the press that I had never paid my taxes. They had a field day with that. "Chris Leben might be retired from MMA, but he's not done fighting. The former UFC star's next big bout is going to be with the IRS," wrote Fox Sports. *Thanks for the heat, Dana,* I remember thinking. *You should have just called the fucking IRS tipster hotline directly.*

Well, at least my tweet about truck driving got Dana's attention. I answered the phone and we immediately went at each other, yelling and cursing. It was as if we were in a competition to see who could shout the word "motherfucker" the most times. Our relationship had had its ups and downs over nine years, so I think it's fair to say we each had some demons to exorcise. After a bit, we calmed down and were able to hash out an understanding like grown men. Dana agreed to have the UFC pay for my carpal tunnel and some counseling. I expressed my gratitude and we hung up. That is the last real conversation we ever had. To be honest, I had always thought the UFC would have done more for me after I was done—maybe give me some kind of pension or a lump sum that would have allowed me to retire comfortably. In the end, it's my fault for putting my faith in someone else's pocketbook.

This incident highlights a hot-button issue that has been at the forefront of MMA headlines for the last few years: fighter compensation. As with PED use, the fighter compensation debate presents all kinds of complexities. To begin, I will offer some of the details of my own career compensation. During my time with the promotion, the UFC paid me something in the range of $1,400,000. That is inclusive of all disclosed purses, performance bonuses, undisclosed "locker room bonuses," and other compensation. Initially, you might think that sounds like a big number. It's not. If you spread that over the nine years of my UFC career, beginning with *The Ultimate Fighter*, then I grossed an average of $155,000 per year. *What are you complaining about?* you may ask. Well, there's more to the story. First of all, in the history of the UFC, I think it is safe to say I was in the top 10 percent of the most popular fighters. My fights put eyes on TVs and asses in seats. What do the most popular basketball, football, hockey, soccer players and boxers earn per year? Generally, many multiples of $155,000. Fuck, even shitty athletes in other sports earn ten times what I did. How about an extreme compensation example? From their highly touted 2015 boxing match, Floyd Mayweather earned approximately $200 million, and Manny Pacquiao earned approximately $120 million. Yes, it was a huge fucking sporting event. But Manny's payday in a losing effort was over 2,300 times the $51,000 purse that I earned per fight at the end of my career.

Additionally, think about where all of my money went. First of all, I had to give 20 percent to my manager and another 10 percent to my head coach. Then I had to pay for the various costs of training and the cost of medical care and physical therapy as needed. Also, I had to fork over money for the travel and accommodations of my cornermen for each fight. I would estimate that, at the end of the day, before paying taxes, I hung onto only about 60 percent of the money the UFC offered me. That drops my annual compensation to around $93,000 per year. And, at the time of writing this book, I think I was ranked in the top twenty-five fight-night bonus winners in the UFC. In other words, relative to my comrades in the organization, I was highly compensated! Do you know who else earns $93,000 per year? Your above-average suburban plumber.

Most UFC fighters in the middle of the pack probably take home less than half of what I earned. Starting pay in spring of 2015 had risen to $10,000 per fight with a $10,000 win bonus. The only problem is that most guys only fight two or maybe three times in a year. At that rate, if you trained year-round and won all of your fights, you'd only see a gross pay of about $60,000. So, I ask you this: for that kind of money, would you be willing to risk life and limb in a very unpredictable business that develops skills transferable to almost no other occupation? Some of you wouldn't fight at any price. Others, I'm sure, would fight for free.

So are Dana White and the Fertitta brothers money-grubbing misers who would rather upgrade their private jets than pay their fighters a decent wage? Some members of the media portray them that way, and, I think, many members of the public accept that portrayal. According to some reports, Dana is worth $300 million, and each Fertitta is worth about $1.5 billion. My feeling is they probably aren't much different from your typical American capitalist. After all, in 2014, Forbes reported that the typical CEO of a Fortune 500 company earns 331 times as much as his average employee. But that kind of imbalance doesn't necessarily justify the level of compensation that the UFC offers its fighters.

I'm not a frigging accountant, and I don't know how to access the Zuffa financial reports. (I wouldn't know how to read them if I did.) So I really can't speculate as to how the UFC uses its money. I don't know what kind of net profits the company churns out. I also don't know exactly how Dana and the Fertittas weigh the various factors that influence what they pay their employees. Sure, they are concerned about their own pocketbooks. But I also have to believe they are concerned with making the wealth distribution across the organization somewhat fair. They are probably also concerned with maintaining control over the heaving beast the UFC has grown into. The guys might look at boxing with its plethora of promoters, its pampered upper-level athletes, and its dwindling fan base, and think that ultra-high levels of compensation could actually lead to major problems within their own promotion. Maybe Dana and the Fertittas have big investments planned for the company that require tons of capital and so they have to hoard their cash a bit. I truly don't know.

However, I do know that in 2014, Forbes estimated the value of the UFC at $1.65 billion. Reportedly, each Fertitta owns around 40 percent of that (around $668 million), and Dana owns 9 percent (around $148 million). I'm not sure how much money is enough. But, it wouldn't hurt them a whole lot to set aside a couple of percent of their ownership as an equity pool for the fighters, would it? Hell, they could give just 2 percent of the company to the fighters and we're talking $33 *million*. They could distribute stock options to the fighters just like Apple and Google and so many other public and private companies do. Then a fighter can earn his equity over time and choose to sell it back to the company for a fair price. I think a plan like that would improve the enthusiasm and loyalty of the fighters . . . and maybe even their performance.

For the past year and a half, I have lived a very modest life in Ocean Beach. Kaleena and I moved into a $1,200-a-month one-bedroom apartment. I took a job as the head MMA coach at Victory MMA. They paid me shit, something like $40,000 a year. But at least the gym was close to my house and I could work with plenty of young aspiring fighters. Actually, my MMA team did damn well. We ran up a combined record of 26–4 during my time at Victory. Often I think I am a better coach than I was a fighter. I can put my heart into the job without having to worry about the physical consequences or the complications that come with my addiction issues. Oddly, a big part of the service I provide to my fight team is psychotherapy. Having spent so much of my life dealing with and overcoming personal demons, I have a lot to offer young people who are confused about their paths in life. I'm continually shocked by how many people share the very intimate details of their lives with me, looking for guidance. Maybe I should hang a shingle somewhere and become a life coach in addition to an MMA coach.

While I did my thing, Kaleena proceeded with her law studies, and for a while we lived a rather uneventful, domestic life. I continued to focus on acceptance—acceptance of disappointments, acceptance of failures, acceptance of myself. Relatedly, although I wouldn't consider myself a religious person, my philosophical viewpoints have become most closely aligned with Buddhism. So I have spent a lot of time exploring the ins and outs of mindfulness and internal peace. I must have listened to at least a dozen books by the Dalai Lama.

I turned to meditation as a way to deal with my issues and calm my spirit. I've spent many nights laying in bed and trying to focus my energy prior to sleeping. This has affected my dreaming and the realizations I have while in an unconscious state. All my life I have been a vivid dreamer. But in recent years, through meditation, I have learned how to train my mind to have lucid dreams—dreams during which I am aware enough to affect the direction and outcome of the dream. Many of these dreams involve me exploring the world or the universe. Some of them seem like premonitions of some kind. Frequently, I am able to clearly recollect the details of the dream after I wake up. I try to understand how I should apply those subconscious messages to my waking life.

All of these spiritual exercises have been helpful. In the past I would often think that one day, all of a sudden, I would figure everything out. I'd read something, or watch a documentary, and have an immediate epiphany about how I should lead my life. But now, I have come to terms with the fact that the path to enlightenment can be a lifelong process. Happiness is found in the journey, not necessarily in reaching the destination.

I do not mean to suggest, however, that I've escaped the kind of emotional madness that I experienced so often in the past. I struggle with this every day. And after retiring I continued to battle with alcoholism and my Suboxone dependency. It was hard on my relationships. At the same time, Kaleena began to struggle with the stress of graduate school. The result was friction. Our little domestic disputes evolved into bitter fights that grew more frequent and intense with time. Our marriage became a time bomb.

In spring of 2015, Kaleena and I had a major verbal blowout over something rather insignificant. Concerned about our relationship and Kaleena's emotional health, I contacted Kaleena's father. I explained the situation to him and suggested we should her to seek therapy for her ongoing anger issues. Well, that was a big mistake. Her father is of Japanese descent, and he's very old school. He felt dishonored by the information I was sharing, especially when I implied that some of her struggles might have to do with the humiliating pressure he put on her earlier in life. He blew up at me, refusing to even consider that his daughter might be partially responsible for the turbulence and pain she and I were experiencing. As far as he was concerned, I was the whole problem.

would be very little he or Robert could do. As I stepped up to the ring, a half-empty beer can hit me in the back and splattered.

Of course, when Otto was introduced, it almost caused an earthquake. You would have thought this guy was the second coming of Elvis Presley. He was sandy-haired, square-jawed, and strapping. He oozed charisma. I, on the other hand, was nervous as hell. I jumped into the ring and stared down at the mat, afraid to look up at the drunk and belligerent crowd that surrounded us. The fans roared and shouted as if they were attending a public hanging.

The fight had a furious pace from the get-go. Otto came straight at me, looking for a takedown and throwing unbridled hooks and crosses. He did not show an ounce of concern for my ability. My guess is that he wanted to please the adoring crowd by finishing the ugly Portland boy as quickly as humanly possible. Within fifteen seconds, he had stunned me with a barrage of punches. Another fifteen seconds later he had put me on my back and was looking to pour on the punishment. I scrambled, but I couldn't keep him off me. He postured and threw heavy hands at my face. Somehow I was able to make it back to my feet, at which point Otto jumped up, latched on a guillotine choke and dragged me back to the ground. It was perfect technique. In fact, he had wrapped his legs around my torso and trapped my left arm. There was almost nothing I could do to escape the hold. I couldn't breathe, and circulation was being cut off from my brain. Darkness closed in from my peripheral vision. The sound of the crowd faded and went silent. Blackness.

*I woke up in my bedroom in my mother's house in Felony Flats. Bright morning sun streamed in through the window. I stood up and noticed I was wearing only the black wrestling shorts I had donned* for the Otto Olson fight. I heard voices whispering in the next room. I opened my door and emerged to find an empty house.

"Mom?!" I yelled. "Tyler?!" No one was there. It was eerily empty. My throat felt strained as I used my voice. I was dizzy.

I stepped out onto the front porch and looked out over the neighborhood. It too, was totally empty. Nobody was around. A few bicycles were abandoned on a neighbor's lawn. In the distance, an old sheet hanging from a clothesline waved in the breeze.

I started to feel numb. The sensation began in my feet and crept upward to my knees, my thighs, my torso, and my head. Finally I felt as if I were detached from my body. It was as if I was completely weightless. I looked at my hands and then down at my feet. I had begun to levitate. I was lifting up off of the ground, slowly at first, then with increasing speed into the sky above Portland. I extended my arms and discovered that, if I concentrated, I could change my speed and direction. I began to soar over Felony Flats, making my way toward Sam Songer's house. Sam and Kim were looking out the window as I flew past. I waved, but they did not see me.

I flew east with increasing velocity, over Gresham and Sandy and Marmot, following the Sandy River. I dropped lower and lower until I was just inches above the water. I reached down and dipped some fingers into it. They left a gentle trailing wake as I continued to fly.

In the distance was Mount Hood. I focused harder and pushed forward, faster and faster over the rolling foothills. I soared above the village and the tilting, dilapidated home that my mother, brother, and I had spent some years in during my childhood. I turned left, up Lolo Pass, and the terrain became steeper. I urged my body forward, the cold wind whipping past me, the peak of Mount Hood rising like a holy beacon into the sky. I raced up the side of the mountain, up past the tree line, and the cliffs, to the very top of its snowcap.

*There, at the peak, stood a man staring off into the distance. I slowed down and came to a soft landing a few feet behind him. I felt a sense of excitement and terror. From my perspective I could tell he was a middle-aged man—balding, pale-skinned, stocky. He stared off into the distance. I reached forward to touch him on the shoulder.*

*Then I heard my name.*

*"Chris."*

*"Chris."*

*"Chris!"*

When I opened my eyes again, I was standing in the middle of the boxing ring facing Otto Olson. My cornermen were screaming. Eddie later explained to me that I had lost consciousness just a few seconds after Otto locked in the guillotine choke. However, although it was obvious from my corner's perspective, the referee did not realize I was out cold. The fight should have been stopped, but it wasn't. So, for about ten or fifteen seconds, Otto continued to apply constrictive pressure to my limp neck. At some point he went to adjust his grip, and my head slipped out. I immediately woke up and, completely disoriented, blindly scrambled back to my feet. By the time I realized what was happening, Otto was bearing down on me. Only then did I understand the fight was still in progress.

The crowd continued to howl and roar, urging their man to finish the job. And as Otto advanced, I could perceive a strange look on his face—part disbelief that I had survived his choke, part anger that I had not yet succumbed to his attacks. Instinctively, I took a deep breath and readied myself. I cocked my arm, and, with all of the strength and fury that I had accumulated in my twenty-three years of life on the edge, fired my heavy, unforgiving fist toward my opponent's chin.

# EPILOGUE

At 10:00 AM on July 24, 2015, I submitted the first full manuscript of *The Crippler* to Skyhorse Publishing. At 10:30 AM my phone rang. It was Chris Leben's manager, my good friend Bobby Cavian.

"What up, Bobbaloo?"

"Have you heard from Chris recently?" Bobby asked with his blended Persian-Swedish accent. He's oddly hard to read. As well as I know Bobby, I'm never quite sure whether he is about to share celebratory or disastrous news. So, this question about Chris elicited a marginal level of concern. It's kind of like when one of my parents—senior citizens now—calls me after 9:00 PM. It might not be a good thing. Did Chris get in to trouble? Did he overdose? Was he pissed at me off about something? I ran through the scenarios in my head before responding.

"I spoke to him a few days ago . . . to wish him a happy birthday. Why do you ask?"

"Are you on speaker phone?"

Now I knew this was going to be something unsettling. "No," I replied.

Bobby hesitated for moment before coming out with it. "Chris is in jail."

"Chris is in jail?"

"Yes," Bobby answered sullenly. "Keep that information to yourself for now."

*Here we go*, I thought to myself.

When I embarked on this writing adventure in early 2014, I truly had no idea of what kind of river I was diving into. As an MMA enthusiast and part-time MMA journalist, I had plenty of awareness of the man they called "The Crippler." Yet, prior to writing this book, I had only interacted with him once, during a brief handshake meeting when I was in Vegas covering *UFC 155*. It was the weekend before New Year's Eve 2012. Bobby, Kaleena, Chris, and a few other folks were having dinner the night before his comeback fight against Derek Brunson. This was his first return to action since his stint in rehab.

"Good to meet, you, man," Chris had said in a manner that was as warm and welcoming as his gruff and gravelly voice would allow.

"The pleasure is mine," I replied. "I've followed your career for a long time, and I'm an old school fan."

Chris chuckled at this. "Good to hear. Good to know that people still care."

I remember being surprised by the humility he exuded. It was sharply at odds with what I had seen on the TV and read about the man. One could have described him as resigned, even deflated at the time. The interaction hardly lasted a minute, but I was emotionally unsettled by it. As I walked away, along the busy and festive thoroughfare of the MGM Grand casino, I actually felt a degree of personal concern for Chris, as if I should go back and give him an extra pat on the back or a pep talk.

In early 2013, shortly after Chris fought his last fight, Bobby first mentioned that they were looking for a writer for his autobiography. For a long time I had been dismissive of Chris as a blowhard and a punk who couldn't handle his liquor. Had the opportunity arisen in 2010 or 2011, I would not have given it due consideration. But, that brief interaction with Chris prior to his Brunson fight had changed my tune. Clearly, there was something deeper to explore. I began to follow his exploits inside and outside of the Octagon much more closely. I often inquired with Bobby about what was happening with Chris—how his training was going, and what kind of personal challenges he was dealing with. I began to research his life and career, and, as the layers of the onion peeled away, I became undeniably engaged in the subject.

There was a constant and unusual sense of intrigue that surrounded Chris, regardless of how he was performing in the UFC. A portion of MMA fandom despised him. Unaware of Chris's true dedication to martial arts, they considered him the epitome of careless irreverence in a sport that deserved the most noble of warriors. But a much more substantial portion idolized Chris and identified with him on a meaningful level. An unrefined punk who was plowing through a crowded field of pedigreed athletes—there was something redeeming in that. Not surprisingly, many working-class young American men viewed the Crippler as the standard bearer for their unheralded movement. And so, he was both savior and villain, both hero and antihero. This is why I pursued the opportunity to write Chris Leben's autobiography. Were Chris an all-American family man who kept his nose clean and his bank account full, I would have had no interest. There's almost no chance I would have committed to writing a book about Georges St-Pierre or Cain Velasquez or Frankie Edgar or even Ronda Rousey for that matter. I am a massive fan of all of those fighters, and I admire them to no end. They are far more accomplished than I expect to ever be. However, in terms of literary and artistic work, it's the combination of the sacred and profane—a mix of beauty and disaster—that most appeals to me. Chris is a walking embodiment of that dichotomy.

Nonetheless, I was not expecting the next year or two of my life to be so steadily impacted and influenced by the trials and tribulations of this remarkable and perplexing man. The saga began when Bobby and I drove the three hours from Los Angeles, where I was living, to Chris's home in San Diego. Upon arriving, I was surprised by how modest Chris's accommodations were. I knew that MMA fighters did not make a lot of money, but this guy was a rock star in that world. I expected something more than the weathered one-bedroom apartment that he and Kaleena were sharing. The place was cramped and, by my estimate, had not been properly cleaned in months. Images of the Buddha adorned the walls, and a faux tiger hide was lain across the carpeted floor. The living room was furnished with a tattered leather futon, a massive, intricately carved wooden coffee table, and, of all things, a mechanical massage chair. When I entered, a gentle little cat limped over to see what was up. It had one foot that was broken sideways and dangled uselessly, though the defect did not seem to pain the animal.

"What's your cat's name?" I asked.

"This is Kickstand!" Chris announced with a smile and laugh. "She was like this when we got her."

*A damaged yet content little critter,* I thought to myself. *How appropriate.*

We were able to complete three or four hours of interviews during that first weekend together, and almost all of it related to Chris's encounter with his estranged father and the drama surrounding his fight with Patrick Côté. I was shocked by the extreme nature of the revelations that Chris offered in those initial interviews. He casually recounted stories involving wild sex, excessive drinking and drug use, and general mayhem as if they were par for the course. But it was Chris's devotion to the truth that really dropped my jaw. Most people, I believe, would be ashamed to admit a good amount of what is unveiled in this book. They would be concerned for the ramifications it would have on their present and future relationships and on their professional prospects. But not Chris. There is something about him that is uniquely unfiltered. To a fault, he is forthcoming about his past and his psyche. In that way (and in other ways), he is like no one else I have ever met. I should say, it was also quite eye-opening that he hid virtually nothing from his wife Kaleena. She typically sat nearby, occasionally contributing the odd detail, while Chris went on about his exploits in madness, hedonism, and the American underbelly. I was envious of the level of openness and trust that they shared.

Needless to say, when that first interview weekend came to a close, I was hooked. As Bobby and I drove back north, I felt a sense of great anticipation for future opportunities to dig into the slanted world that Chris was exposing me to. Working with him, I could tell, would allow me to vicariously experience all kinds of crazy, juicy shit that I had been too reserved to dabble in throughout my life. I grew up in a middle-class suburban Chicago household, attended college on an academic scholarship, and have worked in various capacities within the real estate, finance, and entertainment industries as an adult. The hardest drug I have ever tried is marijuana, and I generally only encounter the police when I forget to renew the sticker on my license plate. I tell my friends that each story that Chris reveals to me is more insane and dramatic than every story I have to offer about my own life . . . combined! Hell, this wasn't just an autobiography that I wanted to write, it was an autobiography that I wanted to read.

As our work progressed, it became increasingly clear that Chris is an unusually complex and multidimensional subject. He's a living, breathing contradiction. To start, his rough-hewn exterior belies an introspective and intellectually curious soul. Chris is fascinated by and well versed in the topics of spirituality, ancient history, philosophy, and science. For example, I once mentioned to him that I was going through a phase in which I was fascinated by quantum physics, of all things. I told Chris that I had watched perhaps a half-dozen documentaries on the subject and was reading a book by a famous Japanese physicist whose name escaped me.

"Is his name Michio Kaku?" Chris asked.

That was, indeed, the name I was trying to recall. Chris then explained that he had listened to a few of Kaku's books on tape and that he had seen all of the same documentaries that I had. He even corrected me when I did not demonstrate a full grasp of, for example, the "observer effect" on subatomic particles.

Another seeming contradiction is that, despite the volatility and instability that characterizes Chris's life, he has numerous deep and long-lasting friendships—relationships that are fuller and more committed, I think, than those that most adult men maintain. I spoke with several of Chris's closest associates during the composition of this book and was impressed, every time, by the concern, appreciation and love that they expressed for him. Yes, some of the guys that appear in this book, including Eddie Herman and Sam Songer, have had to bear the burden of Chris's addiction issues and emotional problems. But, at the same time, they were quick to express to me how important Chris has been in their lives. The general theme is that Chris is the kind of guy who would drop everything and drive across the country just to take a bullet for one of his friends.

One final aspect of Chris's being that is, shall we say, ironic, is his fragility. Here is a man who spent more than a decade engaging in professional fisticuffs with some of the toughest men in the world. He is known for having perhaps the hardest cranium and the most durable chin in the history of the UFC. Yet, Chris is shockingly sensitive and easily hurt by how people treat him. As many of us learned while watching the *TUF 1* series, sticks and stones *rarely* break his bones, but words *often* hurt him. And Chris craves—is even desperate for—affection. When it is denied, he is apt to experience an emotional meltdown. It was painful for me to watch him go through his split with Kaleena. It was torturous for Chris, and, as one might expect, did not end very well.

As you read in the last chapter of this book, Kaleena left Chris in mid-2015 after a somewhat prolonged period of turbulence in their relationship. Given the intensity and unpredictability with which they both live and love, their separation was not a tremendous surprise. And, knowing what I do of Chris's hyper-emotionality and, shall we say, loose interpretation of American law, the fact that this traumatic event culminated with him behind bars was an outcome that did not fall beyond the realm of possibility in my mind. Upon Chris's arrest, the media began reporting a menagerie of information, some of it rather inaccurate and speculative. Only Chris and Kaleena know exactly what transpired, but at the end of the day, Chris had been arrested on a warrant featuring a felony charge and a couple of misdemeanor charges.

I don't know enough to delve too deeply into the details of what led to Chris's arrest. However, as Chris discussed on his ESPN radio show, *Unfiltered MMA*, in September of 2015, it had something to do with him climbing up the side of the apartment building into which Kaleena had moved after their separation, and something to do with the cops arriving to discover an unloaded weapon that he had been storing at that location. As Chris explained on the show, after their initial separation, he and

Kaleena rekindled briefly. He was spending a good deal of time at her new apartment, even, in his words, residing there. But, apparently, after the wall-climbing incident, the court granted a restraining order against Chris, which he unwittingly violated later by texting Kaleena.

Chris originally was faced with an extended stint in the big house—something like three to five years. However, the prosecutor ultimately dropped most of the charges and granted Chris a plea deal that reduced the sentence to a matter of weeks. As I write these words, Chris is doing his time at the San Diego Central Jail with an expected release date in mid-November 2015. As far as I can tell, he is faring well, and, in typical Crippler fashion, is trying to help his lonely cellmate connect with women on the outside. Chris requested a few books from me recently, so I mailed them to him. Here are two of the titles: *The Ancient Secret of the Flower of Life, Volume 2* and *Mastering Astral Projection: 90-Day Guide to Out-Of-Body Experience.*

"Are you, like, *friends* with the Crippler?"

That's the question I often get from my friends who hear some of these stories about Chris. My answer, honestly, is yes. I am proud and happy to say that Chris is my friend. We've had a lot of good times writing this book, and we've had a lot of meaningful conversations. At the same time, I have to acknowledge that our friendship is a little strange, or at least unexpected. I wouldn't begin to consider trying half of the stuff he has done in his life. Furthermore, I don't condone some of his reckless behavior. Some of it even disturbs me, as I am sure some of what you have read in this book disturbs you. There was the time he got drunk and showed me his weapon collection, for example. That wasn't the most at ease I've ever felt in my life. And there was the other time that I woke up on his futon in the middle of the night to find

Chris sitting inches away, naked, muttering to himself. And there was the time that he got up on a Sunday morning at eight o'clock, made a beeline to the kitchen, and filled a Hello Kitty coffee mug with a mixture of vodka and malt liquor.

"What the hell is that?" I asked, referencing the mug.

"Breakfast," he replied before taking a swig.

And, yes, at times I have wondered whether getting wrapped up in his saga might affect my life in a negative way.

But, at this point, I have to say that quite the opposite is true. For one thing, from this experience, I was able to achieve a lifelong goal: I wrote an interesting book about a topic that fascinates me. That's a big deal for me—a tremendous source of pride and satisfaction. Moreover, I've learned a lot about life from interacting with Chris. He's shown me how far a person can go if he believes in himself and stays committed to his dreams. Chris has encouraged me to be less reluctant to take public risks or to show the world exactly who I am, for better or worse. And perhaps most importantly, he has made me more attuned to the fact that I only have one life to live; I should put less emphasis on doing what is expected of me and more emphasis on experiencing as much of this big, beautiful, mad world as I possibly can.

"Don't be afraid to go wild every once in a while," the Crippler would advise.

I think he has a point.

D. Patinkin
October 2015